THE APOSTLE PETER'S THEOLOGY ON CONVERSION

Curtis Braun

New Harbor Press
Rapid City, SD

New Harbor Press 1601 Mt Rushmore Rd, Ste 3288 Rapid City, SD 57701 www.newharborpress.com

Ordering Information: Quantity sales. Special discounts are available on quantity purchases by corporations, associations, and others. For details, contact the "Special Sales Department" at the address above.

The Apostle Peter's Theology on Conversion/Braun —1st ed.

ISBN 978-1-63357-297-3

First edition: 10 9 8 7 6 5 4 3 2 1

Contents

Preface 1

Acknowledgments 5

Dedication and Prayer 7

Prayer 9

Chapter 1: Peter's Pre-Conversion Life – Learning from John the Baptist 11

Chapter 2: Peter's Pre-Conversion Life – Learning from Jesus 57

Chapter 3: Peter's Conversion - The Miraculous Catch of Fish 111

Chapter 4: Peter Hears Jesus Preach on the Narrow Gate and Narrow Way 131

Chapter 5: Peter's Confession, the Church, the Crucifixion and Resurrection, and the Gospel Call to Take Up Your Cross 139

Chapter 6: Peter Hears the Gospel Call for Preeminent Loving Faith Toward the Lord Jesus Christ 191

Chapter 7: Peter's Sermon on Pentecost and Gospel Call 211

Chapter 8: Peter's Sermon in Solomon's Colonnade and Gospel Call 235

Chapter 9: Peter's Sermon to the Sanhedrin 251

Chapter 10: Simon the Sorcerer – Baptized & Believed, but not Saved 265

Chapter 11: Peter's Sermon to Cornelius 279

Chapter 12: Peter's Confession at the Jerusalem Council 287

Chapter 13: Peter's Condemnation of False Teachers 303

Prayer 337

Notes 339

Preface

There is a great burden and zeal I've been given to continue to address Biblical conversion, regeneration, and to defend and proclaim the saving gospel. This is the fifth book written to address sacramentalism in Christianity and the many false teachings on regeneration and conversion. This book is similar in nature to *The Apostle Paul's Theology on Conversion and Condemnation of Sacramental Conversion* and *The Gospel Call and Conversion Theology of James – a Condemnation of Sacramental Conversion and Salvation* where we will look at Biblical conversion and regeneration but through the witness and testimony of the apostle Peter.

The Apostle Peter is proof texted and caricatured as teaching sacramental conversion and salvation in sacramental churches (1 Peter 3:21, Acts 2:38). However, sacramental conversion and salvation was the furthest thing from Peter's theological understanding of true conversion. When Peter is proof texted as one who would teach salvation by sacraments, there is an absolute lack of Biblical consideration of the ritualistic and ceremonial environment that Peter was immersed in. It is troublesome to see how Peter's letters, teaching, and messages in Scripture are twisted in such a way that portray this apostle as teaching sacramental conversion and salvation. In this book, it will be demonstrated that Peter would have put no hope for salvation in circumcision or covenant signs, ceremonial and external washings, law keeping, or any of the like. Rather, Peter understood conversion being repentance toward God and faith in the Lord Jesus Christ.

This is the fifth book I've written on this topic. These books have been written to demonstrate that Jesus, Matthew, Mark, Luke, John, John the Baptist, James, Peter, Paul, and the rest of the Bible speak in one voice. A sinful man is reconciled to holy God through the person and work of the Lord Jesus Christ who calls all men everywhere to repentance toward God and faith in Him.

This book is also written to bring awareness of churches that teach sacramental conversion, and thus, give a false gospel and false assurance of one's salvation. In the books I have written, I've always attempted to replace false doctrine with true doctrine, to explain true regeneration which would expose baptismal regeneration as false, to explain the true gospel which would expose a false gospel, and to explain true conversion which would expose false conversion through sacraments and rituals. In this fifth book, I am seeking once again to explain true conversion through the testimony and witness of Peter and expose the false teaching that conversion and salvation can occur through sacraments, ceremonies, and rituals. A vast majority of churches in the world teach sacramental conversion which leads to massive amounts of false conversions in churches. To sit back and say nothing would be cowardly, disobedient, lazy, inexcusable, and sinful. Love delights in the truth. Adrian Rogers has said this regarding the truth:

"It is better to be divided by truth than to be united by error. It is better to speak the truth that hurts and then heals, than to speak falsehood that comforts but then kills. It is not love and it is not friendship if we fail to declare the whole counsel of God. It is better to be hated for telling the truth than to be loved for telling a lie. It is better to stand alone with the truth than to be wrong with the multitude."

Below is a list of churches that teach sacramental conversion. Saturate these churches with your absence:

- Eastern Orthodox Church
- Oriental Orthodox Church
- Greek Orthodox Church
- Assyrian Orthodox Church
- Lutheran Church
- Anglican Church denominations
- United Methodist Churches
- United Church of Christ
- Many more churches

We will see that Peter warns of false teachers who enter the church, give false gospels, and bring destruction upon themselves and their listeners. Peter's description of these false teaching heretics is astonishing. We'll see that there is not one ounce of grace that Peter gives to false teachers. While it is true that false teachers need to be rescued, the language and utter disdain that Peter uses is inescapable. Peter describes false teachers as false prophets (2 Peter 2:1), bold (2 Peter 2:10), self-willed (2 Peter 2:10), irrational creatures (2 Peter 2:12), blasphemous (2 Peter 2:2, 10), ignorant (2 Peter 3:16), defiled (2 Peter 2:10), deceptive (2 Peter 2:13), covetous (2 Peter 2:3), accursed (2 Peter 2:14), un-submissive (2 Peter 2:1), Lordship scorning (2 Peter 2:10), unrepentant (2 Peter 2:21-22), unceasing from sin (2 Peter 2:14), adulterous (2 Peter 2:14), right way forsaking (2 Peter 2:15), waterless springs (2 Peter 2:17), hell bound (2 Peter 2:17), slaves of corruption (2 Peter 2:19), Scripture twisting (2 Peter 3:16), unestablished (2 Peter 3:16), vomit eating (2 Peter 2:22), excrement wallowing (2 Peter 2:22), and only good when dead creatures who will be eternally destroyed and condemned (2 Peter 2:1, 3, 9, 12).

Lastly, this book is written for the glory of God. The Lord decided and determined to save an adulterous, sexually immoral, loathsome, and selfish sinner such as me. Instead of allowing me to commit suicide, I was given salvation. Rather than continuing on in adultery, I was adopted. Rather than continuing on in pornography, I was pardoned for my transgressions. Rather than continuing on in manipulation, I was monergistically saved. To Him who is the King of the ages, immortal, invisible, the only God, be honor and glory forever and ever. Amen.

Acknowledgments

To Laura, Pax, and Keryx. I love you all very much. Be steadfast, immovable, always abounding in the work of the Lord. Love the Lord your God with all your heart, and with all your soul, and with all your mind, and with all your strength. Stand firm in the faith and let nothing move you. Always give yourself fully to the work of the Lord because you know that your labor in the Lord is not in vain. Be strong in the Lord and His Word. Whatever you do, whether you eat or drink, do it all for the glory of the Lord. Seek the Lord with all your heart. Lastly, repent and put your faith in the Lord Jesus Christ. Deny yourself, take up your cross, and follow after Him.

To Pastor John Macarthur and Pastor Steve Lawson—Thank you for being faithful pastors, able to handle the Word of Truth. Our family continues to be built up in the faith by your ministries.

Dedication and Prayer

Dedicated to Laura, Pax, and Keryx. Trust and follow the Lord Jesus Christ no matter the cost. The fear of man brings a snare, but the one who trusts in the Lord will be protected. Do not fear those who kill the body but cannot kill the soul. Rather fear Him who can destroy both soul and body in hell

Matthew 16:24-26 – *If anyone would come after me, let him deny himself and take up his cross and follow me. For whoever would save his life will lose it, but whoever loses his life for my sake will find it. For what will it profit a man if he gains the whole world and forfeits his soul? Or what shall a man give in return for his soul?*

Prayer

"Father, do the work that I cannot do. In your mercy, use your Word to save the blind and hard-hearted in sacramental churches. Open their eyes, give them the new birth, grant repentance, and author in them saving faith. Do this all for the glory of your beloved Son, the Lord Jesus Christ. Amen."

Chapter 1

Peter's Pre-Conversion Life – Learning from John the Baptist

Acts 10:37 – *You yourselves know what happened throughout all Judea, beginning from Galilee after the baptism that John proclaimed.*

If we are to understand Peter's theology on conversion, it is imperative that we must seek to understand the gospel. If one is wrong about the gospel, they will be wrong on many other biblical doctrines. If one is wrong about the gospel, they will inevitably misinterpret Scripture. If one is wrong about the gospel, they will be wrong about salvation. If one is wrong about the gospel, they will likely have some error on the person and work of Jesus. If one is wrong about the gospel, they will be wrong about the subjective response of repentance and faith to the objective Biblical facts of the person and work of Jesus.

To understand the gospel will help us understand Peter's theology on conversion. For example, what did Peter believe about the bad news of sin, death, and hell? What did Peter believe and understand about sin? What did Peter understand about God's judgment against sin? What did Peter understand about the punishment for sin against God? What did Peter understand about hell?

When it comes to the person of Jesus of Nazareth, what did Peter believe about the person of Jesus? Did Peter believe that Jesus was both God and man? Did Peter believe Jesus was a created being? Did Peter believe that Jesus was the Son of God? Did Peter believe that Jesus was the Son of Man? Did Peter believe Jesus was Lord? Did Peter believe Jesus was the Christ? Did Peter believe that Jesus was the Prophet that was foretold in Deuteronomy? Did Peter believe that Jesus was the King of Israel? Did Peter believe that Jesus was the Creator and Sustainer of the world?

When it comes to the work of Jesus of Nazareth, what did Peter believe about the work of Jesus? Did Peter believe that Jesus was the Savior of the world? Did Peter believe that Jesus Lamb of God who takes away the sin of the world? Did Peter believe that Jesus was the one who would baptize with the Holy Spirit (salvation) and fire (judgment)? Did Peter believe that Jesus was a substitutionary atonement for sin? Did Peter believe that Jesus was sinless or sinful? Did Peter believe that Jesus' miracles provided attestation to His teachings and claims? Did Peter believe that Jesus died? Did Peter believe that Jesus rose from the dead? Did Peter believe that Jesus ascended into heaven? Did Peter believe that Christ would come again and save all true believers while condemning unrepentant men?

When it comes to salvation, what did Peter believe? Did Peter believe that one needed to repent and turn towards Christ? Did Peter believe John the Baptist's message of bearing fruits of repentance? Did Peter believe that one needed to put their faith in Jesus? Did Peter believe that ceremonial and ritual washing or baptism with water gave salvation? Did Peter believe that circumcision gave salvation? Did Peter believe that keeping the Sabbath laws of the Pharisees gave salvation? Did Peter believe that burnt offerings or any offerings under the Levitical system gave salvation? Did Peter believe that law keeping or law observance gave salvation?

To understand Peter's theology on conversion, or rather, repentance toward God and faith in the Lord Jesus Christ, it will be most beneficial to follow a chronological sequence with John the Baptist. We will use the timeline found in the Harmony of the Gospels (1) as we trace Peter's life to understand what Peter comprehended about the gospel and we will follow this timeline through to the book of Acts. By following this timeline, we will see many things such as Peter's first appearance in the gospels, the preaching of John the Baptist that he was exposed to, the teaching and works of Jesus, Peter's sermons, and Peter's statement at the Jerusalem Council. However, before we get started looking at Peter's pre-conversion life, it would be advantageous to become grounded on the bad news of sin and hell as well as the gospel. If we're familiar with the bad news of sin and hell as well as the gospel, we'll be able to identify these elements as we work our way through this book.

The Bad News of Sin and Hell

Man has sinned which is breaking God's law by either not doing what God's law demands (James 4:17) or doing what God's law prohibits (James 2:10) by any thought (Matthew 5:28), word (Matthew 5:22), deed (Matthew 5:39), or intent (Matthew 6:1) which God hates (Psalm 5:5, 11:5), abhors (Psalm 5:6), is angered with (Psalm 7:11), is ready to destroy and punish (Psalm 7:12-13), which is being at warfare with Him (James 4:4), which God considers an abomination (Proverbs 22:12), and which God considers evil (Psalm 7:9). Because God hates sin, He must deal with sin according to who He is. Because God is infinite (1 Timothy 1:17), loving (Psalm 136, 1 John 4:17), just (Genesis 18:25, Deuteronomy 32:4, Job 34:10, Jeremiah 17:10, Ezekiel 18:1–32), good (Psalm 25:8, Mark 10:18), faithful (Lamentations

3:22–23), omniscient (Psalm 147:5, Hebrews 4:13), immutable (James 1:17, Numbers 23:19), omnipresent (Jeremiah 23:23–24), and holy (Isaiah 44:6, 45:5), He must punish sin. For God to leave sin unpunished would violate and act in opposition to His character.

The punishment for sin is hell which is a place of God's full wrath and is a place of blackest darkness (Jude 13, Matthew 22:13), filled with furious and concentrated fire everywhere (Matthew 5:22, 5:29, 13:42, 13:50), where there is weeping and anger against God for the unrepentant Christ-rejecting (Matthew 11:20-24) and Christ-neglecting sinners (Hebrews 2:1-3) where they will spend all eternity paying for every sin they've ever committed (Revelation 20:12) with no hope of escape (Luke 16:26), and only the expectation of excruciating torments to their body, soul, and spirit (Matthew 10:28) and an undying conscience that will haunt them day and night, forever and ever, with no reprieve (Luke 16:25).

The Gospel

The gospel is the good news of salvation that God has authored and owns (Romans 1:1). God had promised this plan of salvation through His prophets and Holy Scripture and has fully revealed the good news of salvation through Scripture (Romans 1:2) which is the authoritative, inspired, inerrant, infallible, and all-sufficient Word of God (2 Peter 1:20-21, 2 Timothy 3:16-17). The good news concerns the person and work of the Lord Jesus Christ. Jesus is the Jewish Messiah and Son of the Living God (Matthew 16:16, Romans 1:1-4). Jesus is God and He is coequal and coeternal with God the Father and God the Holy Spirit (John 5:17-18, 10:30, 10:38, 14:10). Jesus is the eternal, only begotten, one-of-a-kind, Son of God (John 3:16). Jesus is the Anointed One of God (Luke 4:18-19). Jesus is the Savior of the world (Luke 2:11). Jesus is the Creator and Sustainer of the Universe (John

1:1-14). Jesus is the King of Israel (John 1:49). Jesus is the Son of David (Matthew 1:1-16, Luke 3:23-38). Jesus was born of a virgin (Matthew 1:23, Galatians 4:4). Jesus was the Word made flesh (John 1:14). Jesus was physically born into this world as a man (Matthew 1:25). Jesus is thus truly God and truly man (Philippians 2:5-11).

The work of Jesus is that Jesus lived a sinless life (Matthew 26:59-60, 1 Corinthians 5:21) and fulfilled all righteousness found in the law and prophets (Matthew 5:17-20, Luke 24:44-46). He declared Himself to be the Christ (Matthew 16:16), the only begotten Son of the Living God through His teaching (John 3:16, Matthew 22:41-46), which was attested to by His miracles and display of divine power (John 10:37-38). Jesus offered himself as a spotless and blameless sacrifice for sin (John 1:29, 1 Peter 1:19) to propitiate the righteous anger of God by taking all the sins of God's people (John 10:11, Romans 3:25, Isaiah 53, 1 Peter 2:24) and, thus, the full wrath of God that was due to man (Matthew 26:39, 27:45-46, Luke 22:44). His sacrifice propitiated the righteous anger of God and reconciled (Romans 5:10-11) and brought peace from man to God and God to man (Matthew 27:51-53, John 19:30, Romans 5:1, 1 Peter 2:25). His substitutionary sacrifice and death also redeemed sinful man to Holy God by forgiving man's sin (Hebrews 8:12, Ephesians 1:7) and imputing Christ's righteousness to man (1 Corinthians 5:21, Isaiah 53:1-12, Romans 4:3-5). Jesus was resurrected from the dead on the third day by His own power (John 10:18), by God the Father (Galatians 1:1) and God the Holy Spirit (Romans 8:11), which affirmed His person, His teachings, and salvific work for sinners (Romans 4:25). He ascended to the right hand of the Father (Luke 24:51) and is empowered with all authority to bring about the plan of salvation for all His people (Matthew 28:18) by causing them to be born again (John 3:1- 10) and justified by His grace (John 3:16, 3:18, 3:36). He will also return to bring all His own to heaven with Him (John 6:37- 40, 14:1-3) to be glorified

(John 17:24) while also judging and condemning Satan, demons, and sinful man to hell (Matthew 25:31-46, Revelation 20:7-15).

The benefits of the person and work of Christ are available to those who respond to the gospel call of repentance towards God and faith in the Lord Jesus Christ (Mark 1:15, Acts 20:21). Repentance is a gift from God and radical change in mind (Acts 5:31, 11:18, 2 Timothy 2:25) where the sinner understands his sin against God and is thus, poor in spirit (Matthew 5:3, Luke 18:9-14), has godly sorrow and mourns over his sin against God (Matthew 5:4, 2 Corinthians 7:10), and turns away from his sin and sinful former way of life (Ephesians 4:22) and toward God for righteousness and salvation (Matthew 5:5-6, Luke 3:3-17, Acts 17:30, 20:21, 1 Thessalonians 1:9). Saving faith is a gift from God (Ephesians 2:8-9) where a sinner has knowledge of Jesus' person and work where a sinner will respond to Christ's person and work by denying themselves (Matthew 16:24, Mark 8:34, Luke 9:23), picking up their cross (Matthew 10:38, 16:24, Mark 8:34, Luke 9:23), and lovingly (Luke 14:26-27, James 4:7) and obediently (2 Thessalonians 1:8, Romans 1:5) submitting (James 4:6, Matthew 11:28) and committing their life to Jesus (Matthew 10:37-39, 16:24-26, Mark 8:34-37, Luke 9:23-26, 14:25-33) and trusting in Him only for salvation (Romans 10:13, John 3:16, John 3:36, Acts 4:12). Thus, conversion is the turning away from sin in repentance and to the Lord Jesus Christ in faith for salvation (Acts 20:21, 1 Thessalonians 1:9, Ephesians 4:22-24, Colossians 3:9-10, Mark 1:15).

Now that we've gained a brief understanding of the bad news of sin, hell, the person of the Lord Jesus Christ, the work of the Lord Jesus Christ, and the response of the sinner to the person and work of Jesus Christ, let's get started.

John the Baptist Preaches a Baptism of Repentance for the Forgiveness of Sins and Testimony of Christ - Luke 3:3-17

John the Baptist had an extraordinary ministry. John the Baptist was the son of a priest named Zechariah who belonged to the priestly division of Abijah. John's mother was Elizabeth, who was also a descendant of Aaron. Elizabeth was related to Mary, the mother of Jesus, so John the Baptist would have also been related to Jesus. John was the forerunner to Jesus and had the ministry of getting the nation of Israel ready for the Messiah and preparing the way of the Lord. John's ministry was to bring back many of the people of Israel to the Lord their God and to turn the hearts of the parents to their children and the disobedient to the wisdom of the righteous—to make ready a people prepared for the Lord (Luke 1:17). John was to go before the Lord in the spirit and power of Elijah, which means he would be known for being bold and uncompromising in his stand for the Word of God (Luke 1:17). In this section, we will seek to understand John the Baptist's message of repentance and testimony of the Lord Jesus Christ. We'll see that Peter would have been well aware of John the Baptist's message as Peter's brother, Andrew, was a disciple of John the Baptist. We also see Peter make this comment to Cornelius about how widespread John the Baptist's message was in Acts 10:37-38, "you yourselves know what happened throughout all Judea, beginning from Galilee after the baptism that John proclaimed: how God anointed Jesus of Nazareth with the Holy Spirit and with power." We will look at Luke 3:3-17 to understand John the Baptist's baptism of repentance for the forgiveness of sins, Jesus' baptism with John in Matthew 3:13-17, John's testimony of Jesus in John 1:29-34, and Andrew, John the Baptist's disciple, introducing Peter to Jesus (John 1:35-42).

Luke 3:3 – *He went into all the country around the Jordan, preaching a baptism of repentance for the forgiveness of sins.*

John's ministry was one of confrontation with the nation of Israel. It was not only a call to national repentance, but also a call to personal repentance. In ancient times, the herald would go before a king and announce the king's message. The herald would come with the king's message and whether it was an order for the nation's surrender or an edict from the king, the messenger would go throughout the towns and villages and announce the king's message. The herald would not be quiet. The herald would bring forth the message with conviction and all authority of the king. The herald would neither dare to misrepresent the king's message, add to the king's message, leave anything out from the king's message, nor would the herald quietly announce the message. In fact, in ancient times, the herald was to announce the message with a gravity and authority that required the listeners to obey. The herald was not to enter negotiations. The herald was to learn the message and speak the message with the force and conviction of the king himself. The herald would boldly, loudly, and clearly articulate the message of the king to all people with conviction. John the Baptist was no different. His job was to boldly, loudly, and clearly articulate the message with the conviction of the Lord to repent and be baptized. His message was not just a mere change of mind, but a call to prepare one's heart and life to turn away from sin and toward the Messiah. The original word for repentance comes from metanoeo which means "to change one's mind" or "a change of mind." Repentance is certainly a change of mind, but when this change of mind occurs, it is radical. When this change of mind occurs or when there is true repentance, the person realizes they've been wrong about sin. This change of mind leads one to realize they have been wrong about God, wrong about one's salvation, wrong about one's sin, wrong about one's standing before God, wrong about Jesus, wrong about one's worldview, and much more. This change of mind causes one to see their spiritual bankruptcy before a holy God (Matthew 5:3). This change of mind causes one to mourn over their sin against

God (Matthew 5:4). This change of mind causes a person to be meek and submissive unto the Lord (Matthew 5:5). This change of mind causes a person to turn to Christ and hunger and thirst for the righteousness they don't possess (Matthew 5:6). This change of mind causes one to see the heinousness of one's sins, confess one's sins before God, and turn from one's sinful manner and walk of life to Christ (Ephesians 4:22-24). This change of mind causes one to see sin as enormous. This change of mind causes one to see the Biblical Christ as preeminently lovely and worthy above all else. This changing of the mind is not mere intellectual assent, but it also impacts the emotional affections and the volitional will of man. Repentance is not some built up effort performed by man. May it never be! Repentance that leads to life is a gracious and merciful gift which is granted by God (Acts 11:18, 2 Timothy 2:25). His job was to proclaim that all of Israel needed to repent and be baptized for the forgiveness of sins. He did not enter negotiations with anyone. He did not change the King's message. He was not *a reed swayed by the wind,* meaning that he was not a weak man with no convictions (Matthew 11:7). He was a herald and preacher of repentance. The next question that arises is what did this baptism of repentance represent?

There were several ceremonial washings in the Old Testament. However, there was a specific meaning behind John's baptism that would have been especially offensive. Under the old covenant, there was a ceremonial ablution or washing for Gentiles who would convert to Judaism. This ceremonial washing of proselytes was considered purification from heathenism and an initiation or consecration of the convert before his admission to the people of God. Since a Gentile had lived in what was considered heathen pollution and was also considered a heathen and impure, the Gentile would be required to complete a purification process to fully become an Israelite. It was, thus, required of every Gentile to submit to the rite of purification from heathen pollution by immersion. The Babylonian Talmud says that, concerning proselytes, "one is not to be regarded as a proselyte until he has been circumcised and undergone immersion, and as long as he has not undergone immersion, he is still a non-Jew." This was a part of rabbinic regulations for ceremonial purifications and required three witnesses. The candidate, if a male, was first circumcised and when the wound had healed, he was taken to the bath. While he stood in the water, the rabbis once more recited to him some of the great and lesser commandments. The convert would then make a complete immersion and stepped forth as a fully privileged Israelite. In addition to this, the proselyte would be asked questions such as, "What makes thee desire to become a proselyte?" and, if the proselyte would answer, "I am not worthy to give my neck to the yoke of Him who spoke the word and the world came into existence," they would immediately accept him and move forward with the baptism while also reciting commandments.

John's baptism of repentance was a proselyte baptism of repentance for Israel. In other words, John was proclaiming to them with full gravity and conviction that they were not ready for the Messiah. John was telling them that they needed to see themselves as Gentiles. John was telling them that they needed to see themselves as unrighteous as tax collectors, prostitutes, swindlers, whoremongers, fornicators, and outright sinners. John was telling them that their circumcision meant nothing in terms of salvation. John was telling them that their ancestry meant nothing in terms of salvation. John was telling them that their religious rituals meant nothing in terms of salvation. John was telling them that their good works meant nothing in terms of salvation. John was telling them that they were not ready for the Messiah and, if they wanted to receive forgiveness of sins that could be offered by the Messiah, they would need to consider themselves as Gentiles. John was telling them that if they wanted forgiveness of sins as offered by the Messiah, they should consider themselves outside of God's covenant people, that they should consider themselves cut off from God, that they should consider themselves ceremonially unclean to accept the Messiah, that they should consider themselves as equals with the Gentile pagan, and that they should consider themselves unrighteous and damned. This was the meaning of John's baptism of repentance for the forgiveness of sins.

It would have been an extreme shock to the Jews who thought they were the covenant people and were righteous. This message would have turned their world upside down as John not only commanded all of Israel to repent and identify as a Gentile, even the religious leaders and teachers of Judaism were called to this very same repentance. No one in the nation of Israel was excluded from the command to be baptized, repent, identify as a Gentile, confess their sins, and throw themselves at the mercy of the Messiah. This was an extreme message for the Jews to prepare for the Messiah's coming and it was a radical call to turn not only nationally, but also personally, to the Messiah. Isaiah 1:5–6 captures the state of where Israel was just prior to the Messiah's coming where it says, "Why should you be beaten anymore? Why do you persist in rebellion? Your whole head is injured, your whole heart afflicted. From the sole of your foot to the top of your head there is no soundness—only wounds and welts and open sores, not cleansed or bandaged or soothed with olive oil." John proclaimed this very same message to the Jews. They were unsound from the top of their head to the sole of their foot.

Luke 3:4–6—*As it is written in the book of the words of Isaiah the prophet: "A voice of one calling in the wilderness, 'Prepare the way for the Lord, make straight paths for him. Every valley shall be filled in, every mountain and hill made low. The crooked roads shall become straight, the rough ways smooth. And all people will see God's salvation.'"*

John the Baptist has just quoted from Isaiah 40. Although the message and baptism of repentance would have been shocking and offensive as it called for a radical spiritual repentance, John was also citing a promise from Isaiah where God comforts His people. In Isaiah 40, God announces comfort for His people (v. 1), God has said that Jerusalem's penalty has been paid for twice over (v. 2), God promises to tend to His flock like a shepherd (v. 11), God declares His sovereignty and power (v. 15–25), and promises hope for those who trust in Him (v. 29–31). John is preparing Israel to receive their Messiah and he begins to explain repentance through Isaiah 40:3–5.

John's theology of repentance according to Isaiah starts with, "Prepare the way for the Lord, make straight paths for him." John is not calling for a massive demolition and construction of a physical path or road. No, his ministry was to prepare the hearts of the people (Luke 1:17). Therefore, in this short little sentence John is saying that any obstacles that would deter the people from accepting the Messiah must be put away. John is saying that every person needs to clean out their spiritual closet. He is saying that everyone in Israel needs to get rid of their apathy, get rid of their pride, get rid of their distractions, get rid of false religion, get rid of other priorities that interfere with God, get rid of self-reliance, get rid of hypocrisy, get rid of self-will, and get rid of anything that is going to prevent them from accepting the Messiah.

He goes on to state that the crooked roads shall become straight, the rough ways smooth. Once again, John wasn't calling for a road construction project. John was calling for a total self-evaluation. In verse 5, he said, "Every valley shall be filled in, every mountain and hill made low." When John said that *"every valley shall be filled in,"* he was stating that every sin shall be brought up and openly confessed. Take your sins and confess them and do not hold anything back. All the debase sins that you cherish shall be raised up and elevated so that you may be brought low and humbled to receive the Messiah. Notice that he says *"every."* This was a radical repentance. He was saying that the sins that the people knew about in their lives needed to be confessed and rejected. He was saying that all the hidden sins in the valley of one's heart needed to be exposed. Likewise, John said that "every mountain and hill needed to be brought low." He's stating that every righteous act and that every self-exalting accomplishment must be brought low. There was no room for confidence in circumcision. There was no room for confidence in ceremonial washing. There was no room for confidence in Sabbath observance-keeping. He's saying that your sins must be elevated, all your good deeds and religious accomplishments brought low, and every other obstacle in your life must be dealt with and removed. There was no room for religious exaltation, only room for soul-searching repentance and humility and a heart readiness to accept the Messiah as Lord and Savior.

Luke 3:7–8—*John said to the crowds coming out to be baptized by him, "You, brood of vipers! Who warned you to flee from the coming wrath? Produce fruit in keeping with repentance. And do not begin to say to yourselves, 'We have Abraham as our father.' For I tell you that out of these stones God can raise up children for Abraham."*

So, as John is performing his ministry of preparing the nation of Israel for the Messiah, he is also confronting people that do not have true repentance. Here, he calls them "a brood of vipers." Notice that he doesn't call them "Abraham's descendants." He doesn't call them "children of God." He doesn't call them "sons of Israel." No, he calls them a *"brood of vipers."* He is calling them "children of serpents." In Matthew's account, he is speaking specifically with Sadducees and Pharisees, but, in Luke's account, Luke makes no distinction and includes the crowds. He is not calling them "covenant people of God," but "children of the devil." He is warning Israel of divine wrath and judgment.

The people of Israel would have noticed this. They would have known of the serpent in Genesis 3. They would have known that John was telling them they were still under divine wrath and judgment. Notice too that he tells this to the religious Israelites. Israel should have known better that entrance into the kingdom was not a group affair but an individual entrance into the kingdom. They would have known Psalm 1:1–2, "Blessed is the one who does not walk in step with the wicked or stand in the way of sinners or sit in the seat of scoffers, but whose delight is in the law of the LORD, and who meditates on His law day and night." They would have known that this should have been an individual repentance and not just another ritual.

Notice as well that he says, "Who warned you to flee from the coming wrath?" This wrath isn't the wrath of the devil or the wrath of demons or the wrath of men. No, true repentance is an understanding that one is fleeing from the wrath and judgment of God. In other words, John is saying, "So you heard that there was a baptism of repentance and now you're looking to go through a ceremonial rite or ritual to escape God's wrath. Don't do that! Don't think that divine judgment will not fall on you just because you've been baptized. Don't presume that the Jordan River will make you right with God." John further goes on to refine what repentance should look like when he says, "Produce fruit in keeping with repentance." The word *worthy* comes from *axios* and it means "to weigh in keeping with how something weighs in on God's balance-scale of truth." In other words, John is telling them that this ritual means nothing, but what means everything is the heart preparation as it relates to repentance. If the people of Israel do see their offense toward God, have intellectual knowledge of their sins, understand they have no merit before God, mourn over their status before God, and humble themselves to receive the Messiah, they should bring forth fruit that God finds worthy of repentance. If there is no fruit of repentance, there was never a root of true repentance, but rather, a false repentance and dead ritual. John's call for repentance doesn't only apply to the people of Israel, but also applies to all people today. God commands all men everywhere to repent (Acts 17:30).

John was very concerned about false repentance. John knew how wicked the heart was and how man would want the easy road. John knew that not everyone who came to be baptized for repentance would bear fruits of repentance. John was preparing the people for the Messiah and was trying to warn them of a repentance that bore no true fruit. A repentance that bears no fruit is a *dead repentance.* A repentance that doesn't elevate the sins is a *dead repentance.* A repentance that doesn't bring one's pride and righteous accomplishments down low is a *dead repentance.* A repentance that does no soul searching to remove spiritual obstacles from the heart is a *dead repentance.*

John's theology on man's heart would have surely been solid. Surely, John would have known that the heart of a man in its natural state was desperately wicked (Jeremiah 17:9), perverse (Proverbs 11:20), evil (Genesis 6:5), full of madness (Ecclesiastes 9:3), unwashed (Jeremiah 4:14), deceitful and deceived (Jeremiah 17:9), disloyal (Psalm 78:37), straying (Proverbs 7:25), impenitent (Deuteronomy 10:16), unbelieving (Hebrews 3:12), hard (Zechariah 7:12), proud (Proverbs 16:5), covetous (Jeremiah 22:17), murderous (Jeremiah 22:17), foolish (Proverbs 14:1), idolatrous (Ezekiel 14:3), rebellious (Jeremiah 5:23), stubborn (Jeremiah 18:12), and dull (Isaiah 6:10). The job of John was to shock the Jews out of cardiac arrest and bring about a true heart repentance.

In verse 8, he says, "And do not begin to say to yourselves, 'We have Abraham as our father.' For I tell you that out of these stones God can raise up children for Abraham." John is making quite a statement here. He knows that the Jews are inclined to say they are the covenant children of God based on their national heritage. He knows that they are going to say they are circumcised and have the covenant sign. He knows that they are going to say they have the law of Moses, the Levitical system, and more. However, John is telling them not to presume you are righteous just because of your affiliation. Don't presume that because you're a born Israelite that you have right standing with God. Don't presume to say that because you're a priest and have been circumcised in the flesh that you are eternally blessed by God.

Likewise, John's message bears weight today. Today's message to the church would be to say, "Don't presume because you've had a Christian baptism that you possess eternal life. Don't presume because you've made a profession of faith that you have eternal life or the Son. Don't presume because you've gone through confirmation that you have saving faith. Don't presume that because you're a part of a church that teaches biblical and orthodox doctrine that you are in the kingdom of God. No. Rather, you "need to produce fruit worthy of repentance."

Additionally, in verse 8, he says God is able from these stones to raise up children for Abraham. Once again, this was a hard and demeaning message. He has just gotten done calling them snakes and now he is saying that their position is no better than dirt. John is not calling them God's covenant people. He is saying that God can raise up dirt from the ground to be sons of Abraham. No doubt that this would have been incredibly offensive to the nation of Israel, but John's message of repentance was radical and demanded the people's heart be prepared for the Messiah.

Luke 3:9—*The ax is already at the root of the trees, and every tree that does not produce good fruit will be cut down and thrown into the fire.*

John is exhorting the Israelites to earnestly repent, but there is another element to repentance. Notice that John says, "The ax is already at the root of the trees." He is speaking of the urgency of needing to repent. The Israelites would have known what it meant for *the ax to be at the root of the tree*. This means that the one who is chopping down the tree only has one more swing of the ax before the tree falls. His ax has chopped away the bark and made it through the pulp and now there's only one more swing that will complete the fall of the tree. John was speaking of the urgency to repent. Not only had he clarified the nature of repentance, but now he was emphasizing the urgency of repentance. Don't wait one more day. Don't put this off. As John had referenced Isaiah 40, surely the people would have also remembered Isaiah 40:6–8, "All people are like grass, and all their faithfulness is like the flowers of the field. The grass withers and the flowers fall, because the breath of the LORD blows on them. Surely the people are grass. The grass withers and the flowers fall, but the word of our God endures forever." Surely, they would have known that time was of the essence in repentance. Jesus had also emphasized the point of urgently repenting when, in Luke 13:6–9, He gives a parable of a fig tree that has been given care for three years but has shown no fruit. While the man who was growing the fig tree was patient for three years, He gave it one more year to bear fruit otherwise He would cut it down. So, it is today that we must exhort men to repent. We can ascend no higher than John. We have no better message than what John, Jesus, or the apostles said. All men must repent and bear fruit worthy of repentance for their time on earth is short.

The next point John brings up is that a man that bears no fruit of repentance is not saved. The man that says he believes but produces no good fruit of repentance is an unbeliever and is unsaved. The condition of a man who bears no fruit of repentance is evidence that the man was never regenerated. It is evidence that this man never had saving faith. The end of this man is an eternal punishment of fire in hell. Let's also stop and pause to note that John says *"every"* tree that does not produce good fruit is cut down. There is no exception to this. Either a man bears fruits of repentance or he doesn't.

We also see that this fire is an unquenchable fire. In verse 17, He says that His winnowing fork is in His hand to clear His threshing floor and to gather the wheat into His barn, but He will burn up the chaff with unquenchable fire. Once again, John is saying that time is of the essence. The farmer is separating the wheat and the chaff. The wheat has already been harvested. It is no longer growing season, but it is now a time of separation. The wheat is brought into the *barn*, which refers to believers, but the *chaff*, which represents unbelievers, is burned up with unquenchable fire. In those days, the people would have known what John was talking about with "burning the chaff with unquenchable fire." They lived in an agricultural community. The people would have known that when you burn chaff the fire will eventually subside as it runs out of substrate and is quenched. However, John's theology on hell and eternal punishment lines right up with Jesus' theology on hell. Note that John says that *the chaff will be burned up with unquenchable fire,* which means that the fires of hell go on for all eternity. This is a fire that never diminishes, but rather, burns as a raging furnace. This was a fire that would not go out once it had consumed the chaff. No, this fire would persist forever. This fire would not go out. The fire would never be quenched. The chaff would never stop burning. A man that bears no fruit of repentance is on his way to an unquenchable fire that will never go out. Let us etch this in our minds that the Gospel contains many elements, but it must always include divine wrath, divine judgment, and repentance.

Often, we are too quick to say, "Put your faith in Jesus Christ and you will be saved." Let us learn from John that although the Gospel also includes an explanation of the person and work of Christ as well as the subjective elements of human response (i.e., faith), a faithful gospel preacher never leaves out divine wrath, divine judgment, and repentance as he warns men and calls them to the Lord Jesus Christ.

Luke 3:10–11— *"What should we do then?" the crowd asked. John answered, "Anyone who has two shirts should share with the one who has none, and anyone who has food should do the same."*

John continues to expound on his theology of repentance. Notice that John notes what true repentance will look like on the horizontal level or, rather, toward man. True repentance will love your neighbor as yourself. John would certainly have in mind Leviticus 19:18, "Do not seek revenge or bear a grudge against anyone among our people but love your neighbor as yourself. I am the LORD." John is saying that true repentance will show itself in loving your neighbor and meeting your neighbor's needs. He explains that there is not only a negative side to repentance, which is turning away from sin, but also a positive side to repentance, which is turning to righteousness that shows itself in acts of love that the LORD commands. Likewise, the half-brother of Jesus, James, describes a faith that saves and a faith that does not save. James describes a faith that has no care of meeting a neighbor's needs and concludes that a faith that cares nothing for his neighbor and cannot meet his neighbor's essential needs is a *dead faith (James 2:14–17).*

Also, notice in verse 10 that the crowd says, "What should we do then?" Perhaps this was an honest question. Perhaps the crowd was indeed earnest to know what they needed to do. However, one ominous note here is that they needed to ask what to do rather than being deeply convicted. Perhaps they were asking out of deep conviction, but perhaps they really had no conviction at all and were blind to their sins. The main point is that if your sins are brought up to you, confess them, ask for forgiveness, ask for God's help to deliver you from the sin, and repent.

Luke 3:12–14—*Even tax collectors came to be baptized. "Teacher," they asked, "what should we do?" "Don't collect any more than you are required to," he told them. Then some soldiers asked him,*

"And what should we do?" He replied, "Don't extort money and don't accuse people falsely—be content with your pay."

Here, John is expounding even more on true repentance. Here, John tells the tax collectors to be honest in their work and stop stealing. He tells soldiers not to steal and slander. John is talking about the negative side of repentance, which is the aspect of turning from sin. This is further highlighting Leviticus 19:18, which calls us to love our neighbor as ourselves. If we keep this command, we will not only positively love them by doing good to them, but we will also react in a negative sense where we will stop sinning against our neighbor. Not only this but look at the flow of John's theology of repentance. He first explains that there is divine judgment and wrath coming in verses 7–9, which could be considered a vertical repentance toward God, but then also talks about a horizontal aspect of repentance toward men. This is how we must present repentance to all men. We must warn men of the wrath of God that is coming. We must warn men that they must turn from their sin and turn to Christ in faith for salvation. We must also explain that all men must turn from their personal sin against God, but also sinning against man. John's theology on baptism of repentance for the forgiveness of sins was thorough and complete.

Luke 3:15–17—*The people were waiting expectantly and were all wondering in their hearts if John might possibly be the Messiah. John answered them all, "I baptize you with water. But one who is more powerful than I will come, the straps of whose sandals I am not worthy to untie. He will baptize you with the Holy Spirit and fire. His winnowing fork is in his hand to clear his threshing floor and to gather the wheat into his barn, but he will burn up the chaff with unquenchable fire."*

As we mentioned earlier, John is saying that the time of tilling, planting, growing, and harvesting is already done. The farmer has the wheat on his threshing floor. The farmer is throwing the wheat and chaff in the air to separate the two components. The chaff, which is lighter, will blow away and the wheat will fall in the same place. The separation is already occurring. Although there is debate over what *baptize with the Holy Spirit and fire* means, it is helpful to understand this verse in context. In context, to be baptized with the Holy Spirit indicates that this baptism ultimately ends in salvation and would refer to the wheat that is brought into the barn. On the other hand, the baptism of fire should be tied to the chaff as the chaff is ultimately burned up with fire, thus *baptism of fire*. In other words, you are either baptized with the Holy Spirit and saved or baptized with fire and judged unto condemnation. Only Jesus can baptize with the Holy Spirit and save man and He alone can judge men and send them to hell. Thus, true repentance turns away from sin and toward Jesus in faith.

We should also see that John the Baptist was continually telling the people that he could only baptize with water, that he was not the Messiah, and only the Messiah could baptize with the Holy Spirit and fire. The New Testament gives witness from Matthew (Matthew 3:11), Mark (Mark 1:8), Luke (Luke 3:16), the apostle John (John 1:31-33), John the Baptist (John 1:31-33), Jesus (Matthew 3:11–12; Mark 1:8; Luke 3:16, 24:49; John 1:31–33, 7:38–39, 14:15–17, 14:26, 15:26, 16:7; Acts 1:4–5, 2:17–18, 10:44–48, 11:16), Peter (Acts 2:17–18, 10:44–48, 11:16), and Paul (1 Corinthians 12:13, Titus 3:5-6) that man only baptizes with water, but Christ is the only one who baptizes with the Holy Spirit. John was very careful to point away from himself as the Messiah and toward Jesus who was the Messiah (John 1:29). We won't have time to fully develop the understanding of the definition of the *Holy Spirit* so, in lieu of this, a definition of *baptism with the Holy Spirit* could be understood as follows: **The baptism** with the Holy Spirit is the sovereign monergistic work of salvation performed by God the Father, God the Son, and God the Holy Spirit. The Holy Spirit is given from the Father to the Son (John 14:16, 15:26; Luke 11:13) and the Son pours out or gives the Holy Spirit in the Father's name (Matthew 3:11–12; Mark 1:8; Luke 3:16, 24:49; John 1:31–33; 14:16, 26; 15:26; 16:7; Acts 1:4–5, 2:17–18, 10:44–48, 11:16, Titus 3:6). The Holy Spirit then regenerates or causes man to be born again (John 3:3–10, Titus 3:5, Ezekiel 36:25–27) through hearing the Word of God/Gospel (James 1:18, Ephesians 1:13, Romans 1:15–17, 10:17, 1 Corinthians 1:21) which gives spiritual life to the previously spiritually dead man (Ephesians 2:1– 3, Colossians 2:13). God then grants man the ability to repent which is a gift (Acts 11:18, 2 Timothy 2:25) and put saving faith in Jesus Christ which is also a gift (Ephesians 2:8–9, Philippians 1:29, John 7:38–39). Man is then justified by grace through faith in Christ (Titus 3:7), receives and is indwelt by the Holy Spirit (Galatians 3:2, 3:14; Ephesians 1:13; 1 Corinthians 6:19), and the Holy Spirit spiritually unites/immerses man with Jesus Christ and puts the man into the body of Christ (1 Corinthians 12:13, Romans 6:3–4). Baptism with the Holy Spirit is not water baptism, and water baptism is not baptism with the Holy Spirit for only Christ can baptize with the Holy Spirit and man can only baptize with water (Matthew 3:11–12; Mark 1:8; Luke 3:16; John 1:31–33, 3:8, 7:38–39, 14:15–17, 26; 15:26, 16:7; Acts 1:4–5, 2:17–18, 10:44–48, 11:16; 1 Corinthians 1:17). Baptism with the Holy Spirit is a one-time, instantaneous, and salvific work of God (1 Corinthians 12:13).

In John's baptism of repentance for the forgiveness of sins, it would be a colossal mistake to think that the ritual of baptism is what forgave sins. John's message of repentance was radical, and John even warned against treating this baptism of repentance as just another ritual or ceremony. John was calling for heart searching repentance that would bear fruit. If there was no fruit of repentance, but only a baptism, John would have warned that the person who went through the baptism was chaff that was just waiting to be burned with unquenchable fire. A person that desired to confess and reject his sins, reject his spiritual accomplishments, and get rid of the barriers of the heart in preparation for the Messiah would have been characterized as wheat according to John. Now that we understand John the Baptist's message of repentance and the proselyte baptism he was preaching, let us turn our attention to John the Baptist's testimony of Jesus as Jesus comes to him to be baptized.

The Baptism of Jesus – Matthew 3:13-17

As we transition from John the Baptist's message of repentance, we will now observe Jesus' baptism. The apostle Matthew, who was one of the twelve disciples, gives us an account of Jesus' baptism. As Matthew was one of the twelve disciples (Matthew 10:3), it would be very reasonable to assume that Peter would have possessed the same knowledge as Matthew. Additionally, since we know that Andrew was also one of the twelve disciples of Jesus (Matthew 10:2), was also a disciple of John the Baptist (John 1:35-40), and lived with Peter (Mark 1:29), it would be reasonable to believe that Peter would have known these details of Jesus' baptism.

Matthew 3:13-14 – *Then Jesus came from Galilee to the Jordan to John, to be baptized by him. John would have prevented him, saying, "I need to be baptized by you, and do you come to me?"*

As we noted earlier, John's message of repentance was to turn the hearts of the people from sin and to the Messiah. John's message was confrontational and bold and was given to sinners. So, when Jesus came to be baptized by John we begin to see some confusion by John. At this point, it's unclear how John would have identified Jesus as the Christ. Perhaps John knew based on the testimony of Elizabeth, John's mother, where Elizabeth said to Mary in Luke 1:43, "And why is this granted to me that the mother of my Lord should come to me?". Here, we have a testimony from Elizabeth that the baby in Mary's womb was Elizabeth's Lord. Perhaps this is how John knew that Jesus was the Christ. We know that when Mary visited Elizabeth, she stayed with Elizabeth for three months (Luke 1:56). Perhaps during the three months, Mary told Elizabeth how the baby was conceived by the Holy Spirit (Luke 1:31, 35, Matthew 1:20). Perhaps Mary told Elizabeth that her son would be called Immanuel (Matthew 1:23). Perhaps, Mary told Elizabeth that this child would be named Jesus (Luke 1:31). Perhaps Mary told Elizabeth that the baby Jesus would be called Son of the Most High (Luke 1:32). Perhaps Mary told Elizabeth that Jesus would be given the throne of David, rule over the house of Jacob, and His kingdom would have no end (Luke 1:33). Perhaps Mary told Elizabeth that Jesus would be called the Son of God (Luke 1:35). Perhaps John the Baptist's parents told John these truths about Jesus.

However, there appears to be a better explanation of how John recognized that Jesus was sinless and the Messiah. In Matthew 3:5-6 it says, "Then Jerusalem and all Judea and all the region about the Jordan were going out to him, and they were baptized by him in the river Jordan, **confessing their sins**." Mark 1:5 says something similar where it says, "And all the country of Judea and all Jerusalem were going out to him and were being baptized by him in the river Jordan, **confessing their sins**." Both Matthew 3:6 and Mark 1:5 say that the people were confessing their sins. The word for "confessing" comes from *exomologeó*. It is a compound word with *ek* meaning "wholly out from" which intensifies *homologéō* which means "to say the same thing." Properly, *exomologeó* means to "fully agree and to acknowledge" or "to openly confess and declare without reservation." Thus, all of the people from Jerusalem and Judea were openly confessing their sins as they were baptized. However, when Jesus would come to be baptized, there were no sins to be confessed by the Messiah for He was and is without sin. Therefore, as Jesus was coming to be baptized, it may have shocked or caught John off guard that Jesus confessed no sins as there were no sins to repent of. Perhaps this absence of confessing sins by Jesus is what caused John to identify Jesus as the Messiah. It can be certain that Jesus would not have lied and confessed any sins as such an act by Jesus would have been a lie and a sin. The absence of a confession of sins would likely have led John to understand this truth about Jesus. Regardless, John was baptizing many people, and he distinguished and discerned that there was something different about Jesus.

As Jesus would approach John the Baptist for His baptism, John was preventing Jesus from being baptized. In fact, the word for "hindered" is *diakóluó* which is a compound word and it means to "obstinately prevent" or "utterly prohibit." John wasn't just suggesting that Jesus not be baptized, he was actively preventing Jesus from this baptism. John's reason for not baptizing Jesus is abundantly clear where he said to Jesus, "I need to be baptized by you, and do you come to me?" Essentially, John had enough knowledge to know that he was a sinner and Jesus was sinless. John saw Jesus as sinless which is why John was trying to prevent Jesus from being baptized. The thought of Jesus, who was and is sinless, being baptized by a sinner who preached a gentile, proselyte, heart-turning repentance made no sense to John.

Matthew 3:15 – *But Jesus answered him, "Let it be so now, for thus it is fitting for us to fulfill all righteousness." Then he consented.*

We begin to understand why Jesus needed to be baptized by John. Let's notice that Jesus said this baptism was needed to fulfill all righteousness. This baptism was not for Jesus' sins as Jesus is holy, blameless, pure, and set apart from sinners (Hebrews

7:26). This baptism was part of Christ fulfilling all righteousness (Matthew 3:15, 5:17-20). Part of Christ's righteousness included submitting to His Father's will to be baptized by John the Baptist. This is an important point that Christ is making. In some religious denominations, water baptism is considered as God working as the agent in baptism and, thus, is not a work. However, Christ categorizes water baptism as a work. Christ's water baptism was a part of His perfect obedience and sinless life. Therefore, Matthew is making a point that this baptism was part of Christ's perfect obedience, sinless life, and fulfillment of all righteousness.

When Jesus explained to John that His baptism was needed to fulfill all righteousness, we see John agrees to baptize Jesus knowing that he is a sinner and Jesus is sinless. Perhaps, at this point, John knew that although he didn't fully understand why Jesus needed to be baptized, he realized that he was standing in the way of Jesus fulfilling all righteousness which was to stand in the way of God's purposes. Therefore, we see that Jesus' explanation was sufficient for John to stop prohibiting Jesus from fulfilling all righteousness and standing in the way of God's will and purpose.

Theologians give many points on the purpose of Christ's baptism. Many would say that this was part of Christ's perfect obedience to the Father's will and fulfilling all righteousness. Many would say that Christ was identifying Himself with sinners. Many would say that this was the launch of His earthly ministry. Many would say that this pre-figured what water baptism was meant to symbolize. All of these points are valid and help explain Christ's baptism.

Matthew 3:16 – *And when Jesus was baptized, immediately he went up from the water, and behold, the heavens were opened to him, and he saw the Spirit of God descending like a dove and coming to rest on him.*

After Jesus was baptized, Matthew notes that the heavens were opened to Him and John saw the Holy Spirit descending on Jesus as a dove and resting on Him. Much could be made of the Holy Spirit resting on Jesus as a dove. Some would suggest that the dove was a symbol as a sacrificial animal. The bull was a sacrificial animal for the rich, the lamb was the sacrificial animal for the middle class, and the dove was the sacrificial animal for the poor (Leviticus 1:14).

However, the main point that should be emphasized is that the Holy Spirit had anointed Jesus for His earthly ministry. In Jesus' first message to His hometown in Nazareth, He read Isaiah 61:1 which says, "The Spirit of the Lord God is upon me, because the LORD has anointed me to bring good news to the poor; he has sent me to bind up the brokenhearted, to proclaim liberty to the captives, and the opening of the prison to those who are bound" and then proclaimed that this prophecy was fulfilled, meaning that He was the Anointed One of God to proclaim the gospel (Luke 4:18-21). Peter saw and proclaimed this very truth to the household of Cornelius where he said this in Acts 10:38, "how God anointed Jesus of Nazareth with the Holy Spirit and with power. He went about doing good and healing all those who were oppressed by the devil, for God was with him." Therefore, let us see that John saw the Holy Spirit descend on and anoint Jesus which was Jesus' inauguration of His earthly ministry.

Matthew 3:17 – *and behold, a voice from heaven said, "This is my beloved Son, with whom I am well pleased."*

Here, we see the Father giving a testimony of His only begotten, one-of-a-kind Son. The Father's testimony was that Jesus was and is the Son of God. Additionally, we see that Jesus is the beloved Son of God with whom the Father is well pleased. The word "beloved" comes from *agapétos* which properly means "divinely loved." To be the Son of God is to be of the same substance of God and co-equal and co-eternal with God. Thus, when the Father calls Jesus His Son, He is stating that Jesus is His Son and possess all of the qualities and attributes of God meaning Jesus is eternal, omnipotent, merciful, kind, good, loving, omniscient, faithful, immutable, omnipresent, all-wise, wrathful, and holy. Likewise, just as the Son is co-eternal and co-equal with the Father, we see that the Holy Spirit is also co-equal and co-eternal with the Father and shares the same substance with the Son and the Father and is thus, God the Holy Spirit.

Additionally, we see that Jesus is the Father's Son with whom He is well pleased. This is to say that the eternal Son of God was and is well-pleasing to the Father. God cannot look on sin with favor (Habbakuk 1:13). Because God is love (1 John 4:8), He hates sin and cannot look on it with favor (Genesis 3). Because God loves righteousness (Psalm 11:7), He is not pleased with wickedness (Psalm 5:4). Therefore, God the Father's testimony of His Son is one where He affirms Jesus' deity and sinlessness. All three members of the Godhead are present at Jesus' baptism. The Son begins His earthly ministry as the sinless Messiah. The Holy Spirit anoints the Son for His ministry. The Father attests to the deity and sinless nature of His Son.

As we close this section, let us keep in mind this testimony of Christ. John the Baptist is witness to these events. Andrew, Peter's brother, is a disciple of John the Baptist. Matthew, one of the twelve disciples of the Lord Jesus Christ wrote this under the inspiration of the Holy Spirit. This is all to say that Peter would have had knowledge of these events. After Jesus' baptism, He is led out into the wilderness to be tempted by Satan for forty days (Matthew 4:1, Mark 1:12).

John the Baptist's Testimony of Jesus - John 1:29-34

As we transition back to John's testimony of Jesus, we see John give a testimony to the priests and Levites from Jerusalem.

John openly gives a testimony of who he is. John testifies that he is not the Christ (John 1:20). John testifies that he is not Elijah (John 1:21). John testifies that he is not the prophet foretold by Moses in Deuteronomy 18 (John 1:21). However, John confessed that he was the prophecy of the voice of one crying in the wilderness to prepare the way of the Lord as spoken by Isaiah (John 1:23). The priests and Levites then ask John why he is baptizing since John is not the Christ, not the prophet, and not Elijah (John 1:25). John will reply that he baptizes with water, but there is one who is greater and whose sandal strap he's unworthy to untie (John 1:26). John was essentially giving testimony that he was commissioned by God for this ministry to prepare the way for the Messiah.

John 1:29 – *The next day he saw Jesus coming toward him, and said, "Behold, the Lamb of God, who takes away the sin of the world!*

Jesus has just returned from being tempted forty days in the wilderness by the devil. For the purposes of this book, we won't go into the details of the temptation of Jesus. However, Matthew and Luke both demonstrate Jesus' sinless nature in that Jesus resists Satan's temptation to distrust God in the dangerous wilderness, without food and drink, and all while being tempted for forty days. However, we see that Adam was in the Garden of Eden, with food and drink, enjoying communion with God, but fell to the temptations of the devil by not trusting God's command and eating fruit from the tree of the knowledge of good and evil. Thus, Jesus has returned from His temptation demonstrating that He is holy, innocent, unstained, and separate from sinners (Hebrews 7:26). This is where we'll pick up John's testimony of Jesus.

We see that John will give a testimony on the person and work of the Lord Jesus Christ. John sees Jesus coming toward him and recognizes Him and says, "Behold, the Lamb of God, who takes away the sin of the world!" John has just made a testimony of epic proportion and one of massive theological depth. Notice that John doesn't call Jesus the one who will dash the nations and rulers in pieces like a potter's vessel (Psalm 2:9). Although Jesus is the King of heaven and earth (Psalm 47:6-7), John calls Jesus the "Lamb of God who takes away the sin of the world!", which is a testimony to Jesus' sinless nature, Jesus being God's chosen servant, and Jesus being a sacrificial lamb that will provide forgiveness of sins. This testimony of John should have brought the Jews right back to the Levitical sacrificial system. This testimony should have triggered the Jews to understand the purpose of Jesus' ministry. To understand the significance of John's statement, let us turn to Leviticus 1:1-9 to understand the burnt offering. Leviticus 1:10-13 will give the instructions for sacrificing a lamb, but for the sake of depth, we'll review Leviticus 1:1-9 which are the instructions for sacrificing a bull.

The book of Leviticus was to teach the people that they were sinful and God was holy. We see this in Leviticus 11:45 where the LORD told the Israelites, "I am the LORD, who brought you up out of Egypt to be your God; therefore be holy, because I am holy." The LORD was teaching His people that He was separate from everything created and He was certainly separate from sinful man. The LORD was to be worshipped differently than all other gods of the pagan nations. He was teaching the Israelites that they were sinful and could not approach Him or worship Him on their own terms because He was and is a holy God. Chapters one through seven of Leviticus help us understand how the offerings were to typologically represent Christ. The burnt offering was to represent Christ's atonement and sinless nature (Leviticus 1:3–17, 6:8–13). The grain offering was to represent Christ's dedication/consecration and the complete dedication and devotion to the Father's will and purposes (Leviticus 2:1–16, 6:14–23). The fellowship offering was to represent Christ's reconciliation/fellowship and the peace He had with God. The sin offering was to represent Christ's propitiation for sin and His substitutionary death for sinners (Leviticus 4:1–5:13, 6:24–30). The guilt offering was to represent Christ paying the ransom and redemption for sin (Leviticus 5:14–6:7; 7:1–10). As we examine the burnt offering, it is important to note and identify the several aspects of worship that the LORD was instructing His people through this offering as Peter was able to look back at the sacrificial system and make the connections to how Christ fulfilled the sacrificial system (2, 3, 4, 5).

Leviticus 1:1–2—*The LORD called Moses and spoke to him from the tent of meeting, saying, "Speak to the people of Israel and say to them, When any one of you brings an offering to the LORD, you shall bring your offering of livestock from the herd or from the flock.*

The *tent of meeting* or the *tabernacle* was where God would meet with His people and receive worship. It is where the glory of the LORD would rest and dwell or reside among the Israelites (Exodus 25:22). It was a place where the Israelites would come and hear God's commands.

First, we learn that the burnt offering was an offering to the LORD. This was not an offering to Satan, nor to Molech, nor to Dagon, nor to the priests, nor to man, nor to the nation of Israel, nor to any other false god. This was an offering that was given directly to the LORD. This was an offering that needed to please the LORD. This offering needed to be brought on His terms. This offering could not be brought on man's terms, but only on the LORD's terms alone for God is a consuming fire (Deuteronomy 9:3). We see this in Leviticus 1:13 that when offered on the LORD's terms, "It is a burnt offering, a food offering, an aroma pleasing to the LORD." In fact, we see in Amos 5:21 that when the worshipper did not bring the burnt offering to God according to His prescribed instruction, He was not pleased with them where He says, "I hate, I despise your feasts, and I take no delight in your solemn assemblies. Even though you offer me your burnt offerings and grain offerings, I will not accept them. And the peace offerings of your fattened animals, I will not look upon them." Additionally, we see that when an offering was given, but the one offering the gift lived in opposition to God's will and ways, He was not pleased with the offering where He says in Jeremiah 6:20, "What use to me is frankincense that comes from Sheba, or sweet cane from a distant land? Your burnt offerings are not acceptable, nor your sacrifices pleasing to me." Here, we can see that simply offering the burnt offering, but living in opposition to God, is not what He desired. So, if there was no sacrifice, there was no access to fellowship with God. In fact, the root word for *offering* is *qarab* which can also mean "to come near." Thus, we see that to draw near to the LORD required a sacrifice or offering that was given to the LORD on His terms or prescribed instruction.

Second, we learn that the burnt offering was to be a submissive or domesticated animal from one's own herd. The regulation excluded horses, dogs, pigs, camels, donkeys, lions, and birds of prey that were used in other pagan sacrifices. It was to be a sacrifice from one's own cattle, sheep, goats, or non-predatory bird. Only domestic animals could be sacrificed. Only defenseless animals that needed to be defended were brought. This was to ultimately be a picture of the humble and submissive sacrifice of the Lord Jesus Christ. Christ didn't go to Calvary as a roaring lion or the Lion of the tribe of Judah. Rather this pictured an animal as in Isaiah 53:7, "He was oppressed, and he was afflicted, yet he opened not his mouth; like a lamb that is led to the slaughter, and like a sheep that before its shearers is silent, so he opened not his mouth."

Leviticus 1:3— "*If his offering is a burnt offering from the herd, he shall offer a male without blemish. He shall bring it to the en-*

trance of the tent of meeting, that he may be accepted before the LORD.

Third, we see that the burnt offering had to be without blemish. The LORD provided provisions on what a defect was. It was not to be blind, injured, maimed, have warts, have festering sores, have running sores, be deformed, be stunted, have bruised testicles that were crushed, torn, or cut, and it must be of a certain age (Leviticus 22:17–33). They were to pick a sacrifice that was their best. They were to learn to give the best and most valuable livestock to the LORD. They were to learn that the sacrifice was to have no defects and only the best sacrifice with no blemishes was fit to be offered to the LORD. In fact, Israel would be reminded that offering a blemished animal was an affront and a sin. The LORD confronts the priests and people for offering blemished offerings in Malachi 1:6–14, where He says this:

> *"A son honors his father, and a servant his master. If then I am a father, where is my honor? And if I am a master, where is my fear? says the LORD of hosts to you, O priests, who despise my name. But you say, 'How have we despised your name?' By offering polluted food upon my altar. But you say, 'How have we polluted you?' By saying that the LORD's table may be despised. When you offer blind animals in sacrifice, is that not evil? And when you offer those that are lame or sick, is that not evil? Present that to your governor; will he accept you or show you favor? says the LORD of hosts. And now entreat the favor of God, that he may be gracious to us. With such a gift from your hand, will he show favor to any of you? says the LORD of hosts. Oh that there were one among you who would shut the doors, that you might not kindle fire on my altar in vain! I have no pleasure*

> *in you, says the LORD of hosts, and I will not accept an offering from your hand. For from the rising of the sun to its setting my name will be great among the nations, and in every place incense will be offered to my name, and a pure offering. For my name will be great among the nations, says the LORD of hosts. But you profane it when you say that the Lord's table is polluted, and its fruit, that is, its food may be despised. But you say, 'What a weariness this is,' and you snort at it, says the LORD of hosts.* You bring what has been taken by violence or is lame or sick, and this you bring as your offering! *Shall I accept that from your hand? says the LORD. Cursed be the cheat who has a male in his flock, and vows it, and yet sacrifices to the Lord what is blemished. For I am a great King, says the LORD of hosts, and my name will be feared among the nations.*

The burnt offering with no blemish was to foreshadow Christ. Peter calls Christ the spotless lamb in his letter in 1 Peter 1:18- 19 where he says, "knowing that you were ransomed from the futile ways inherited from your forefathers, not with perishable things such as silver or gold, but with the precious blood of Christ, like that of a lamb without blemish or spot." Peter also says this about Christ's sinless nature when he references Isaiah 53:9 in 1 Peter 2:22 where he says, "He committed no sin, neither was deceit found in his mouth." Paul said it another way in 1 Corinthians 5:7, where he says, "For Christ, our Passover lamb, has been sacrificed." Peter and Paul saw that Christ was the sinless lamb without blemish. Peter and Paul saw that the lamb without blemish was to be sacrificed for sin. Peter and Paul saw that God chose the very best sacrifice for sin that could be offered, His only beloved Son, the Lord Jesus Christ. Therefore, the burnt offering was to be spotless and without blemish as it foreshadowed the sinless and perfect nature of the Lord Jesus Christ.

Leviticus 1:4—*He shall lay his hand on the head of the burnt offering, and it shall be accepted for him to make atonement for him.*

Fourth, we learn that the burnt offering was to be an acknowledgment of sin. The symbolic gesture of placing one's hand on the head of the animal was to show the transfer of sins from the one sacrificing the animal to the sacrificial animal. This symbolic gesture was also meant to bring about repentance. The transferring of sin to the sacrificial animal was to bring about sorrow for sin against the LORD and teach His people that there was a penalty of death for sin.

Fifth, we learn that with the burnt offering the LORD was teaching that there was to be a substitutionary atonement. This substitutionary sacrifice would prefigure Christ. Isaiah 53:11–12 captures this substitutionary atonement where it says, "Out of the anguish of his soul he shall see and be satisfied; by his knowledge shall the righteous one, my servant, make many to be accounted righteous, and he shall bear their iniquities. Therefore, I will divide him a portion with the many, and he shall divide the spoil with the strong, because he poured out his soul to death and was numbered with the transgressors; yet he bore the sin of many and makes intercession for the transgressors." The LORD was teaching that sin was going to be dealt with through a substitutionary atonement that took the punishment for sin.

Sixth, we learn that the burnt offering was to be an atonement. We learn this when it says, "It shall be accepted for him" and "to make atonement for him." The word *atonement* comes from *kaphar* and means "to cover over" or "propitiate." This prefigured Christ in that Christ would ultimately be the once-for-all atonement for sin (Hebrews 7:26–27, 9:24–28). This atonement was to show God's people that there would be a substitutionary atonement that would cover the sacrificer's sin so God could no longer see it. Isaiah 43:25 expresses this idea of atonement where it says, "I, I am he who blots out your transgressions for my own sake and I will not remember your sins." Isaiah 44:22 also conveys this idea of covering sins where it says, "I have blotted out your transgressions like a cloud and your sins like mist; return to me, for I have redeemed you." Micah 7:19 captures this as well on how a substitutionary atonement would cover sin, "He will again have compassion on us; he will tread our iniquities underfoot. You will cast all our sins into the depths of the sea." We see that David counts the blessedness of one whose sins the LORD does not count against him where he says this in Psalm 32:1–2, "Blessed is the one whose transgression is forgiven, whose sin is covered. Blessed is the man against whom the LORD counts no iniquity, and in whose spirit there is no deceit." Peter saw this atonement and the covering of sins where he identifies Christ as the only propitiation for sinners where he says this in 1 Peter 2:24, "He himself bore our sins in his body on the tree, that we might die to sin and live to righteousness. By his wounds you have been healed." Peter eventually saw that the Father had punished His only Son with the wrath that sinners deserve, and Christ was the atonement or propitiation for sin.

Leviticus 1:5–8—*Then he shall kill the bull before the LORD, and Aaron's sons the priests shall bring the blood and throw the blood against the sides of the altar that is at the entrance of the tent of meeting. Then he shall flay the burnt offering and cut it into pieces, and the sons of Aaron the priest shall put fire on the altar and arrange wood on the fire. And Aaron's sons the priests shall arrange the pieces, the head, and the fat, on the wood that is on the fire on the altar;*

Seventh, we learn that sin was to be a vivid picture of the ugliness of sin. Everything about the sacrifice was to show how grotesque sin was. The one offering the sacrifice was to put his hands on the head of the animal and then slaughter the animal. The one sacrificing the animal was to see the effects of his sin passed on to the animal. The one sacrificing the animal would slit the throat of the bull and then start seeing the ugliness of sin and death. The one sacrificing the animal would hear the horrific noise of the animal as the animal would scream in pain. The one sacrificing the animal would see blood gush out of the animal and the one sacrificing would see the animal's life ebb away. The one sacrificing the animal would the smell the horrible smell of blood. This was all meant to shock the senses of the one sacrificing. This was to be a brutal picture of the horrendous nature of sin. The one sacrificing was to picture himself as the one deserving the animal's fate. This was an event that should have left the one sacrificing the offering aghast at his sin. This should have drove a sword straight to the heart of the one sacrificing. It would not be out of line of the one sacrificing to say something like this, "LORD, I see my sin. I see that you cannot look at me or accept me based on any merit. I see that you are angry and abhor my sin. I see that I should be the one who should be slaughtered. I see that I am the one who should have my throat slit. I see that if I were to enter your temple, you would need to strike me dead because I am loathsome and you are holy." This was to be the most graphic picture of the ugliness of sin.

The priest was then to sprinkle the blood against the altar. The one sacrificing the burnt offering would be bloody. The priest would be bloody. The LORD was showing to the Israelite nations and the Gentile nations that He was the God that could not tolerate sin. Again, this hearkens us back to Leviticus 11:45, "So you shall be holy, because I am holy." The LORD was showing the sinfulness of man and the holiness of God. Paul saw the ugliness of sin. Peter saw the devastation of sin. Peter saw that God the Father had but one Son. Peter could look back on the cross and see that the Father punished His one and only Son with divine wrath (1 Peter 2:24). Peter saw that Jesus was the sacrificial Lamb who committed no sin (1 Peter 1:19, 2:22), was reviled (1 Peter 2:23), suffered (1 Peter 2:23), bore the sins of His people on the cross (1 Peter 2:24), and ransomed His people with His precious blood and sacrificial and substitutionary death (1 Peter 1:19).

Leviticus 1:9—*but its entrails and its legs he shall wash with water. And the priest shall burn all of it on the altar, as a burnt offering, a food offering[a] with a pleasing aroma to the LORD.*

Ninth, we understand that in the burnt offering the LORD wanted to show that the internal motives, intentions, and will needed to be pure and clean. The LORD commanded that the entrails and legs be washed with water. Commentators will vary on this and they will note that the entrails and legs needed to be washed with water to ensure there was no excrement that was put on the altar. However, we can know that the LORD desires a circumcised heart and a heart that loved Him totally as He says in Deuteronomy 10:12, 16, "And now, Israel, what does the LORD your God require of you, but to fear the LORD your God, to walk in all his ways, to love him, to serve the LORD your God with all your heart and with all your soul . . . Circumcise therefore the foreskin of your heart, and be no longer stubborn."

The LORD was not only wanting a sacrifice that was without blemish, but He was also wanting one that was fully devoted to Him. Of course, this points to Christ. Christ did nothing of His own will and fully submitted to the will of His Father. This is captured in John 5:19, where it says, "So Jesus said to them, 'Truly, truly, I say to you, the Son can do nothing of his own accord, but only what he sees the Father doing. For whatever the Father does, that the Son does likewise.'" The Lord Jesus Christ lived His perfect and sinless life in full and total submission to His Father. Thus, we see that the LORD desired purity from the inside and Christ Jesus did this perfectly. He looked not to His own needs, but fully submitted Himself to the will and purpose of the Father.

Tenth, we see that the burnt offering was to undergo divine judgment. The fire that was used to burn up the sacrifice was to represent divine judgment on behalf of the sinner. The one sacrificing the offering was to see himself as one deserving divine judgment. As we know, Christ fulfilled this as the perfect, blameless, and spotless sacrifice for sinners. Isaiah 53:10 captures this divine judgment of the Suffering Servant where it says, "Yet it was the will of the LORD to crush him; he has put him to grief; when his soul makes an offering for guilt, he shall see his offspring; he shall prolong his days; the will of the LORD shall prosper in his hands." God the Father treated His own Son like the burnt offering and pronounced divine judgment on His Son in place of sinners. The LORD was teaching His people and the Gentile nations that a substitutionary sacrifice needed to be slaughtered and undergo divine judgment in the place for sinners. Peter talks about this divine judgment in 1 Peter 2:24 where he says, "He himself bore our sins in his body on the tree, that we might die to sin and live to righteousness. By his wounds you have been healed." Paul says a similar statement in Galatians 3:13 where he says, "Christ redeemed us from the curse of the law by becoming a curse for us—for it is written, 'Cursed is everyone who is hanged on a tree.'" Therefore, we know that Peter understood that when Christ "bore our sins in his body on the tree," he knew that Jesus was being cursed as if He was the sinner, though He had done no wrong.

Christ was cursed with every curse that had been promised to sinners (Deuteronomy 28:15–68). Christ taught what this curse would look like in the Beatitudes. Since a curse is the opposite of a blessing, we can see how Christ was cursed. Christ was cursed as one being refused entrance into the kingdom of God (Matthew 5:3). Christ was cursed as one receiving divine pain and retribution rather than divine comfort (Matthew 5:4). Christ was cursed as being cut off from His Father's inheritance rather than receiving the Father's inheritance (Matthew 5:5). Christ was cursed as one who would receive misery and wretchedness rather than divine satisfaction (Matthew 5:6). Christ was cursed as one receiving divine punishment rather than divine mercy (Matthew 5:7). Christ was cursed as one who was forsaken and cut off from His Father rather than one who would see God (Matthew 5:8). To be cursed by God was to undergo the white-hot wrath of God the Father. The only people that have an idea of what this wrath is like are those who are suffering in hell. Upon the cross, the Father poured out His full furious and fiery wrath on the Lord Jesus Christ and turned His face away from His Son (Matthew 27:46).

In Matthew 25:31-46, Jesus explains how everyone will be judged. In this explanation, He states that the goats, or rather, those who refuse to repent and put their faith in Christ are cursed and the sheep, or rather, those who repent and put their faith in Christ are blessed. So how does the Lord treat the unrepentant and unbelieving goats? He says this of the goats in Matthew 25:41, "Depart from me, **you cursed**, into the eternal fire prepared for the devil and his angels." In Galatians 3:13 it says, "Christ redeemed us from the curse of the law by **becoming a curse for us** – for it is written, 'Cursed is everyone who is hanged on a tree'". When Jesus Christ was on the cross, He was treated as a cursed sinner. The punishment for sin is hell. Christ suffered this punishment on the cross for the elect. Only an eternal God could suffer an eternal punishment. Only the Son of God and Son of Man could propitiate the righteous wrath of God the Father. One cannot even comprehend the wrath that was poured out on the Son. Just one lustful intent is enough to damn a man's soul and cast him into hell for all eternity (Matthew 5:28). Upon the cross, Jesus absorbed the full fiery wrath from His Father for the sins of all who would be saved. If one sin is not paid for, man would remain damned. If one sin were left unpunished, man would remain cursed. If one sin is not propitiated, man would remain indebted and damned. If one sin is not atoned for, man would remain condemned. Imagine if a father could take the sun, which at its core is 27 million degrees Fahrenheit, and lift it up and cast it down on his son to crush him and then turn his back on his child as the child was left to suffer. Imagine the father crushing his son with the full weight and heat of the sun, turning his back on his son, and saying, "I cannot and will not look upon my beloved son with favor as I curse him and crush him." This is but a pathetic example of the wrath that the Father poured out on His Son. The Father's wrath for sin is far greater than we will ever know. The purposeful, eternal, rich and bountiful love that was demonstrated by God the Father to curse His Son on the cross in place for sinners who rebel against Him is unfathomable to the human mind. On the cross, God punished Jesus for every sin of every person of human history who would be redeemed with His all-knowing and all-powerful wrath.

Eleventh, we see that when the burnt offering is offered up to the LORD on His terms, it is an aroma pleasing to Him. As we noted earlier, atonement was used to talk about the LORD making a covering for sin. The word *atonement* had been translated to *propitiation* in the Septuagint. *Propitiation* was used to describe an offering by which the wrath of a deity had been appeased. Therefore, we can see that the burnt offering allowed the LORD to be satisfied because an animal without defect had been selected by the worshipper sacrificing to Him and had acknowledged that their sin was so vile and loathsome that it deserved to be punished by death and undergo divine judgment. Therefore, the LORD's wrath was propitiated, and it was an offering that was a food offering that was a pleasing aroma to the LORD. Therefore, we can understand that Peter came to know of Christ's substitutionary atonement for sinners by taking the wrath of God in the place of sinners. Peter saw that Christ was the fulfillment of the Levitical sacrificial system where he says this in 1 Peter 1:18-19, "knowing that you were ransomed from the futile ways inherited from your forefathers, not with perishable things such as silver or gold, but with the precious blood of Christ, like that of a lamb without blemish or spot." Peter saw that animals were sacrificed in the morning and evening every day. Peter may have seen the mass sacrificing of animals in Jerusalem during Passover which could range in the tens of thousands to hundreds of thousands. Peter eventually saw Christ as the sacrificial, once for all, Passover Lamb.

This is what the Jews should have understood. They should have understood John's claim that Christ was the sacrificial Lamb that would take away sins. They should have understood that their sins needed to be forgiven. They should have understood the substitutionary nature of the burnt offering. They should have understood that the sacrificial animal needed to be sinless and without blemish. They should have understood the sacrificial animal needed to be killed. They should have understood the ugliness of sin. They should have seen the divine punishment for their sin of an animal being burnt up. John's testimony of Jesus being the Lamb of God who takes away the sins of the world carried the full weight and truth of Christ being the sinless, spotless, blameless, and chosen Lamb of God who would need to undergo divine judgment, divine wrath, and death to propitiate the righteous wrath of God to forgive sinful men.

John 1:30 – *This is he of whom I said, 'After me comes a man who ranks before me, because he was before me.'*

John now gives a testimony of Christ's preeminence. John is not stating that Jesus came before him in birth. In fact, Elizabeth, John's mother, was in her sixth month of pregnancy when the angel Gabriel announced to Mary that she would give birth to Jesus (Luke 1:26-31). Therefore, Jesus did not come before John in birth. Jesus was born after John. Therefore, John is simply testifying to the eternality and preeminence of Jesus. Jesus ranks ahead of John because Jesus is the Lamb of God (John 1:29), the Anointed One (John 1:32), the baptizer with the Holy Spirit (John 1:33), and the Son of God (John 1:33). Jesus ranks ahead of John because the One who is co-equal and co-eternal with God the Father and God the Holy Spirit is greater than John. John was constantly pointing people to the Lord Jesus Christ.

John 1:31 – *I myself did not know him, but for this purpose I came baptizing with water, that he might be revealed to Israel."*

Although there appears to be a contradiction in John's testimony, this can easily be understood with our exposition of Matthew 3:13-14. It is true that John was sent to baptize with water so that Jesus could be revealed to Israel. Since John was in the wilderness of Judea (Matthew 3:1), it is likely that he did not have a close relationship with Jesus, and thus, didn't know or recognize Him.

The most likely explanation behind John's comment is that he did not know or recognize Jesus as the Messiah, up until Jesus came for His baptism. John was continually baptizing all the people from Jerusalem and Judea who were openly confessing their sins as they were baptized. However, when Jesus would come to be baptized, there would be no sins to be confessed by the Messiah for He was and is without sin. Therefore, as Jesus was coming to be baptized, it may have shocked or caught John off guard that Jesus confessed no sins as there were no sins to repent of. It is most likely that John didn't recognize Jesus as the Messiah until he saw Jesus' absence of confessing sins for Jesus would be a liar and a sinner if he confessed sins. The absence of a confession of sins would likely have led John to identify the truth of who Jesus was.

Therefore, as Jesus came to be baptized, John saw that there was no confession of sin from sinless Jesus. Upon this recognition, John realized that he was in need of being baptized by Jesus (Matthew 3:13-14). However, when Jesus explained that this needed to be done to fulfill all righteousness, John agreed to the baptism of Jesus that would reveal Him as the Anointed One (Matthew 3:15).

John 1:32-34 – *And John bore witness: "I saw the Spirit descend from heaven like a dove, and it remained on him. I myself did not know him, but he who sent me to baptize with water said to me, 'He on whom you see the Spirit descend and remain, this is he who baptizes with the Holy Spirit.' And I have seen and have born witness that this is the Son of God."*

John's testimony of Jesus hearkens back to the good news he was continually preaching as well as the testimony of God the Father at Jesus' baptism. We see that Jesus was anointed by the Holy Spirit at His baptism. We see that John's ministry was given to Him by the Father. When John says, "He who sent me," he is testifying that the Father commissioned him for ministry to preach and baptize with water. We see that Jesus is the one who baptizes with the Holy Spirit. The baptism with the Holy Spirit is a sovereign work of salvation which only God can perform. Jesus would later clarify this in His discussion with Nicodemus where He says, "The wind blows where it wishes, and you hear its sound, but you do not know where it comes from or where it goes. So it is with everyone who is born of the Spirit." Essentially, Jesus was explaining that the Holy Spirit could not be controlled, coerced, or commanded by man. The Holy Spirit operates by divine sovereignty. Lastly, we see that John testifies that Jesus is the Son of God. Therefore, in just five verses, John proclaims the following:

- Jesus is the sacrificial Lamb of God who will take away the sins of the world
- Jesus is preeminent and eternal
- Jesus is the Anointed One of God, or rather, the Christ or Messiah
- Jesus is the only one who will baptize with the Holy Spirit
- Jesus is the Son of God

Let us keep this in mind as we transition to Andrew introducing Peter to Jesus as Andrew was one of John the Baptist's disciples. Therefore, we can understand that Andrew, Peter's brother, with whom he shared a house, would have surely shared John the Baptist's testimony of Jesus with Peter.

Chapter 2

Peter's Pre-Conversion Life – Learning from Jesus

John 3:7 – *Do not marvel that I said to you, 'You must be born again.'*

As we begin this next chapter, we will see that there is a transition where John the Baptist will point His disciples to Christ. One of the disciples that will follow Christ will be Andrew, Peter's brother. This chapter will connect everything we learned about John the Baptist to Jesus to demonstrate that Peter would have had significant knowledge of John the Baptist's message and ministry as he started following Jesus. We will also examine Jesus teaching Nicodemus on the new birth and salvation, John the Baptist's final testimony of Jesus, and Jesus' sermon to His hometown of Nazareth. By doing this, we will come to understand that Peter would have learned much about regeneration, salvation, and more on the person and work of the Lord Jesus Christ.

Andrew Introduces Peter to Jesus, the Messiah – John 1:35-42

John 1:35-37 – *The next day again John was standing with two of his disciples, and he looked at Jesus as he walked by and said, "Behold, the Lamb of God!" The two disciples heard him say this, and they followed Jesus.*

The very next day, we see that two of John's disciples are with him as John points out Jesus as the Lamb of God. John was continually pointing people toward Christ. As John would look at Jesus and testify that Jesus was the Lamb of God, this triggers John's disciples to follow Jesus. As we'll learn shortly, one of the disciples is Andrew, Peter's brother.

John 1:38-39 – *Jesus turned and saw them following and said to them, "What are you seeking?" and they said to him, "Rabbi" (which means Teacher), "Where are you staying?" He said to them, "Come and you will see." So they came and saw where he was staying, and they stayed with him that day, for it was about the tenth hour.*

John has pointed two of his disciples to Jesus and these two disciples are now following Jesus. Here we see something of the character and qualities of Andrew and the other disciple, who was most likely the apostle John. Jesus saw that they were seeking. The word "seeking" comes from *zéteó* which properly means "to investigate to reach a binding (terminal) resolution" or "to search to get to the bottom of a matter." Both disciples of John heard the teaching and claims of John and were seeking to learn more of Jesus whom John was pointing to.

The disciples respectfully called Jesus, "Rabbi," and asked where He was staying. Most likely, they were desiring to learn more of Jesus, whom John was pointing to. John claimed that Jesus was the Lamb of God, anointed by the Holy Spirit, the baptizer with the Holy Spirit, and the Son of God. Jesus allowed both of these disciples to follow Him and see where He was staying. Since it was the tenth hour, it was about 4PM so the disciples would have been able to follow Jesus, be taught by Him, and ask Him questions. The Bible gives us no indication what was discussed during this time, but based on what we know, it would be reasonable to ask Jesus the subsequent questions such as, "What did John mean that you're the Lamb of God who takes away the sin of the world?", "What did John mean when he said you would baptize with the Holy Spirit and fire?", "What did it mean when John saw the Holy Spirit descend and remain on you?", "Are you truly the Son of God?". The seeking disciples were following Jesus to learn from Him.

John 1:40-42 – *One of the two who heard John speak and followed Jesus was Andrew, Simon Peter's brother. He first found his own brother Simon and said to him, "We have found the Messiah" (which means Christ). He brought him to Jesus. Jesus looked at him and said, "You are Simon the son of John. You shall be called Cephas" (which means Peter).*

We read that Andrew went and found his brother, Simon, and explained that they had found Jesus, the Messiah. It's helpful to understand at this point that Andrew has been discipled by John and sat under his preaching and he has enough knowledge to tell his brother, Peter, that they have found the Messiah. Therefore, it is reasonable to believe that although Andrew may not have fully understood everything that was being preached, he had a good sketch of the gospel by his testimony to Simon that they had found the Messiah.

Andrew would have known that John was preparing the hearts of the people in Israel through a baptism of repentance (Luke 3:3). Andrew knew that the sins of one's heart needed to be brought up and all self-righteousness needed to be brought low (Luke 3:5-6). Andrew knew that John preached the wrath of

God (Luke 3:7). Andrew knew that John called for repentance in one's life (Luke 3:8). Andrew knew that the people were not to treat the baptism as another ritual or depend on their ancestry, lineage, or ceremonialism (Luke 3:8). Andrew knew that there was an immediate need to bring forth fruits of repentance (Luke 3:9). Andrew knew that one who bore no fruits of repentance would be cast into hell (Luke 3:9). Andrew knew that John was calling everyone to repentance from the most religious leaders (Matthew 3:7), to tax collectors (Luke 3:12), to those who were not loving their neighbors as themselves (Luke 3:11), to soldiers who were practicing extortion (Luke 3:14). Andrew knew that John was pointing to the Christ and the Christ would baptize with the Holy Spirit and with fire (Luke 3:16). Andrew knew that the Christ would save the repentant but would judge and condemn the unrepentant in eternal fire (Luke 3:17). Andrew knew that Jesus was the Lamb of God who takes away the sin of the world (John 1:29). Andrew knew that Jesus was anointed by the Holy Spirit (John 1:32). Andrew knew that Jesus was the Son of God. Therefore, we can be certain that when Andrew told Peter they had found the Messiah, he considered and carefully assessed all of these testimonies by John.

Andrew humbly brings Peter to Jesus and Jesus says, "You are Simon the son of John. You shall be called Cephas." At this point, there are many theologians that would claim that Peter was converted at this point. Although there could be a theological basis for this claim, I don't believe this is where Peter's conversion took place as there is stronger Biblical evidence of Peter's conversion at a later point in time. Additionally, when Jesus says that Simon will be called Cephas, the word "called" is written in the future tense and indicative mood. This is simply meaning that Simon would be called Peter in the future. At this point in time, we see that Andrew, Peter, and the other disciple are following and learning from Jesus.

As we close this section, the hope is that we can see the connection between Andrew and Peter. Thus, we are able to see the depth of knowledge that Andrew possessed and would likely have shared with Peter. Peter would have known of John's teaching as John's ministry was well known (Acts 10:37-38).

The Miracle in Cana and Jesus Clears the Temple at Passover

In this section, we will just briefly highlight Jesus' first miracle in Cana and Jesus clearing the Temple at Passover. However, before we do so, there has been one more testimony that is noteworthy. Nathanel, also known as Bartholomew, has made the following testimony of Jesus in the presence of Philip and Jesus in John 1:49 after beholding Jesus' omniscience where he says, "Rabbi, you are the Son of God! You are the King of Israel!." Therefore, we have another testimony that Jesus is the Son of God and we have a testimony that Jesus is the King of Israel.

We'll transition to Jesus' first miracle where Jesus' disciples, including Peter, attend a wedding at Cana in Galilee. During this event, they witness Jesus turn approximately 120 to 180 gallons of water into wine. Not only was this a miracle of power and creation, but it was also a demonstration of compassion and mercy. It would have been a major social embarrassment for the bridegroom to run out of wine at a great celebration. However, when it says in John 2:11, that Jesus "manifested his glory", it was a manifestation of His attributes and a demonstration that He was the Christ, the Son of the Living God which was a demonstration that He was the all-powerful Creator, the all-merciful God, and the all-compassionate God.

Additionally, it says in John 2:11, "his disciples believed in him." This statement by John indicates that the disciples had faith in Jesus at this point, which would include Peter. Although this statement by John indicates that these disciples had faith in Jesus, Scripture would support that Peter's conversion occurs later. For example, in John 12:42 it says this of the authority's faith in Jesus, "Nevertheless, many even of the authorities believed in him, but for fear of the Pharisees they did not confess it, so that they would not be put out of the synagogue." The faith in John 12:42 was a faith that believed in Jesus but would not confess Him. The apostle John is demonstrating that such a faith that would not confess Jesus because of the fear of man would certainly not be a saving faith. In Hebrews 11:8 it says this of Abraham's faith, "By faith Abraham obeyed when he was called to go out to a place that he was to receive as an inheritance. And he went out, not knowing where he was going." Therefore, we know that Abraham was called by the LORD to leave his country by faith in Genesis 12:1 and we also see that Abraham was not justified by faith until Genesis 15:6 where it says, "And he believed the LORD, and he counted it to him as righteousness." In fact, when Paul makes a point to demonstrate that one is justified or legally and forensically declared righteous by faith, he quotes Genesis 15:6 in Romans 4:3 and Galatians 3:6 to defend the doctrine of justification by faith. Therefore, although Abraham responded to the LORD's call to leave his land by faith, he had a non-justifying faith in Genesis 12 and then was granted or gifted a justifying faith in Genesis 15:6. Abraham was trusting God in Genesis 12, but he had not yet been converted. So, although Peter would have believed in Jesus at this point, Scripture will support that his conversion came later.

One more event that took place was Jesus cleansing the temple. It was the time of the Passover and many Jews would travel to Jerusalem to observe Passover. Josephus, the Jewish historian, estimates that with such a large number of people going to Jerusalem, there may have been the slaughter of 250,000 animals. As part of the Passover, the people needed to sacrifice an animal. Because they could come from long distances, they would purchase the animal once they got to Jerusalem. Therefore, to be able to sacrifice an animal that met the worship regulations and would not be rejected, it would be more convenient to buy the animals in Jerusalem rather than to bring one's own animals and have them be rejected. Therefore, there was the selling of animals in the Temple area. There were also exchange tables for exchange rates of different currency. Thus, there was the opportunity for money changers to charge a fee for exchanging currency, and thus, profit from the currency exchange. What Jesus saw was the Temple that was meant to bring the worshipper to reverence, repentance, humility, and praise was turned into a marketplace for greed and corruption. Jesus reacted in white-hot divine fury and drove them all out. His zeal was for the glory of God. To see God's temple being treated as a place of greed and corruption is what caused the Son of God to react with such wrath. His disciples, including Peter, recalled Psalm 69:9 where it says in John 2:17, "His disciples remembered that it was written, 'Zeal for your house will consume me.'" Jesus' reaction was a display of His divine attributes. He was not zealous for overthrowing the Roman government. He was zealous for God's glory.

Jesus Teaches the Teacher of Israel on Regeneration and Salvation - John 3:1-16

Jesus' teaching on the new birth is critical to our understanding of Peter's theology on conversion. Peter lived during a time of widespread ceremonialism, ritualism, legalism, and dead orthodoxy. Jesus would confront the Pharisees on their Sabbath restrictions, ceremonial external washings, and much more. Nicodemus was the teacher of Israel and was honored and esteemed. Therefore, for Jesus to teach the teacher of Israel on the new birth and salvation is critical to our understanding of salvation. We'll spend a fair amount of time understanding Jesus' teaching on the new birth and salvation as we'll see that the Lord's teaching on the new birth was comprehended and understood by Peter (1 Peter 1:3, 1:23).

John 3:1—*Now there was a man of the Pharisees named Nicodemus, a ruler of the Jews.*

Pharisees were the religious teachers during the time of Christ. At the time of Christ, Josephus records that there were about 6,000 Pharisees in Israel. The term *Pharisee* comes from the term "separated." Pharisees are depicted in a very negative light in the New Testament, but during this specific time in Israel, they were seen as the conservative religious leaders. They were zealous to keep the law and they were the experts on Scripture. Pharisees were meticulous about preserving both the Old Testament Scripture as well as oral tradition. Nicodemus was not only a Pharisee, but he was also a member of the Jewish Sanhedrin. There were two classes of Jewish courts which were called *Sanhedrin.* There was the Great Sanhedrin and the Lesser Sanhedrin. A Lesser Sanhedrin of twenty-three judges was appointed to sit as a tribunal in each city, but there was only supposed to be one Great Sanhedrin of seventy-one judges which, among other roles, acted as the Supreme Court. The Great Sanhedrin would take appeals from cases which were passed to them by lesser courts. To put it in modern terms, there were state Supreme Courts and Federal Supreme Courts, and Nicodemus was a member of the Federal Supreme Court. There were seventy-one judges on the Great Sanhedrin in the case of an even vote so that the seventy-first member could be the tiebreaker. In the modern American era, judges that are on the Supreme Court have not only attended the best law schools, but they have also served on smaller circuits, gained experience and are considered experts in the law. In the same way, Pharisees were experts in Old Testament Scripture and the law. They were knowledgeable in Scripture and were considered the premier teachers in Israel.

Nicodemus would have also had an upbringing that was strong in preserving and teaching Judaism. Jewish women were very important in the life of the child. If Jewish women were faithful to their religion, they would know of many of the noble Hebrew mothers and would seek to follow their example. The children would be trained from infancy to recognize God as their Father and as Maker of the world. They were trained to have knowledge of the laws from earliest youth and to have these impressed in their souls or, rather, engraven on their souls. This would have been a command from Deuteronomy 6:6–7, "And these words that I command you today shall be on your heart. You shall teach them diligently to your children, and shall talk of them when you sit in your house, and when you walk by the way, and when you lie down, and when you rise," and Deuteronomy 11:18–19, "You shall therefore lay up these words of mine in your heart and in your soul, and you shall bind them as a sign on your hand, and they shall be as frontlets between your eyes. You shall teach them to your children, talking of them when you are sitting in your house, and when you are walking by the way, and when you lie down, and when you rise." The children were brought up learning, exercised in the laws, and made acquainted with the acts of their predecessors to imitate them.

However, while the earliest religious teaching would, of necessity, come from the mother, it was the father who was "bound to teach his son." He was to impart to his child the knowledge of the Torah with great spiritual clarity as if he had been the one to receive the law from Mount Horeb. Every engagement was to be a time where he could teach his child, even at the necessary mealtime. The men were to see this as serious labor that would not prove fruitless. In fact, men who had sons and had failed to bring them up in the knowledge of the law were considered profane and vulgar. Therefore, the man had a high duty and calling to instruct his child.

When the child learned to speak, his religious instruction was to begin. Such instruction would begin with verses from Scripture which could include Jewish liturgy, such as the Shema, which would have certainly included Deuteronomy 6:4–5, "Hear,

O Israel: The LORD our God, the LORD is one. You shall love the LORD your God with all your heart and with all your soul and with all your might." There was special attention given to memory since forgetfulness might prove fatal in its consequences as this might lead to ignorance or neglect of the law.

Very early, the child would be taught what might be called his *birthday text,* which was some verse of Scripture beginning with, ending with, or at least containing the same letters as his Hebrew name. This verse would be inserted in the child's daily prayers. There were also hymns they were taught which would be the Psalms for the days of the week, or festive Psalms, such as the Hallel (Psalms 113–118).

Regular instruction would begin when the child reached the age of five or six years (according to strength). This is when the child would be sent to school. There are several references to schools existing throughout the land and almost every period. The existence of higher schools and academies would not have been possible without a primary education. Tradition ascribes to Joshua the son of Gamla the introduction of schools in every town and the compulsory education in them of all children above the age of six. In fact, it was deemed unlawful to live in a place where there was no school and it was thought that such a city deserved to be destroyed.

The education that took place was marked by extreme care, wisdom, accuracy, and a moral and religious purpose as the end goal. The children could be gathered in synagogues or schoolhouses where they stood or sat in a semicircle, facing the teacher. The teacher was generally the *hazan*, the leader of the synagogue or was an officer of the synagogue. The teacher was to impart to the children the precious knowledge of the law with constant adaptation to their capacity, with unwearied patience, intense earnestness, strictness tempered by kindness, but above all, with the highest object of their training in view. He was to keep the children away from contact with vice; to train them to gentleness, even when the bitterest wrong had been received; to show sin in its repulsiveness, rather than to terrify by its consequences; to train to strict truthfulness; to avoid all that might lead to disagreeable or indelicate thoughts; and, to do all this without showing partiality, undue severity, or laxity of discipline. He was to teach with judicious study and work and with careful attention to thoroughness in acquiring knowledge. This was the ideal set before the teacher and made his office of high esteem in Israel.

It was held that the Bible should be the exclusive textbook up to ten years of age. From ten to fifteen years of age, the child was to learn the Mishnah, or traditional law. After this, the child would enter theological discussions which occupied time and attention in the higher academies of the rabbis. However, this progression was not always made. If the child had been taught and entered into Mishnaic studies and not shown any aptitude, there was little hope that was given to his future.

The *Mishnah* is a written collection of Jewish oral tradition that is reflective of how the Jews interpreted the Old Testament. After the Mishnah, there was supplementation to the oral traditions and so there were commentaries created called the *Gemara*. So, there was the Mishnah, which contained the oral tradition and then the Gemara, which was the commentary on the Mishnah, and these were combined to make the Talmud. There was and is both a Babylon Talmud and a Jerusalem Talmud. After this came the *midrash* which was a collection of interpretation on the books of the Bible.

The child would start his learning with the book of Leviticus which was done to teach the child of their guilt and the need of justification. After this, the child learned other parts of the Pentateuch, then the Prophets, and, finally, the Hagiographa, which included Ruth, Psalms, Job, Proverbs, Canticles, Lamentations, Ecclesiastes, Daniel, Esther, Ezra, and Chronicles. He would learn the Gemara which was the commentary on the Mishnah and would be taught the Talmud which was taught in the academies. There was care taken not to send a child too early to school and, thus, overwork them. Therefore, school hours were fixed and attendance shortened during the summer months.

The teaching in school would be aided by the services of the synagogue as well as the influences in the homelife. Not every home would have the whole Old Testament in Hebrew, but if there were some portions of the Word of God in the house, it would be the most cherished treasure of a pious household. The academies would hold copies of Holy Scripture and there was great care taken to preserve the integrity of the text and it was deemed unlawful to make copies of small portions of a book of Scripture. This was to prevent misquotes and misinterpretations in Scripture (6).

In summation, Nicodemus is an expert in Scripture and the law and has attained one of the highest positions in Jewish culture and religion. He is considered "the teacher of Israel." This title of being "the teacher of Israel" carries with it the full weight and force of what the Pharisees were teaching during the life and times of Jesus. Nicodemus was well-versed on teachings that circumcision was necessary for salvation. Nicodemus was well-versed on the pervasive and ubiquitous ceremonial handwashing, dish washing, pots and pans washing, and Mikvah purification immersion washing that was being taught. Nicodemus was well-versed on the restrictive extrabiblical Sabbath regulations that were taught. Nicodemus was "the teacher of Israel" who was on a crash course to learn about salvation and regeneration from Jesus.

John 3:2—*This man came to Jesus by night and said to him, "Rabbi, we know that you are a teacher come from God, for no one can do these signs that you do unless God is with him."*

Nicodemus, a member of the Sanhedrin, comes to Jesus in the cover of night. There may be many speculations made on why

Nicodemus came by himself at night. Most likely it was because he was concerned over his salvation. Christ graciously welcomed Nicodemus. Though the Lord would go on and oppose the Pharisees numerous times, Christ still made time for a teacher coming at night. Nicodemus approaches Jesus in a respectful manner and calls Him "Rabbi." Nicodemus acknowledges that the Pharisees know that Jesus is a teacher that has come from God. Although Jesus was early on in His ministry, by this time Jesus had turned water into wine and had cleared the temple courts at the time of the Jewish Passover. The miracle of turning water into wine had never been performed. Therefore, Nicodemus knew that Jesus must have been sent by God given these signs.

John 3:3—*Jesus answered him, "Truly, truly, I say to you, unless one is born again he cannot see the kingdom of God."*

It seems odd that Jesus doesn't answer or respond to Nicodemus' greeting, but rather launches into a teaching and explanation of being born again. It is very likely that Jesus knew Nicodemus' heart and his thoughts since Jesus knew all people and knew what was in mankind (John 2:24–25). Therefore, it is reasonable to surmise that Nicodemus had come to Jesus because he had questions on salvation and perhaps even his own salvation. Jesus begins His teaching on regeneration by saying "Truly, truly," or rather, "Amen, amen." The lexicon describes "*amen*" by stating that *amen* means that "what is about to be said is sure and certain." It is also used at the beginning of a statement to introduce something of pivotal importance. As R. C. Sproul has said, "Whenever we read in the text of Scripture our Lord giving a statement that is prefaced by the double 'amen,' it is time to pay close attention and be ready to give our response with a double amen to it."

What does Jesus mean by being *born again*? In the original language, *born again* is "*gennethe anothen.*" *Gennethe* is derived from *gennao* which means "to beget, or to bring forth." It is used to describe being born. The Greek word *anothen* can also be translated as "from above." When putting both words together, *born again* can also be translated as "born from above." The word *anothen* is referring to something coming from God or heaven. In James 1:17, the author says, "Every good and perfect gift is from **above**, coming from the Father of the heavenly light, who does not change like shifting shadows." Therefore, Jesus is referring to a birth that comes from above or from heaven.

The next phrase to dissect is *cannot see.* In the original language, it says "*ou dynatai idein.*" The word *ou* is translated as "not." *Dynatai* is derived from the root word *dunamai* which means "to be able" or "to have power." The last word, *idein,* is derived from the root word *horao* which means to "see," "perceive," "discern," or, metaphorically, "to spiritually see with inward spiritual perception." The translation into English "*cannot see*" is a very good translation. Another way to accurately translate the whole phrase "*ou dynatai idein*" would be to say, "has no power or ability to see or perceive."

The kingdom of God is the sphere of salvation over which God rules. Since it is God's kingdom, He is the King over all those who enter His kingdom. The kingdom of God and the kingdom of heaven carry the same meaning and describe the spiritual realm over which the Lord reigns as King in this context.

So, let's put all these phrases together in verse 3. Jesus says, "Truly, truly, I say to you, unless someone is born again he cannot see the kingdom of God." I will take some liberty to say the same thing but in a different way that carries the same meaning:

- Most assuredly and most certainly, unless you are born from above, you have no power to see the sphere of salvation.

- This is the truth, unless you are born from above, you cannot spiritually understand how to enter the spiritual realm over which the Lord reigns.
- Pay attention to this important truth, unless you are born from above, you have no ability to see and understand how to be saved.
- Most assuredly and most certainly, unless you are born from above, you have no ability to see how to enter the kingdom of heaven through saving faith in Christ.

Notice here that being born from above is a necessity to enter the kingdom of God. Without spiritual regeneration, no man can see the call of repentance and faith (Mark 1:15). Also note that unless you are born from above, or have a spiritual rebirth, you can't see the kingdom of heaven and, thus, won't be able to enter the kingdom of heaven. Also note that this is a personal spiritual rebirth. Nicodemus should have asked himself the following questions: What ability do you have to be born from above? What role did you have in your physical birth? What role did you have in your conception? If you had no role in your physical birth or conception, what role do you have in your spiritual birth? The undeniable answer is that just as you had no role in your physical birth, you have no role in your spiritual birth.

Also pay attention to what Jesus just told Nicodemus. Nicodemus was at the highest religious level in Judaism and Jesus tells him that he must be born again before he can even perceive or see the kingdom of God. In other words, He's saying, "Nicodemus, all your religious achievement, all your education, all your knowledge, all your righteous works, all your ceremonies, all your Sabbaths, all your sacrifices, all your law keeping, all your prayers, all your Passovers, all your rituals, and all your efforts to enter into the kingdom amount to nothing. Nicodemus, weren't you paying attention to John the Baptist's message? You need to start all over again because what you have falls short.

God is not impressed by your religious achievements. All your years of apostate Judaism is worth nothing. If you want to enter the kingdom of God, you need to start all over and be born from above." This is what Jesus is telling Nicodemus.

Also take care to note that if you have not been born from above, you are spiritually dead. If you have not been born from above, you will not have spiritual life when you die.

John 3:4—*Nicodemus said to him, "How can a man be born when he is old? Can he enter a second time into his mother's womb and be born?"*

Nicodemus understands what Jesus just said. Nicodemus understands that Jesus is using a physical example to explain a spiritual reality. Nicodemus understands that it is impossible to be physically born a second time. There is no example of anyone ever being physically born again so Nicodemus knows that physical rebirth is impossible. Therefore, Jesus' example is showing Nicodemus that if physical rebirth is impossible, how much more impossible is it to be born from above? How can a man make physical rebirth happen? Likewise, what can a man do to be born from above? What prayer can he pray? What sacrament can he partake in? What law can he keep? What good work can he do? What ceremonial or sacramental washing can he partake in? What Sabbath observance can he observe? He could also ask more questions about physical rebirth: What role did he play in his first birth? Did he have any say when he was conceived? Did he have any say what day he was born? Did he have any say in his gender? Did he have any say on how long he stayed in the womb?

When looking into Scripture, surely Nicodemus would know Psalm 139:13–15, "For you created my innermost parts; you wove me in my mother's womb. I will give thanks to You, because I am awesomely and wonderfully made; wonderful are your works, and my soul knows it very well. My frame was not hidden from You when I was made in secret, and skillfully formed in the depths of the earth. Your eyes have seen my formless substance; and in Your book were written all the days that were ordained for me, when as yet there was not one of them." So, just as Nicodemus had no part in his physical birth, he would surely have no part in a spiritual birth. Jesus is showing that being born from above is simply a monergistic work of God that man has no control over and Nicodemus understands the impossibility of rebirth by Jesus' question.

John 3:5—*Jesus answered, "truly, truly, I say to you, unless one is born of water and the Spirit, he cannot enter the kingdom of God."*

Jesus is about to make another statement that is of critical importance. As we learned earlier, it is time to pay attention because what He is about to say is an essential truth as triggered by the double amen. Jesus says, "Unless someone is born of water and the Spirit, he cannot enter the kingdom of God." Since we have taken time to understand what the kingdom of God is, we need to understand what it means to be born of water and the Spirit. Commentaries from different theologians and denominations look to this passage as clear evidence that this is a reference to Christian baptism. This is the furthest thing from the mind of Christ.

In fact, ceremonial washings during this time were widespread. There were washings for hands, cups, pots, copper vessels, and dining couches (Mark 7:1–7). The Mishnah contains several regulations on handwashing such as how much water can be used, what kind of vessel could be used to pour water over one's hands, how to handle cases of doubtful impurity for handwashing, and more. Not only these, ritual pools called *mikvahs* were used for ceremonial cleanliness. There were regulations on how much water was needed to make a mikvah, what type of water made a mikvah, what happened if objects fell into a mikvah, rules for immersion, and more. Jesus was not insinuating that regeneration was brought on by some sort of ceremonial washing. May it never be! Nicodemus would not have been thinking that he just needed to undergo one more ceremony or ritual, or perform one more good work, as Jesus is emphasizing being born from above. Nicodemus would have been very familiar with all the Old Testament water purification rituals. Nicodemus would have been very familiar with the Mikvah water purification rituals and ceremonial cleansings. Nicodemus would have been very familiar with the Mikvah purification rituals as these relate to converting to Judaism.

Jesus has just gotten done explaining that you must be born from above to see the kingdom of God and Nicodemus understands that this second birth is out of his control. Jesus is about to double down on the emphasis of the new birth being a monergistic act of God. John the Baptist said in Luke 3:16, "John answered them all, 'I baptize you with water. But one who is more powerful than I will come, the straps of whose sandals I am not worthy to untie. He will baptize you with the Holy Spirit and fire.'" In fact, Matthew, Mark, Luke, John, Jesus, John the Baptist, and Peter all note that Christ is the only one who can baptize with the Holy Spirit and that man can only baptize with water (Matthew 3:11–12; Mark 1:8; Luke 3:16; John 1:31–33; 3:8; 7:38–39; 14:15–17, 26; 15:26; 16:7; Acts 1:4–5, 2:17–18, 10:44–48, 11:16).

So, what is Jesus trying to say? Remember that Nicodemus was advanced in Judaism and, as Jesus said in verse 10, "You are the teacher of Israel." Jesus says, "Nicodemus, you are *the* teacher," using a definite article. Jesus says, "You are not *a* teacher," which is an indefinite article, but "*the*" teacher. Jesus is telling Nicodemus to follow along. Jesus is saying, "You should know what I'm saying when I say, 'born of water and the spirit.'" Jesus is pointing Nicodemus to the New Covenant promise of Ezekiel 36. Although the scripture of Ezekiel 36 is being spoken to Israel, it is true for every believer. Ezekiel 36:24–27 says, "For I will take you from the nations, and gather you from all the lands; and I will bring you into your own land. Then I will sprinkle clean **water** on you, and you will be clean; I will cleanse you from all your filthiness and from all your idols. Moreover, I will give you a new heart and put a new spirit within you; and I will remove the heart of stone from your flesh and give you a heart of flesh. And I will put my **Spirit** within you and bring it about that you walk in My statutes, and are careful and follow My ordinances." This is most certainly where Jesus is pointing Nicodemus.

Nicodemus would have and should have been aware of this passage of Scripture as it pointed to Israel's restoration, and he should have been aware of the personal pronouns in this portion of Scripture. In these four short verses, the LORD uses the personal pronoun "*I*" seven times. He is indicating that this salvation will strictly be a work of God. This work of salvation will be a one-sided affair. The LORD God is going to perform a mighty act of salvation for His name's sake. To understand Jesus' statement of being born of water and the Spirit, it is important to understand Ezekiel 36:24–27.

Ezekiel 36:24 – *I will take you from the nations and gather you from all the countries and bring you into your own land.*

In this section, the LORD is pointing to separation or holiness. This is to say that when God justifies, God also sanctifies. It is to say when God gives the man the gift of faith and repentance and brings him through the narrow gate, God immediately places that man on the narrow road (Matthew 7:13–14). Let us firmly remember Ezekiel 36:23 where the LORD says, "And I will vindicate the holiness of My great name which has been profaned among the nations, which you have profaned among them. Then the nations will know that I am the LORD, declares the LORD God, when I show Myself holy among you in their sight." When God regenerates and saves a man, He is proven holy among men and the nations. That is to say that the salvific work of God is so holy and amazing that, although unregenerate man may not fully understand the salvation that took place, they will marvel and awe at the transforming and regenerative work of God who puts the life of God in the soul of a man. It is to say that God always acts first! You can almost hear Jesus saying, "Nicodemus, aren't you familiar with Ezekiel 16:1–8?"

> *"The word of the Lord came to me: 'Son of man, confront Jerusalem with her detestable practices and say, "This is what the Sovereign Lord says to Jerusalem: Your ancestry and birth were in the land of the Canaanites; your father was an Amorite and your mother a Hittite. On the day you were born your cord was not cut, nor were you washed with water to make you clean, nor were you rubbed with salt or wrapped in cloths. No one looked on you with pity or had compassion enough to do any of these things for you. Rather, you were thrown out into the open field, for on the day you were born you were despised." 'Then I passed by and saw you kicking about in your blood, and as you lay there in your blood I said to you, "Live!" I made you grow like a plant of the field. You grew and developed and entered puberty. Your breasts had formed and your hair had grown, yet you were stark naked.' "Later I passed by, and when I looked at you and saw that you were old enough for love, I spread the corner of my garment over you and covered your naked body. I gave you my solemn oath and entered into a covenant with you, declares the Sovereign Lord, and you became mine."*

It is as if Jesus is telling Nicodemus, "It has always been about God acting on His own initiative and will." It is as if Jesus is saying,

"You've never done anything to earn my favor. Nicodemus, don't you see that you were not a nation, until I made you a nation? Nicodemus, don't you remember when I spoke to Elijah and told him that I have reserved 7,000 in Israel—all whose knees have not bowed down to Baal and whose mouths have not kissed him (1 Kings 19:18)? Nicodemus, don't you know that I'm the one who set apart Israel for Myself? Nicodemus, don't you see that I alone separate men unto Myself?"

Ezekiel 36:25—*I will sprinkle clean water on you, and you shall be clean from all your uncleannesses, and from all your idols I will cleanse you.*

Once again, notice the personal pronoun of *"I."* **I** will sprinkle clean water on you and **I** will cleanse you. The question to ask is: What is this reference to water? It is a reference to forgiveness. After David had been confronted for his sin of adultery and murder by the prophet Nathan, he penned Psalm 51, which gives us insight into this water and cleansing reference. In Psalm 51:1–2, he says, "Be gracious to me, God, according to Your faithfulness; According to the greatness of Your compassion, wipe out my wrongdoings. Wash me thoroughly from my guilt and cleanse me from my sin." In verse 7, he says, "Purify me with hyssop, and I will be clean; cleanse me, and I will be whiter than snow." No theologian would *exposit*, or try to reason, that David is asking the LORD for a bath, a shower, or a ceremonial washing. No, the washing that David is asking for is the washing away and cleansing of sins. He is asking for personal forgiveness from the LORD. He is asking that the LORD would not look at his sins but turn away from them and forgive them. He is asking the LORD for mercy and compassion and not to deal with him according to justice. He is also asking to be cleansed. In the Hebrew, this word is *taher*, which means "to be clean or pure." In context, David is saying, "Cleanse me and purge me from my immorality. Only

You can make me morally clean. Only You can cleanse my murderous and adulterous heart. I don't need a physical bath, LORD! I need You to cleanse the filth in my heart and forgive me."

In Psalm 51:10, David cries out for the same thing, "Create in me a clean heart, God, and renew a steadfast spirit within me." Once again paraphrasing David, "LORD, I have no ability to change my heart. I have no ability to keep Your laws. LORD, without You cleansing my heart and renewing my spirit, I am hopeless." In verse 25 of Ezekiel, the LORD is saying this very thing. The LORD is saying that He is the one who will act to forgive sins. He is the one who will purify us from our sins. He is the one who will cleanse us from our filthiness and idols. Note here that this is not just a reference to forgiveness of sins. This is also a promise to purify us morally from our sins and idols. Again, what the LORD is saying is that this cleansing and purification is not just forgiveness of sins, but a continual work of God to rid one's life of sin. Nicodemus should have known this. You can almost hear Jesus saying to Nicodemus, "Nicodemus, don't you know that it is God who forgives sins? Nicodemus, don't you know that it is God who cleanses people from their sins? Don't you know that unless God cleanses someone from the inside, he cannot be clean before God? Nicodemus, don't you know that external water cannot take away the stain of sin, but only God can remove the stain of sin? Nicodemus, won't you learn from David and see that the cleansing you really need is from the heart? Nicodemus, God is the one who sprinkles the clean water and who cleanses you."

Ezekiel 36:26—*And I will give you a new heart, and a new spirit I will put within you. And I will remove the heart of stone from your flesh and give you a heart of flesh.*

Let's remember that Jesus just said to Nicodemus that you must be born of water and the Spirit. Verse 25 captures the water and verse 27 captures the Spirit but sandwiched in between the water and the Spirit is verse 26 that talks about the LORD giving a new heart and a new spirit. So, what does this mean? When the LORD says He will give a new heart and a new spirit, He is saying that He isn't going to help man be a better person, or become more moral, or to help him love Him just a little more. No, He is saying that He is going to change man's very nature and who man is. Oftentimes, the heart and the spirit encapsulate man's intellect, emotions/affections, and will (i.e., his whole being). What the LORD is saying is that He is going to change man's intellect so man will know the LORD. He will change man's emotions and affections so that man's affections will be toward the LORD and what the LORD loves. What the LORD hates, man will hate and what the LORD loves, man will love. The LORD will also change man's will so that man's disposition will be inclined to do the will of the LORD.

What is a heart of stone? A *heart of stone* is an inanimate object. A heart that has no life. You can kick a stone, you can shock a stone, you can scream at a stone, but the stone will not respond. The heart of stone does not respond to divine stimuli or God's Word. A *heart of flesh* is a heart that is alive. The heart of flesh is responsive. The heart of flesh has a pulse. The heart of flesh responds to divine stimuli or God's Word. What then is the spirit? The *spirit* is the innermost part of man. In Genesis 6:5, it says, "The LORD saw how great the wickedness of the human race had become on the earth, and that every inclination of the thoughts of the human heart was only evil all the time." That is the inclination of man. That is man's heart and spirit. Man's heart and spirit is only evil and inclined toward evil all the time.

In Jeremiah 13:23, the LORD says, "Can an Ethiopian change his skin or a leopard its spots? Neither can you do good who are accustomed to doing evil." Once again, the LORD is saying man cannot change his evil disposition no more than a leopard or an Ethiopian can change his skin. It is not possible. The LORD says of man's heart in Jeremiah 17:9, "The heart is deceitful above all things and beyond cure. Who can understand it?" Once again, verse 26 is sandwiched between water and the spirit and Jesus is drawing Nicodemus to this sovereign act of God which changes a man's very being and imparts spiritual life.

Ontology is the study of being or the nature of being. A man will follow his nature. A pig will always lay in its filth. A bird will fly south when winter comes. A man will always choose evil because that is his nature. The changing of one's being is only accomplished by the sovereign work of God. Man can't change his nature. In fact, Ezekiel 11:19–20, 36:24–27 and Jeremiah 24:7, 31:33–34, 32:38–40 capture this very idea of God changing man's intellect, emotions, and affections, will, and nature so man is inclined to repent and trust in Jesus Christ. Notice the "I will" statements which highlight the act of God monergistically acting on His own to save. Notice the changes to the "spirit," "heart," and "mind" which highlight God changing man from the inside. Notice the new covenant language of *"they will be my people, and I shall be their God"* which explains how God makes a right relationship with man; by changing the inside of a man:

> *And* I will give them one heart, *and* put a new spirit within them. *And* I will remove the heart of stone from their flesh *and* give them a heart of flesh, *so that they will walk in My statutes, and keep My ordinances and do them. Then they will be My people, and I shall be their God (Ezekiel 11:19–20).* I will also give them a heart to know Me, *for I am the LORD; and they will be My people, and I will be their God, for they will return to Me wholeheartedly (Jeremiah 24:7). They shall be My people, and I will be their God; and* I will give them one heart and one way, *so that they will fear Me always, for their own good and for the good of their children af-*

> *ter them.* I will make an everlasting covenant *with them that* I will not turn away from them, to do them good*; and,* I will put the fear of Me in their hearts, *so that they will not turn away from Me (Jeremiah 32:38–40). For* I will take you from the nations, *and gather you from all the lands; and,* I will bring you into your own land. *Then,* I will sprinkle clean water on you, and you will be clean*;* I will cleanse you from all your filthiness and from all your idols. *Moreover,* I will give you a new heart and put a new spirit within you*; and,* I will remove the heart of stone from your flesh and give you a heart of flesh. *And,* I will put My Spirit within you and bring it about that you walk in My statutes, and are careful and follow my ordinances *(Ezekiel 36:24–27).* For this is the covenant which I will make with the house of Israel *after those days, "Declares the LORD:* 'I will put My law within them and write it on their heart*; and* I will be their God, *and they shall be My people. They will not teach again, each one his neighbor and each one his brother,' saying, "Know the LORD," for they will all know Me, from the least of them to the greatest of them,' declares the LORD, "for* I will forgive their wrongdoing, *and* their sin I will no longer remember" *(Jeremiah 31:33–34).*

It is as if Jesus is telling Nicodemus, "Nicodemus, don't you know that in your fallen nature, you are only prone to evil? Nicodemus, don't you remember that your heart is only wicked all the time? Nicodemus, don't you understand that your heart is deceitful and beyond cure? Nicodemus, God needs to remove your heart of stone from your flesh and give you a heart of flesh and give you a new spirit. Nicodemus, you don't perform this work, God does it. Nicodemus, don't you remember that God is the one that writes His law on your heart and mind? Nicodemus, don't you realize that when you receive this new heart and new spirit, God's laws will be written on them as well? Nicodemus, how do you earn getting a new heart and a new spirit? Nicodemus, don't you see that the old covenant was written on stone tablets and the promised new covenant will be written on the heart of flesh? Nicodemus, don't you know that it is God who must completely change your intellect, affections, and will?"

Ezekiel 36:27—*And I will put my Spirit within you, and cause you to walk in my statues and be careful to obey my rules.*

As part of this new covenant promise, the LORD promises that He will put His Spirit in us to walk in His ways. So let's recap. The LORD is saying that He will forgive our sins. The LORD will cleanse us from our impurities and sins. The LORD will write His law on our heart and mind. The LORD will give us a new heart and spirit and completely change us. Finally, the LORD will give us His Spirit so that we will be careful and able to obey Him. It is as if Jesus is telling Nicodemus, "Nicodemus, it is God who forgives our sins. It is God who cleanses us from our sin. It is God who gives us a new heart, new spirit, and completely changes our nature and will. It is God who writes His law on our heart. It is God who writes His law on our mind. It is God who gives us a heart of flesh. It is God who puts His Spirit in us. It is God who gives a heart to fear Him. It is God who gives us the new heart to return to Him wholeheartedly. Nicodemus, don't you know that salvation is from the LORD and not from ceremonies, rituals, law observance, ceremonial washings, and the like? Nicodemus, it is God who causes you to be born from above. It is God who gives you the gift of faith. It is God who gives you the gift of repentance. It is all about God monergistically saving man." Jesus is emphasizing that salvation and regeneration are the sovereign monergistic work of God to Nicodemus and He seeks to remind Nicodemus of this by drawing him to the new covenant promise in Ezekiel 36.

John 3:6—*That which is born of the flesh is flesh, and that which is born of the Spirit is spirit.*

It is as if Jesus is telling Nicodemus that he needs to go back and study his theology of man. Jesus is telling Nicodemus to go back and study man's total depravity and inability to please God on his own merits. You can almost hear Jesus telling Nicodemus to recall the depravity of man (Ecclesiastes 7:20, Psalm 51:5, Jeremiah 17:9, Psalm 14:2-3, Genesis 6:5).

Jesus is telling Nicodemus that the only thing that man can produce is flesh and wickedness. Man can do nothing that produces any spiritual life. If flesh can only produce flesh, then flesh can only produce sin. Flesh can only produce spiritual death. Flesh is incapable of producing righteousness. Jesus also says that the Spirit gives birth to spirit. Once again, Nicodemus should have known what this meant, and Jesus seeks to remind him that only by the Spirit can man live. Only by the Spirit can man have spiritual life. Judaism had reached a terrible level of legalism and rituals. Jesus shut the door to works, actions, rituals, and externality, which were emphasized by the Pharisees. Jesus declared that these things did not give you entrance into the kingdom of God. Entrance to the kingdom of God was by the regenerating work of God the Holy Spirit.

John 3:7—*Do not marvel that I said to you, 'You must be born again.'*

Jesus reiterates the same truth to Nicodemus that He stated in verse 3. In verse 3, Jesus says you must be born from above to even see the kingdom of God. In other words, you can't even see how to be reconciled with God and be saved unless you have been born from above. Jesus is saying this to Nicodemus a second time as He is emphasizing this important point to teach Nicodemus of the sovereign monergistic work of God. In fact, He tells Nicodemus, "You should not be surprised." The original language translates this word *thaumases* or *thaumazo*, which means "to wonder at, be amazed (i.e., astonished out of one's senses, awestruck), or to regard with amazement." In other words, this

teaching of being born from above should not have been a new or amazing teaching.

Let's also notice in this verse that Jesus says, "You must be born again." Jesus is saying that "you" must be born from above again. There are two important words here. The first word of importance is *you*. Here, Jesus is saying this is a personal birth from above. This is not a group birth but a personal birth from above that must occur. Just as you came into the world at a certain location and at a certain time, so it is with your spiritual birth. Unless a man is born from above, he will not enter or see the kingdom of God. Second, Jesus says, "You **must** be born again." The original word *dei* means that it is necessary. This second birth is a necessity. Without a second birth, you have no spiritual life. Without a second birth, you are dead in trespasses, alienated from God, and an enemy of the Lord. Jesus is emphasizing the importance and necessity of the new birth to enter the kingdom of God.

John 3:8—*The wind blows where it wishes, and you hear its sound, but you do not know where it comes from or where it goes. So it is within everyone who is born of the Spirit.*

If we are closely following along with Jesus, we see that He is saying you must be born from above which is something that God controls and not man (v. 3). Jesus is saying that we must be born of water and the Spirit which is in reference to Ezekiel 36, where God is sovereignly acting to give man a new heart, a new spirit, and put His Spirit within man (v. 5). He has stated that man in his depraved state can only produce flesh and sin, but the Spirit gives birth to spirit and life (v. 6). Jesus states again the necessity of being born from above to Nicodemus (v. 7). Thus far, we have Jesus making four statements that man's entrance into the kingdom of God is a work from God the Holy Spirit where the Holy Spirit monergistically acts to change man and give him spiritual life. Jesus is going to give another earthly analogy to explain a spiritual reality. This time, He chooses the wind as a metaphor. Jesus' first statement is that the wind blows where it pleases. This is to draw Nicodemus to the following understanding:

- What can you do to start the wind?
- What can you do to stop the wind?
- What can you do to influence the wind?
- What can you do to control the wind?

The answer to these questions is nothing. Just as man cannot control the wind, so man cannot control the Spirit. There is nothing done by man to influence the wind. There is nothing done by man to control the wind. There is nothing done by man to command the wind. The Spirit operates freely and totally by Divine will. This is Jesus' first point.

The second point Jesus makes with the wind metaphor is that you can hear its sound, but you cannot tell where it comes from or where it is going. So, it is with everyone born of the Spirit. Here Jesus is saying that when the Spirit operates, you hear His sound. Another way of restating this is, when the Spirit operates, you will know that there was work done by the Spirit. When the Spirit operates, it will be obvious that a work of God was done to change a man. When the Spirit operates, you will see a man with a new nature and new affections. You will not know where the Spirit came from or went, but it will be obvious that someone was operated on by the Spirit. Jesus' analogy of the way the wind works being analogous to the Spirit cannot be mistaken. He is emphasizing the monergistic work of God and the transformational outcome. We can't control the wind or the Spirit, but we will be able to tell when the Spirit has been at work. Just like we can't control a tornado or a hurricane, we will see when there has been a tornado or a hurricane and we will see the evidence of it. Everyone born of the Spirit has undergone a sovereign monergistic work of God the Holy Spirit and, where God the Holy Spirit has acted, it will be clear that there will be a person with a new heart, a new spirit, and the Spirit of God working in that person.

John 3:9–10—*Nicodemus said to him, "How can these things be?" Jesus answered him, "Are you the teacher of Israel and yet you do not understand these things?"*

Nicodemus has still not understood the meaning of the second birth and Jesus is unveiling the spiritual depth to which Israel and one of Israel's premier teachers has fallen. A better translation of "*You are Israel's teacher*" could be as follows, "You are **the** teacher of Israel and these things you do not know?" This is a definite article. Jesus is not saying you are a teacher, but the teacher. In other words, Nicodemus is the premier teacher of Judaism in Israel, and he has not grasped the understanding of the new birth and God's Spirit bringing life to spiritually dead men. Nicodemus should have known the new covenant promise in Ezekiel 36. Nicodemus should have known the new covenant promise in Jeremiah 33 where God writes His laws on man's heart and mind. Nicodemus should have known the total depravity of man's sinful state. Nicodemus should have known that man's good works are like filthy rags. Nicodemus should have known that man can't give himself spiritual life. Jesus is telling "the" teacher in Israel that he needs to start all over because he doesn't understand the sovereign saving work of God and needs to start over and be born from above to enter the kingdom of God. Jesus is telling Nicodemus that salvation has always been from God and not from man. How far Israel had fallen. No wonder Jesus was moved with compassion in Matthew 9:36 as He saw that His covenant people were harassed and helpless, like sheep without a shepherd. We can, thus, come away with a definition of *regeneration* which is: **the sovereign monergistic work of God the Holy Spirit in giving spiritual life to spiritually dead and sinful man so that man is enabled to repent and respond in saving faith to Jesus Christ.**

John 3:16—*For God so loved the world, that he gave his only Son, that whoever believes in him should not perish but have eternal life.*

Jesus would continue to instruct "the teacher of Israel." Pharisaical Judaism was ceremonial, legalistic, ritualistic, cold, mechanical, and unloving. Jesus would further instruct Nicodemus on the character of God and salvation.

First, we see that God the Father was the one to act out of love. God the Father didn't wait for man to come up with a plan of salvation. No, God the Father was the one who would initiate and execute this plan of salvation. God the Father was the sovereign creator and author of the gospel. Paul would say it this way in Romans 1:1 that this gospel was from God and not from man where he says, "Paul, a servant of Christ Jesus, called to be an apostle, set apart for the gospel of God." The gospel is God the Father's. This gospel was determined in eternity past between the Godhead of the Father, Son, and Holy Spirit.

Second, we see the indescribable love of God the Father. God the Father loved the world. This is the very world that has rebelled against Him. This is the same God who **hates** sin and those who practice it (Psalm 5:5). This is the same God that **abhors** the bloodthirsty and sinful man (Psalm 5:6). This is the same God that is **angry** with wicked sinners (Psalm 7:11). This is the same God that is ready to **destroy** wicked and unrepentant sinners (Psalm 7:12–13). This is the same God that **hates** the wicked who love violence and sin (Psalm 11:5). This is the same God that considers sin as being in **warfare with Him** (James 4:4). This is the same God that considers sin an **abomination** (Proverbs 22:12). This is the same God that considers sin as **evil** as well as everyone who commits sin (Psalm 7:9). God the Father's soul hates the wicked. In fact, there was nothing redeemable in man which would elicit love from God the Father. There was nothing redeemable in man that God should love. This love of God the Father was a predetermined love that occurred in eternity past and will continue in eternity future for God does not change like shifting shadows (James 1:17). This love of God the Father is lavish (1 John 3:1). This love of God the Father is rich (Ephesians 2:4). This love of God the Father is described as loving kindness (Titus 3:4). This love of God the Father endures forever (Psalm 136). God determined in eternity past to love the very ones who rebelled against him, waged war against him, violated his law, rebelled against his commands, and proved that they so hated God that they would crucify His Son.

Third, let's note that God loved the world. God didn't just love the Jews. God the Father loved a great multitude of people from every nation, from every tribe, and from every language (Revelation 7:9). God's love wasn't just confined to the Jews or even the elite Jews who were advanced in knowledge. God's love extended past the Jews. Jesus loved and came to save the Jew, the Greek, the circumcised, the uncircumcised, the barbarian, the Scythian, the slave, the free, women, children, the Samaritan, and all mankind (John 4, Colossians 3:11).

Fourth, note that God so loved the world that He gave His one-of-a-kind Son. The word *Only Begotten* has been translated from *monogenés* which properly means "one and only" or "one of a kind," literally, "one of a class and the only of its kind." Jesus is the "only one-of-a-kind" Son of God. God the Father didn't give the world another animal sacrifice. God the Father didn't give more rules that needed to be followed in order for man to save himself. No, God the Father gave His Son, His only Son whom He had loved from all eternity past. God the Father gave His only Son whom He loved and with whom He was well pleased (Matthew 3:17, 17:5; Mark 1:11). A parent who loves their child knows the pain of what it would be like to give up just one of their children. A parent is sinful and their children are sinful. God the Father who is perfect (Matthew 5:48) gave His only Son who was also perfect (John 5:17–18).

Fifth, note too that God so loved the world that He gave up His one and only Son to die and suffer His wrath in man's place. When Jesus tells Nicodemus that God gave His only Son, this is a reference to John 3:14 where Moses lifted up the snake for the Israelites. Just as the snake was lifted up on a pole for all to look at the snake and live, so Christ would be lifted up on the cross as a substitutionary sacrifice for the sins of men so they may live and not perish. God unloaded His full unbridled wrath on His Only Begotten Son. God the Father cursed His perfect and beloved Son on the cross as if Christ was the vile, loathsome, wicked, malicious, and abhorrent sinner (Galatians 3:13). Upon the cross, God the Father poured out His white-hot wrath on His Son (Matthew 26:39). Upon the cross, the Father poured out His full furious, omnipotent, and fiery wrath on the Lord Jesus Christ and turned His face away from His Son (Matthew 27:46).

Sixth, let us see that God the Father offered up His Son that whoever would believe upon Him should not eternally perish but have eternal life. Unlike the harsh, cold, and burdensome rules the Pharisees laid upon the Jews, the Father gave His Son that whoever would have faith in His Son should not suffer the punishment of hell but would have a new quantity of life and a new quality of life which is eternal life. Unlike the harsh rules that the Pharisees gave the people which could never save, God gave His Son that whoever would repent and have faith in Him should be saved. Nicodemus' heart should have been plowed by the preaching of John the Baptist. Nicodemus should have paid attention to John's message that works and self-righteousness needed to be brought down low and the sins must be confessed and repented of in preparation to receive the Messiah through faith.

As Jesus would close His dialogue with Nicodemus, He would say the following in John 3:19–21, "And this is the judgment: the light has come into the world, and people loved the darkness rather than the light because their works were evil. For everyone who does wicked things hates the light and does not come to the light, lest his works should be exposed. But whoever does what is true comes to the light, so that it may be clearly seen that his works have been carried out in God." As Jesus would claim to be the Light of the World later in His ministry (John 8:12), He would also ominously claim that those who would not come to Him for salvation remained in darkness.

As we close this section, we see how Nicodemus "the teacher of Israel," needed much instruction. Nicodemus needed instruction on the new birth or regeneration. Nicodemus needed correction on the depravity of man's sin. Nicodemus needed correction on where salvation came from. Nicodemus needed correction on the terms of salvation, repentance toward God and faith in His Son, the Lord Jesus Christ. Nicodemus needed correction on the attributes of God. Nicodemus needed much humbling. "The teacher of Israel" needed to humble himself before the Lord, for the Lord had showed Nicodemus his error and the false apostate Judaism he was propagating. Nicodemus should have been afflicted for leading Israel astray.

Did Peter learn a lesson on regeneration? Was Peter convinced that regeneration was a sovereign monergistic work of God to give spiritual life to spiritually dead men? How do we know that Peter came to know and understand regeneration or the new birth? Peter states it this way in 1 Peter 1:3, "Blessed be the God and Father of our Lord Jesus Christ! According to his great mercy, he has caused us to be **born again** to a living hope through the resurrection of Jesus Christ from the dead." Peter talks of this new birth or regeneration again in 1 Peter 1:23

where he says, "since you have been **born again**, not of perishable seed but of imperishable, through the living and abiding word of God." When Peter talks about this new birth or being born again in his epistles, it carries the full weight and force of Jesus' teaching to Nicodemus on the new birth. Therefore, we see that Peter was also influenced by the Lord's teaching on the new birth, being born again, or regeneration.

John the Baptist's Testimony of Jesus (John 3:22-36)

As John's ministry is winding down, his disciples are noting that people are now following Jesus and not him. In fact, Jesus' disciples are baptizing people (John 3:22-26, 4:2). We see that John humbly answers this way in John 3:27, "A person cannot receive even one thing unless it is given him from heaven," which is an acknowledgment that John's ministry was simply given to him by the Lord. It was John's time to fade away and time for Christ's ministry to begin. John acknowledged that he was not the Christ and reiterated that he was simply the friend of the bridegroom (John 3:28-29). As Christ's ministry was coming to the forefront, John says this about the importance of Christ in John 3:30, "He must increase, but I must decrease." His ministry was all about preparing the hearts to repent and receive Jesus, the Messiah. John will fade out of the scene and give a closing testimony of Jesus.

First, John will testify that Jesus is from above, or rather, from heaven. This means that Jesus' knowledge is heavenly and not of the earth (John 3:31). Second, John will bear witness that Jesus' testimony is superior because His testimony is from heaven (John 3:32). Third, John will bear witness that the testimony of God is true concerning His Son (John 3:33). The Father's testimony about Jesus in Matthew 3:15 is that, "This is my beloved Son, with whom I am well pleased." The Father's testimony is true because God cannot lie (Hebrews 6:8). You must accept the testimony of God because God cannot lie. Therefore, John is saying that those who receive the testimony of God, affirm that God has told the truth about His Son. Fourth, we see that the Father loves the Son and has given Jesus all things including the plan of redemption (John 3:35). Fifth, we see that John believed in the Triune Godhead (John 3:34–35). Lastly, John ends with this statement about damnation, salvation, and faith in Jesus in John 3:36, "Whoever believes in the Son has eternal life; whoever does not obey the Son shall not see life, but the wrath of God remains on him."

As John's ministry fades away, we see some staggering truths about John. John believed that Jesus was the Christ (John 3:28–36). John believed Jesus was the Lamb of God who took away the sin of the world (John 1:29). John believed that Jesus was the Christ (John 1:32-33). John believed Jesus was the one who would baptize with the Holy Spirit and with fire (John 1:31-33, Luke 3:16). John believed that Jesus was the Son of God (John 1:34). John believed in God the Father (John 3:35). John believed in the Holy Spirit (John 3:34). John believed that one must repent and believe upon Jesus for salvation (Luke 3:3–18, John 3:36). John believed that if one did not believe in Jesus Christ, the wrath of God remained on the one who remained in unbelief (John 3:36).

John had fulfilled his ministry. Jesus would tell His disciples that among those born of women there had arisen no one greater than John the Baptist (Matthew 11:11). Jesus told His disciples that John was the Elijah who is to come (Matthew 11:14). As we move on, let's keep in mind the deep theological groundwork and gospel message that John had given to prepare Israel to receive Jesus Christ, the Lamb of God who takes away the sin of the world.

Jesus Begins His Ministry (Mark 1:14-15)

For the purposes of this book, we will not cover Jesus' visit with the woman at the well (John 4:1-45). However, it would be helpful to point out a couple of truths. Jesus testifies that true worshipers would worship the Father in spirit and truth (John 4:23-24). This testimony essentially states that there had now come a time where true worshipers would worship the Father from the heart with love, with truth, and according to the Word of God. The Samaritan people would believe in Jesus because of the woman's testimony and would give a confession that Jesus, "is indeed the Savior of the world."

Just as John had preached a baptism of repentance for the forgiveness of sins, Jesus picked up where John left off. Jesus' would begin His ministry by proclaiming and preaching, "The time is fulfilled, and the kingdom of God is at hand; repent and believe in the gospel." The message that Jesus was proclaiming was that God's kingdom was near and that to enter this kingdom, one needed to repent and believe in the gospel, or rather, the truth of Jesus for the forgiveness of sins. The heart turning message of repentance of John the Baptist was the same heart turning message of repentance from Jesus. in Matthew 4:17, it says, "From that time Jesus began to preach, saying, 'Repent, for the kingdom of heaven is at hand.'" The word *repent* is in the present tense, infinitive mood, and active voice, meaning Jesus was preaching repentance and continued to preach repentance wherever He went. In Mark 1:15, the words "repent" and "believe" are in the present tense and imperative mood. This simply means that the one desiring to enter the king of God was to understand that to enter the kingdom of God, they would need to enter the kingdom of God knowing that they would commit and live the rest of their lives repenting and believing the truth about the person and work of Jesus.

If we combine John the Baptist's message with Jesus' message, we could see the good news of repentance that was preached by both men which could be paraphrased below:

"You need to see yourselves as no better than the Gentile pagans, as outside God's blessing, as outside God's Covenant people (Luke 3:3). You must elevate your sins and wickedness, confess them, and repent of them (Luke 3:4–5). You must bring down low all spiritual pride, self-righteousness, and self-reliance (Luke 3:5). You must see that you are under God's wrath (Luke 3:7). You must bear fruits of repentance (Luke 3:8). You must see that if you do not repent, you will be cut down and cast into hell (Luke 3:9). You must bear fruits of repentance in your life (Luke 3:10–14). You must prepare your hearts to receive the Messiah because He will save you and bring you to heaven or judge you and cast you into the fires of hell (Luke 3:15–17, John 3:27–36). You should see that Jesus is the Anointed One or the Christ (Luke 4:18–19). You should see that Jesus is the Lamb of God who takes away the sin of the world (John 1:29). You should see that Jesus is the Son of God (John 3:36). You should repent and believe Jesus' message (Mark 1:15). You must repent and believe in Jesus for the forgiveness of sins and salvation (John 3:36, Matthew 4:17)."

Therefore, we see that the message of repentance kicked off Jesus' ministry, and as we'll see later, was a recurring message proclaimed throughout His ministry. This was Jesus' ministry. As we see in Luke 4:15, He went around teaching and preaching this message where it says, "And he taught in their synagogues, being glorified by all."

Jesus' Sermon in Nazareth – Luke 4:16-30

Jesus' sermon that He delivers to His hometown of Nazareth is important to the gospel writer, Luke. Luke's gospel is unique in that he has an emphasis on repentance. In fact, in the New

Testament, Luke uses the term *metanoeó* and *metanoia* twenty-five of the fifty-eight times in the book of Luke and Acts. Luke is very concerned about the nature of true repentance. In Jesus' sermon at Nazareth, Luke is careful to demonstrate that salvation is for the destitute. Luke carries this same theme throughout his gospel noting that Jesus has not come for the healthy, but for the sick (Luke 5:31). Jesus has not come for the righteous, but for sinners (Luke 5:32). Jesus has not come for those who justify their sins before men and who exalt themselves, but rather, for those who are humbly repentant (Luke 16:15, 18:9-13). Jesus has come to seek and save the lost (Luke 19:10). In this event, Luke will highlight the mission of the Messiah and the tragedy of spiritual pride and self-righteousness. We will go through an exposition of Luke 4:16-30 to understand that salvation is for the destitute and the danger and devastation of those who are religious yet spiritually proud.

Luke 4:16 – *And he came to Nazareth, where he had been brought up. And as was his custom, he went to the synagogue on the Sabbath day, and he stood up to read. And the scroll of the prophet Isaiah was given to him. He unrolled the scroll and found the place where it was written*

As recorded in Luke, after Jesus had been presented at the temple for purification and consecration, He was brought back to Nazareth where He was raised and reared (Luke 2:22-40). On this day, Jesus would deliver a message at His home synagogue in Nazareth. Synagogues were an extremely important part of the Jewish life. In fact, it may be argued that this was the most important institution of the Jewish life. The Jewish life would have centered around the synagogue and, as we learned earlier, the teacher who taught the children would most likely have been the synagogue leader or an officer of the synagogue.

The worship that took place in a synagogue took place every Sabbath, or every Saturday. The Sabbath was from Friday at sundown to Saturday at sundown. They would also have special services every festival day. The format of the service would include a reading of the Law (Torah), a reading of the Prophets, and then there were prayers offered by the leader along with responses by the people. The people would respond with amens or various praises to God. After this, there would be an exposition of some text of the Scripture. If there was a visiting dignitary or a visiting rabbi, he would be given the right to speak the exposition (6). As we see in the book of Acts, this is exactly what Paul did where he would travel and then preach in a synagogue or place of worship and it's exactly what Jesus did in His ministry (Luke 4:44). Thus, Jesus would have certainly been able to deliver an exposition in the synagogue as reports about Him went out throughout the surrounding country and He was being glorified by all (Luke 4:14-15). He would give His exposition on Isaiah 61:1 which is a Messianic text.

Luke 4:18-19 – *"The Spirit of the Lord is upon me, because he has anointed me to proclaim good news to the poor. He has sent me to proclaim liberty to the captives and recovering of sight to the blind, to set at liberty those who are oppressed, to proclaim the year of the Lord's favor." And he rolled up the scroll and gave it back to the attendant and sat down. And the eyes of all in the synagogue were fixed on him. And he began to say to them, "Today this Scripture has been fulfilled in your hearing."*

First, we should see in this text that this Messianic text prophesied that the Messiah would be anointed by the Holy Spirit or rather, the "Spirit of the Lord." As we learned earlier, at Jesus' baptism, the Spirit descended upon Him as a dove and remained on Him and God the Father testified that "This is my beloved Son, with whom I am well pleased." John the Baptist testified this same truth about Jesus in John 1:29-34. Therefore, we can clearly see that this prophecy was fulfilled in the Lord Jesus Christ at His baptism.

Second, we should see that the Messiah would preach good news or the gospel to a very finite group of people. It is true that the gospel call rings out to everyone and the gospel invitation is to be declared to everyone. However, what this Messianic prophecy declares is that there is good news proclaimed to a people that are poor, captives, blind, and oppressed. Please notice that the text does not proclaim good news to those who are well and have no need of a physician (Luke 5:31). Please notice that the text does not proclaim good news to those who are already righteous (Luke 5:32). Please note that the text does not proclaim good news to the rich in spirit (Luke 6:24). Please note that the text does not proclaim good news to those who are spiritually satisfied with themselves (Luke 6:25). Please notice that the text does not proclaim good news to those who will not weep and mourn over their sin and spiritual condition (Luke 6:25) Please notice that the text does not proclaim good news to those who justify themselves before men (Luke 16:15). Please notice that the text does not proclaim good news to those who trust in themselves that they are righteous (Luke 19:9). Please notice that the text does not proclaim good news to those who don't believe they're lost (Luke 19:10). No, this good news is for the poor, captives, blind, and oppressed.

Third, we should see that the "poor" are those that are poor in spirit. Matthew 5:3 says this regarding those who are poor in spirit, "Blessed are the poor in spirit, for theirs is the kingdom of heaven." When Jesus was giving His Sermon on the Mount, He started by giving the attitudes of those who were part of His kingdom. It is important to note that Jesus pronounces blessing for all those who exhibit these attitudes. The word *blessed* comes from *Makarios* which means "happy," "blessed," or "to be envied." This word describes a believer in an enviable or fortunate position where they receive God's favor and grace. This is the kind of happiness that comes from receiving divine favor. John Macarthur has said of this word, "It is a divine pronouncement, the assured benefit of those who meet the conditions God requires. It is a state of existence to God in which a person is blessed from God's perspective even when he or she doesn't feel happy or is experiencing good fortune. This does not mean a conferral of blessing or an exhortation to live a life worthy of blessing; rather, it is an acknowledgement that the ones indicated are blessed. Negative feelings, absence of feelings, or adverse conditions cannot take away the blessedness of those who exist in such a relationship with God." Therefore, we can know that the Beatitudes are the attitudes of those who have been divinely blessed by the Lord.

The opposite of being blessed would be to be cursed. When Jesus denounced towns or the Pharisees, He would give them "woes." *Woe* is translated from *ouai* and this word can be said as "alas!" or "woe" and uttered in grief or denunciation. It is an *onomatopoeic word*, an imitation of the sound, which serves as an interjection expression or a cry of intense distress, displeasure, or horror. In the Septuagint, it can be a funeral lament, which is used eight times in this expression; it can mean a cry to get attention, which is used four times in this expression; or, it can mean an announcement of doom, which is used forty-one times in this expression. Therefore, let us note that those who are blessed by God will have kingdom attitudes and those who are cursed will not possess kingdom attitudes.

When Jesus preached on the Beatitudes, He gave them in a very specific and sequential order. The first attitude was to be the attitude that would set into motion the rest of the Beatitudes. The first attitude was to be the catalyst that started a chain reaction. The first attitude was to be the very basic foundation and starting point of the Christian faith. To put it another way, one will never be spiritually rich until they are spiritually poor. One will never mourn over sin if he cannot see his spiritual bankruptcy.

One will never show obedient meekness unless there is spiritual brokenness. One will never hunger and thirst for righteousness if they remain satiated and pleased with their sinful condition. Everything starts with being poor in spirit.

We should see that blessedness from the Savior comes from bankruptcy in spirit. The first attitude Jesus pronounces a blessing over is being *"poor in spirit."* The word *poor* is translated from *ptóchos* which means to "crouch, cringe or cower down and hide oneself for fear." It is a picture of a person reduced to total destitution who crouched in a corner begging as he held out one hand for alms and hid his face with the other hand because he was ashamed of being recognized. There are different words to describe being in poverty and the Lord used the word that pictured absolute poverty and destitution. *Ptóchos* does not simply refer to honest poverty and the struggle needed to make ends meet, it refers to abject poverty which literally has nothing and which is in imminent danger of real starvation. In fact, this word is used to describe Lazarus who was so poor that he was desiring to eat whatever fell from the rich man's table because he was so destitute. There are two words in Greek which are used to describe being poor. *Penēs* describes a man who had to work for a living while struggling. It is a word to describe the working man who is not rich but is not destitute either. Instead of *penēs*, Matthew chooses to write *ptóchos* which is the man who crouches, cowers, hides his face, and holds out his hand for help because he has absolutely nothing.

Please note that the Lord announces blessing over bankruptcy in spirit. This is not bankruptcy of wealth. This is not bankruptcy of good friends. This is the bankruptcy of the inner man. This is the bankruptcy of the inner man's spirit. This is bankruptcy of the inner man's spirit over sin. To commit one sin is to be rich in trespasses. To commit one sin is to be rich in wickedness. To commit one sin is to be rich in abomination against the Lord. To commit one sin is to be the wealthiest owner of what God hates. To commit one sin is to be at enmity with God. To commit one sin is to be the commander-in-chief of an army at enmity with God. To commit one sin is to be the crowd that cried out, "Crucify Him, crucify Him!" To pray one prayer out of selfish intent is to be the chief of sinners. To compare your own righteousness against someone else's and not against the righteousness of God is self-righteousness worthy of eternal hell.

To be poor in spirit is to say that you have no righteousness to offer God. To be poor in spirit is not to say that you have a little bit of something, but rather, that you have a whole lot of nothing. To be poor in spirit is to acknowledge that you're rich in sin and worthy of hell. To be poor in spirit is to acknowledge that you're rich in wickedness and worthy of judgment. There is not one denarius of righteousness. There is not one mite of righteousness. However, there are talents upon talents and denarii upon denarii of sin. To be poor in spirit is to beat your breast, turn your face away from heaven and say, "God be merciful to me the sinner." To be poor in spirit is to say what David said in Psalm 51:4, "Against you, you only, have I sinned and done what is evil in your sight."

When Jesus is pronouncing blessing on the poor in spirit, He is announcing blessing on those who realize their spiritual bankruptcy before the Lord. John the Baptist would say that these are the ones who have filled every valley, or rather, elevated and confessed their sins before God and brought down every mountain and hill, or rather, rejected all spiritual accomplishments and pride before the Lord. These are the ones who are smitten and shattered by their sin against God. There is no righteousness of water baptism for the poor in spirit. There is no righteousness of confirmation for the poor in spirit. There is no righteousness of giving to the church for the poor in spirit. There is no righteousness of good works for the poor in spirit. There is no righteousness of being a prayer warrior for the poor in spirit. There is no righteousness of church attendance and membership for the poor in spirit. There is no righteousness of being a Sunday school teacher for the poor in spirit. Poverty of spirit does not mean having the right view of human sexuality, having the right view of marriage, taking communion, or any of the like. No! Being poor of spirit is to be brokenhearted over sinning against God and the realization that one stands with no righteousness to claim before God. Having an attitude of self-righteousness, self-importance, being a religious achiever, or having good morality is to be rich in spirit, but it is not the attitude of the poor in spirit. For the poor in spirit, there is simply a lowliness that is brought on by one's own sin and absolute spiritual destitution.

Oswald Chambers has said of this first beatitude, "As long as we have a conceited, self-righteous idea that we can do the thing if God will help us, God has to allow us to go on until we break the neck of our ignorance over some obstacle, then we will be willing to come and receive from Him. The bedrock of Jesus Christ's kingdom is poverty, not possession; not decisions for Jesus Christ, but a sense of absolute futility, 'I cannot begin to do it.' . . . The knowledge of our own poverty brings us to the moral frontier where Jesus Christ works." Martyn Lloyd-Jones has said this regarding being poor in spirit, "It means a complete absence of pride, a complete absence of self-assurance and of self-reliance. It means a consciousness that we are nothing in the presence of God. It is nothing, then, that we can produce; it is nothing that we can do in ourselves. It is just this tremendous awareness of our utter nothingness as we come face-to-face with God." J. C. Ryle has said this of poverty of spirit, "He means the humble, and lowly-minded, and self-abased; he means those who are deeply convinced of their own sinfulness in God's sight: these are people who are not 'wise in their own eyes and clever in their own sight ' (Isaiah 5:21). They are not 'rich ' and have not 'acquired wealth '; they do not fancy they ' do not need a thing'; they regard themselves as ' wretched, pitiful, poor, blind and naked ' (Revelation 3:17). Blessed are all such! Humility is the very first letter in the alphabet of Christianity. We must begin low, if we want to build high."

We should also see that blessing is pronounced by the Lord on such people who have the right view of sin, who have the right view of their helpless depraved state, and who have the right view of the exalted holiness of God. Sinclair Ferguson has rightly said this about poverty of spirit, "There is much teaching on how to be filled with the Spirit, but where can we learn what it means to be spiritually emptied—emptied of self-confidence, self-importance, and self-righteousness? The sad truth is that we know so little of the blessing of which Christ speaks (and which He gives) because we are all too often full of ourselves and our own means of blessing. In fact, there is no sadder commentary on our lack of this spiritual poverty than the readiness so many of us have to let others know what we think. But the man who is poor in spirit is the man who has been silenced by God and seeks only to speak what he has learned in humility from Him." It is important to understand that poverty of spirit is an ongoing attitude and not just a one-time attitude. This is simply to say true believers don't escape or graduate past an attitude of being poor in spirit. Being smitten over sin and seeing oneself as helpless and dependent on the Lord is the absolute start of the Christian life.

There is not one milligram of grace from heaven that falls on those who are not poor in spirit. To not be poor in spirit is to receive no grace. To not be poor in spirit is to be outside the kingdom of heaven. To not be poor in spirit is to be under the prince of the power of the air. To not be poor in spirit is to be going through the broad gate and walking the broad path to destruction. However, for those that have seen their sin as God sees it, have seen the punishment that they rightly deserve, and declare their utter bankruptcy before God, they are those who become rich. Those who become poor in spirit, will become rich in God's kingdom. Those who have poverty in spirit become those who inherit every spiritual blessing as Paul says in Ephesians 1:3, "Blessed be the God and Father of our Lord Jesus Christ, who has **blessed us in Christ with every spiritual blessing** in the heavenly places." Those who are poor in spirit are in the kingdom of heaven. It means that those who are poor in spirit are in the kingdom of heaven over which God reigns. They are blessed because in the kingdom of heaven, they are rich in mercy, peace, joy, wisdom, love, joy, peace, and goodness. To be the subject of the eternal Lord, God, and King is where true happiness and blessedness spring from. Thus, we see that there is good news for the poor in spirit.

The good news proclaims that there is deliverance to the captives. The word for "captive" is *aichmalótos* and properly means "a prisoner of war." The word for "deliverance" comes from *aphesis* and can also mean "letting go," "remission," or "forgiveness." John 8:34-36 captures this where it says, "Jesus answered them, 'Truly, truly, I say to you, everyone who practices sin is a slave to sin. The slave does not remain in the house forever; the Son remains forever. So if the Son sets you free, you will be free indeed." Jesus came to proclaim good news to those who were prisoners of sin and knew it. Peter captures the essence of this in 1 Peter 2:10 where he says, "Once you were not a people, but now you are God's people; once you had not received mercy, but now you have received mercy." Jesus' ministry was one of redemption, ransom, and rescue. Therefore, this good news is for the poor in spirit who understand their spiritual bankruptcy and captivity to sin.

The good news proclaims that there is recovery of sight to the blind. The blind that are being spoken of are those that are spiritually blind, unregenerate, and unconverted. Jesus said it this way to the Pharisees who refused to repent and believe in Him in John 9:39-41, "'for judgment I came into this world, that those who do not see may see, and those who see may become blind.' Some of the Pharisees near him heard these things, and said to him, 'Are we also blind?' Jesus said to them, 'If you were blind, you would have no guilt, but now that you say, 'We see,' your guilt remains." Therefore, Jesus came to the poor in spirit, those who knew they were captive to sin, and to restore sight to those who were spiritually blind and give them sight to see Him as the Light of the world (John 8:12).

The good news proclaims that there is deliverance to the oppressed. The word "oppressed" comes from *thrauó* which means "crushed," "broken," or "shattered." These are those who are crushed, broken, and shattered by their sin and unrighteousness. Jesus says it wonderfully in Matthew 12:20 on how He will tenderly deal with such broken people where He says, "a bruised reed he will not break, and a smoldering wick he will not quench." Matthew Barnes says this about the Lord's comments in Matthew 12:20, "A bruised, broken reed is an emblem of the poor and oppressed. It means that he would not oppress the feeble and poor, as victorious warriors and conquerors did. It is also an expressive emblem of the soul broken and contrite on account of sin; weeping and mourning for transgression. He will not break it; that is, he will not be severe, unforgiving, and cruel. He will heal it, pardon it, and give it strength." Therefore, Jesus came to proclaim good news to the poor in spirit, to those who knew they were captive to sin, to the blind, and to those who were crushed, broken, and shattered by their sin.

When Jesus proclaimed that "Today this Scripture has been fulfilled in your hearing," He was stating that He was the Anointed One who would proclaim good news of forgiveness and deliverance to the poor in spirit, prisoners of sin, spiritually blind, and those shattered by their sin. This was the favorable year of the Lord and salvation had come to Israel.

Luke 4:22 – *And all spoke well of him and marveled at the gracious words that were coming from his mouth. And they said, "Is not this Joseph's son?"*

Initially, Jesus' message was well received. As we learn later on in Scripture, we learn that at the end of the Sermon on the Mount that crowds were astonished at His teaching because He taught as one who had authority and not as their scribes (Matthew 7:28-29). We learn Jesus' teaching possessed authority (Luke 4:32). We learn that at the Festival of Tabernacles, the temple guards who were to bring Jesus back to the chief priests and Pharisees, were amazed by Jesus where they said this in John 7:46, "No one ever spoke the way this man does." Thus, we see that the people were amazed at His teaching and astonished at His wisdom (Mark 6:2).

Although the people were amazed at Jesus' teaching, they also asked, "Is not this Joseph's son?" In other words, the people at Nazareth knew of Jesus and that His mother was Mary. They knew He was the carpenter's son, and His brothers were James, Joseph, Simon, and Judas (Matthew 13:55). They were very also aware of the mighty works He was doing (Matthew 13:54).

Luke 4:23 – *And he said to them, "Doubtless you will quote to me this proverb, '"Physician, heal yourself.' What we have heard you did at Capernaum, do here in your hometown as well.'"*

When Jesus quoted the proverb to the people, He knew they would want to see miracles. Another way of saying "Physician, heal yourself" would be to say, "Show us more miracles." In other words, Jesus knew that the people were desiring to see miracles. Jesus had turned water into wine (John 2:1-12). Jesus had healed an official's son (John 4:46-54). They would not and could not be satisfied with the miracles they had heard about and that He had performed. The testimony of John the Baptist, the accounts of His miracles, and the wonder of His teaching was not enough for them. The people thought that the problem was that they needed to see more miracles. However, they couldn't accept the testimony and accounts that had been given or Jesus proclaiming that Isaiah 61:1 had been fulfilled in Him.

The biggest problem the people had was that they couldn't see themselves as poor, prisoners, blind, and oppressed. The problem was their view of sin. The problem was their self-righteousness. The problem was they refused to see themselves as sinners. As we noted earlier, Jesus came to call sinners to repentance, not those who were well and in no need of a physician.

Luke 4:24-26 – *And he said, "truly, I say to you, no prophet is acceptable in his hometown. But in truth, I tell you, there were many widows in Israel in the days of Elijah, when the heavens were shut up three years and six months, and a great famine came over all the land, and Elijah was sent to none of them but only to Zarephath, in the land of Sidon, to a woman who was a widow."*

The people would not accept Jesus' testimony because they were familiar with Him and believed Him to simply be one of their own and nothing more. Jesus would then give them two stories. The first story was about a widow who lived in Zarephath which was a Gentile city in Sidon. It was a time when Ahab was king of Israel, Jezebel was killing the LORD's prophets (1 Kings 18:4), and Baal worship was widespread in Israel (1 Kings 18:18-21). The LORD had directed Elijah to go to a Gentile widow during a famine (1 Kings 17:8-9). Elijah came to a widow and asked her for water and bread, but the widow replied that there was only a handful of flour and a little oil left and that she was going to go back, make it and die which demonstrates the severity of the famine during that time (1 Kings 17:10-12). However, Elijah commanded her to make him some cake and bring it to him and then afterward make something for herself and her son (1 Kings 17:13). Elijah promised that the jar would not be spent and the jug of oil would not be empty until the LORD sent rain on the earth (1 Kings 17:14). Therefore, the woman had a choice. The woman and the boy were on the verge of death due to the famine and drought. She had a choice to give up and trust the prophet, or hang on to the very little she had left. The widow decided to trust Elijah. Therefore, the jar of flour and jug of oil did not become empty (1 Kings 17:16). The widow was poor and starving and had little hope. The only hope she had was to give the very last of what she had to Elijah and trust the prophet of the LORD would help her. The point is that she needed to make a sacrifice and trust before she would ever see a miracle. She had nothing left and was already poor and oppressed, but yet, she sacrificed and trusted. This is what Jesus was getting at. Just like the widow, the people at Nazareth needed to see themselves as the poor, blind, oppressed, and prisoners, and reach out to Him who could forgive and set them free. Jesus gave them a story to show that they were in danger of God showing mercy to a Gentile woman who acknowledged her desperate state, sacrificed, and trusted God's Word from the prophet. Just like the widows in Israel during the time of Elijah, they were in jeopardy of being passed over because of their unwillingness to see themselves as poor, prisoners, blind, and oppressed.

Luke 4:27 – *And there were many lepers in Israel in the time of the prophet Elisha, and none of them was cleansed, but only Naaman the Syrian.*

Jesus would end with one more story. This story was of Naaman, a high-ranking commander of the King of Syria who had been given much success by the LORD, but was a leper (2 Kings 5:1-2). Naaman learns that there is a prophet in Israel that can cure his leprosy and he seeks out Elisha (2 Kings 5:3-9). Elisha sends a messenger to Naaman to go wash himself seven times in the Jordan and his flesh would be restored, and he would be clean (2 Kings 5:10). However, Naaman is angry because he is not healed immediately and complains that the Abana, Pharpar, and Damascus rivers are better than the waters of Israel and intends to leave in anger (2 Kings 5:11-12). However, a servant comes to him and says, "My father, it is a great word the prophet has spoken to you; will you no do it? Has he actually said to you, 'Wash, and be clean'?" Naaman needed to be humbled so he went and dipped himself in the Jordan River seven times and he was clean and restored (2 Kings 5:14). Essentially what Jesus is getting at is that just as a Gentile commander needed to be humbled, so the people of Nazareth needed to be humbled. Naaman had no other options to be healed but to trust the word of the man of God. So, just like Naaman, the people of Nazareth needed to be humbled, see themselves as poor, prisoners, blind, and oppressed, and trust the Word of God.

What would have been so painful for the people of Nazareth is that they had just been given two examples of Gentiles who saw their hopeless state and trusted the words of the prophets. However, they had a prophet from their own town and they stubbornly and self-righteously refused to see themselves as poor, oppressed, blind, and prisoners. They would not and could not be humbled.

Luke 4:28-30 – *When they heard these things, all in the synagogue were filled with wrath. And they rose up and drove him out of the town and brought him to the brow of the hill on which their town was built, so that they could throw him down the cliff. But passing through their midst, he went away.*

The people of Nazareth knew what Jesus said. He finished demonstrating how two Gentiles could see and admit their hopeless state and trust the prophets. They saw that God saved the poor, prisoner, oppressed, and blind Gentiles. They saw through the stories that God saved the helpless and not the self-righteous, self-willed, and highly religious. The people of Nazareth refused to see themselves as sinners, as spiritually poor, in need of forgiveness, in need of deliverance, in need of sight. This is what angered them. This is what caused them to desire to kill Jesus. Just one sermon from Jesus of Nazareth caused them to turn murderous and cast Jesus out of their synagogue and throw Him off the brow of the hill. The self-righteous, spiritual elite, and hyper-religious synagogue attending people wanted to kill Jesus, the Christ, the Messiah, the Anointed One, the Lamb of God because they could not be humbled and see their sin.

This is the tragedy of an unrepentant heart. This is the tragedy of covering oneself with religious activity but no regeneration of the inner man. This is the tragedy of having a low view of sin and a high view of self. This is the tragedy of self-righteousness. This is the tragedy of a works-based salvation that gives comfort to the sinner rather than confrontation of sin. Those that cannot repent, cannot see their sin, and cannot humble themselves will never come to Christ in faith. Jesus came to save sinners. Jesus came to save the worst sinners. Jesus came to call the sick. Let us keep this in mind as we transition to Peter's conversion account.

Jesus would leave Nazareth and head to Capernaum in Galilee and will fulfill prophecy. He would, thus, fulfill prophecy from Isaiah 9:1-2 which is captured in Matthew 4:15-16 where it says, "The land of Zebulun and the land of Naphtali, the way of the sea, beyond the Jordan, Galilee of the Gentiles – the people dwelling in darkness have seen a great light, and for those dwelling in the region and the shadow of death, on them a light has dawned." There was the darkness of apostate Judaism. There was the darkness of the souls of the unconverted. However, the light that had shown was Jesus, the Son of God, the Messiah, the Lamb of God, the Anointed One. Jesus had come full of grace and truth (John 1:14). He would go to Capernaum to continue His ministry.

CHAPTER 3

Peter's Conversion - The Miraculous Catch of Fish

Luke 5:8 – *But when Simon Peter saw it, he fell down at Jesus' knees, saying, "Depart from me, for I am a sinful man, O Lord."*

There is much debate and theory written on when Peter was converted or born again. The purpose of writing this chapter is not in and of itself to definitively answer the exact moment when Peter was converted. Rather, the purpose of this chapter is to identify the fruits of true repentance and saving faith which are the result of regeneration. To try and be as unbiased as possible, we will briefly explore other suggestions on when Peter was born again and converted.

- Suggestion #1 - John 1:35-42 – Andrew and Peter begin following Jesus and Jesus tells Simon that he will be called Peter. Although there could be a theological basis for this claim, Biblical evidence would suggest that Peter's conversion took place at a later point in time (See John 1:35-42 in Chapter 2). Additionally, when Jesus says that Simon will be called Cephas, the word "called" is written in the future tense and indicative mood. This is simply meaning that Simon would be called Peter in the future. At this point in time, we see that Andrew, Peter, and another disciple are following and learning from Jesus.

- Suggestion #2 - John 2:1-11 – The disciples, including Peter, see Jesus' first miracle and believe in him. Although Peter was following and believed in Jesus at this point, Scripture would still suggest that Peter's conversion came later. For example, in Hebrews 11:8 it says this of Abraham's faith, "By faith Abraham obeyed when he was called to go out to a place that he was to receive as an inheritance. And he went out, not knowing where he was going." Therefore, we know that Abraham was called by the LORD to leave his country by faith in Genesis 12:1 and we also see that Abraham was not justified by faith until Genesis 15:6 where it says, "And he believed the LORD, and he counted it to him as righteousness." In fact, when Paul makes a point to demonstrate that one is justified or legally and forensically declared righteous by faith, he quotes Genesis 15:6 in Romans 4:3 and Galatians 3:6 to defend the doctrine of justification by faith. Therefore, although Abraham responded to the LORD's call to leave his land by faith, he had a non-justifying faith in Genesis 12 and then was granted and gifted a justifying faith in Genesis 15:6. At this point in Peter's walk, Scripture would suggest that Peter was following and believing in the Lord with a non-saving faith.
- Suggestion #3 – Matthew 4:18-22 – Jesus calls Peter, James, John, and Andrew to follow Him. Some theologians would contend that this was a deeper calling to follow Jesus. Others may contend that this is where Peter may have been converted. Still, stronger Scriptural evidence will point to a later time of Peter's conversion or regeneration.

- Suggestion #4 – Matthew 16:16-18 – Peter confesses that Jesus is the Christ and Jesus declares blessing on him and calls him Peter. Some would contend that Peter had not yet been converted as Jesus tells his disciples that they must become like little children to enter the kingdom of heaven (Matthew 18:1-4). Others would contend that Peter was converted at a previous point.
- Suggestion #5 – John 20:22 – After Jesus' resurrection, He appears to His disciples, breathes on them as says, "Receive the Holy Spirit." Some would contend that this is when Peter was converted. However, we understand that the disciples did not receive the Holy Spirit until Jesus was glorified (John 7:39) and until the day of Pentecost (Acts 2:1-4).
- Suggestion #6 – John 21 – Peter is recommissioned. Some theologians would contend that Peter was converted after Jesus recommissioned him and would use Luke 22:32 to support this where it says, "but I have prayed for you that your faith may not fail. And when you have turned again, strengthen your brothers." Thus, some believe that Jesus recommissioning Peter was Peter's conversion.

Although all these suggestions on Peter's conversion warrant consideration, we can eliminate suggestion #5 and #6 and any suggestions after John 13. We see in John 13:8-11 that Jesus says this regarding Peter and the disciples with the exception of Judas Iscariot:

"Peter said to him, 'You shall never wash my feet.' Jesus answered him, 'If I do not wash you, you have no share with me.' Simon Peter said to him, 'Lord, not my feet only but also my hands and my head!' Jesus said to him, 'The ***one who <u>has bathed</u> does not need to wash,*** *except for his feet, but is completely clean. And* ***<u>you are clean</u>****, but not every one of you.' For he knew who was to betray him; that was why he said, 'Not all of you are clean.'"*

When Jesus is saying that those who have bathed are clean, He is declaring to His disciples that they are saved. In fact, when Jesus is saying "have bathed," this word "bathed" is written in the perfect tense meaning that an action took place in the past, but still affects the present. Therefore, Jesus is declaring that the disciples are all cleaned or saved, except Judas Iscariot. How is it that the disciples became cleaned or saved? Jesus answers this in John 15:3 where He says, "Already **you are clean** because of the word that I have spoken to you." They are not clean because they went through an external washing. No, they are clean because of the revealed gospel truth that Jesus had spoken to them which they have received (John 17:8), believed (John 17:8), and kept (John 17:6). In fact, Jesus will confirm this truth in His High Priestly prayer where He says they belonged to the Father (John 17:6-9), they have not been lost (John 17:12), and they are not of the world (John 17:14, 16). Therefore, we can be certain that suggestion #5 and #6 and anything proceeding after John 13 cannot be Peter's conversion. Therefore, Peter's conversion would have had to take place some time between John the Baptist's ministry and John 13.

As we come to Luke 5:1-11 in Jesus' ministry, the Harmony of the Gospels (1) would suggest that Jesus has already called His disciples from their fishing occupation (Matthew 4:18-22, Mark 1:16-20) as this call is distinctly different from the Luke 5:1-11 call and account. With that being said, it is most likely that Peter has witnessed Jesus casting out a demon in the synagogue which demonstrated His kingdom and power was greater than Satan's (Mark 1:21-28, Luke 4:31-37). Peter would have also witnessed Jesus healing his mother-in-law and casting out many demons who shouted, "You are the Son of God!" (Matthew 4:14-17, Mark 1:29-34, Luke 4:38-41). Additionally, Peter saw Jesus continuing to preach and heal every disease, sickness, paralysis, and demon-possession (Matthew 4:23-25).

As noted above and as we enter this chapter, the goal in and of itself is not to identify exactly when Peter was converted. Rather, the goal of writing on Peter's conversion is to understand true repentance and saving faith in the Lord Jesus Christ which are the result of regeneration or the new birth. Scripture will demonstrate that we'll find such an account in Luke 5:1-11.

Luke 5:1 – *On one occasion, while the crowd was pressing in on him to hear the word of God, he was standing by the lake of Gennesaret*

On this occasion, we see that the crowd is pressing upon Jesus to hear Him speak. We know that Jesus was proclaiming the gospel of the kingdom as well as healing every disease and affliction (Matthew 4:23). In fact, when it says He was "going" throughout all of Galilee teaching in the synagogues and proclaiming the gospel, the word "going" is in the imperfect tense and indicative mood. This simply means that Jesus had the habitual ministry of preaching, teaching, and healing. Additionally, in Luke 4:43, it says this of Jesus and the primary purpose of His ministry, "I must preach the good news of the kingdom of God to the other towns as well; for I was sent for this purpose." Therefore, we see that Jesus' primary mission was to proclaim the good news of the kingdom of God. The many miracles He was performing substantiated His claims and His teaching. Because of this ministry, it says that news of Him spread throughout all Syria and great crowds followed Him from Galilee and the Decapolis, and from Jerusalem and Judea, and from beyond the Jordan (Matthew 4:24-25). Those that followed Him were from everywhere and the crowds that followed were massive. They knew His teaching carried authority, they saw His power over illness and disease, and that He had command over demons (Mark 1:27-34). They were all excited and desired to learn from Jesus and see His miracles.

Luke 5:2 – *and he saw the two boats by the lake, but the fishermen had gone out of them and were washing their nets*

Since it was daytime, fishermen would use the days to clean their nets, fix their boats, and all other equipment. The nighttime was the time when fishermen would typically fish as the fish would come to the surface to feed. As the sun came up and temperatures rose, the fish would dive deeper as the sun warmed the surface of the water. Therefore, fishermen would not have fished at this time as the conditions would have been less favorable.

Luke 5:3 – *Getting into one of the boats, which was Simon's, he asked him to put out a little from the land. And he sat down and taught the people from the boat.*

We see that the Lord has gotten into Simon's boat and is going to teach the crowds. So, what exactly would Jesus have been preaching? It would be logical to say that Jesus would have preached the same message as John the Baptist as well as the good news that had been revealed thus far which could include this paraphrased message:

You need to see yourself as no better than the Gentile pagans, as outside God's blessing, and outside God's Covenant people (Luke 3:3). You need to repent by elevating, renouncing, and confessing your sins and wickedness (Luke 3:4–5). You must bring down low all spiritual pride, self-righteousness, and self-reliance (Luke 3:5). You must see that you are under God's wrath (Luke 3:7). You must bear fruits of repentance (Luke 3:8) for if you don't, you will be cut down and cast into hell (Luke 3:9-14). You are to prepare your hearts to receive the Messiah because He will save you and bring you to heaven or judge you and cast you into the fires of hell (Luke 3:15–17, John 3:27–36). You must see that Jesus is the Lamb of God who takes away the sin of the world, the Anointed One of God, the baptizer with the Holy Spirit, and the Son of God (John 1:29-34). You should see that God has so loved the world that He has given His one and only Son that whoever would believe in Him should have eternal life (John 3:16), but if you will not repent and believe upon Him, the wrath of God remains on you (John 3:36). You should see yourselves as the poor, prisoners, blind, and oppressed and that there is deliverance and forgiveness of sins in God's Messiah, Jesus, the Son of God (Luke 4:18). You must repent and believe the good news of the person and work of Jesus Christ for the forgiveness of your sins (Mark 1:15, Matthew 4:17).

The message that Jesus preached would have certainly included the bad news of sin and hell. It would have included the good news of the person and work of Jesus Christ. The message would have also called for repentance and faith in Jesus and that forgiveness of sins, deliverance, and eternal life would be given to those who would come to Jesus in repentance and faith. Peter was getting a front row seat to Jesus' teaching.

Luke 5:4-5 – *And when he had finished speaking, he said to Simon, "Put out into the deep and let down your nets for a catch." And Simon answered, "Master, we toiled all night and took nothing! But at your word I will let down the nets."*

After Jesus finished teaching the crowds in Peter's boat, Jesus tells Peter to put out into deeper water for a catch of fish. As we noted earlier, the daytime would not be the ideal time for catching fish so it might have been surprising for Peter to have Jesus finish teaching the people and then command him to cast his net to catch fish. Peter will explain that they had been toiling all night and caught nothing. The word for "toiling" comes from *kopiaó* and it means "exhausting labor" or "to labor until worn-out or depleted." They had been working hard through the whole night, yet they had caught nothing.

The net in this verse is called a *diktuon* which is a generic term for any type of fishing net. The type of net that Peter was using was most likely not a one-man net as a one-man net would be used in shallow waters and the Lord commanded Peter to put out into the deep. So, the net that was used may have been a two-man net. Additionally, the noun "nets" is written in the plural form which gives further evidence that this was a large net, possibly made of many nets.

Let's also notice that Peter calls Jesus "Master" or *epistates. Epistates* can mean "master," "chief," or "commander." It can be used to refer to a master in charge. Although Peter didn't believe that casting a net would yield a catch of fish, he was obedient to his master and let down the nets.

Luke 5:6-7 – *And when they had done this, they enclosed a large number of fish, and their nets were breaking. They signaled to their partners in the other boat to come and help them. And they came and filled both the boats, so that they began to sink.*

We see that the catch of fish was a very large catch. The word for "large number" comes from *plethos* which means "multitudes" or "great numbers." The catch was so large that their nets began breaking and caused both boats to begin sinking. There is an academic article that has been written called "An Estimate of the Value of Two Boatloads of Fish, as Recorded in Luke 5:1-11" (7). This article looks at the estimated value of the catch of fish given the historical considerations such as size of the boat, physics of buoyancy, weight of water displacement, weight of the boat, surface area of the boat, estimated weight of occupants and gear, estimating the weight of the fish, estimating the value of the fish in 301 AD, estimating yearly wages of workers, calculating days worked per year, and calculating what each partner received. Given these factors, the estimate is that there was a total of 62,696 pounds of fish filled between the two boats. A wage and commodity price law from 301 AD indicates this gave each of the four fishing partners 24.5 to 36.4 years' salary at general laborer rates or 12.1 to 18.2 years at the skilled labor rates, depending on the fish's quality. Thus, it is estimated that this catch was large enough to let the fishermen live comfortably for many years.

Luke 5:8 – *But when Simon Peter saw it, he fell down at Jesus' knees, saying, "Depart from me, for I am a sinful man, O Lord."*

This is where we'll transition into understanding Peter's conversion or regeneration. As mentioned above, some or many theologians may disagree with this, but Scripture appears to give the strongest indication that this is where Peter was born again and converted. We will go through the evidence provided by Luke to demonstrate that this is the most probable point where the apostle Peter was converted. In Luke 5:8-10, we will see fruits of repentance and in Luke 5:11, we will see fruits of faith toward the Lord Jesus Christ.

First, let's notice the purposeful name change Luke uses in his gospel for Peter. Luke is purposeful to call Peter "Simon" five times preceding this event (Luke 4:38, 5:3, 5:4, 5:5). Prior to this event Simon is never called "Peter" in Luke's account. Although Peter is called "Simon" later on in this same gospel (Luke 5:10, 6:14, 22:31, 24:34), this event marks the first time that we see Simon called "Simon Peter" in Luke's account of the gospel. Luke appears to be intentional to call Peter "Simon" up until this event and he appears to be intentional to call Peter "Simon Peter" at this point in his gospel account.

Second, we see Peter fall down at Jesus' knees in worship. This is a sign of worship and reverence. In Psalm 95:6 it says this of worship, "Oh come, let us worship and bow down; let us kneel before the LORD, our Maker!." In the book of Revelation, we're given a picture of worship in heaven. In Revelation 5:14, we see this type of worship in heaven where it says, "And the four living creatures said, 'Amen!' and the elders fell down and worshiped."

Additionally, we see that the devil was desiring this type of worship from Jesus when Jesus was being tempted in the wilderness. The devil said this to Jesus in Matthew 4:9 regarding worship to him, "All these I will give you, if you will fall down and worship me." Let us notice that Peter wasn't running away from Jesus saying, "Depart from me." No, Peter fell before the Lord Jesus Christ in reverent worship knowing that he didn't deserve to be in the presence of the Lord God Almighty. Therefore, we see that Peter's act of falling down at Jesus' knees is an act of worship toward the Lord.

Third, we see that Peter is overcome with the reality of his sinfulness before the Lord. John Calvin has made these two statements in the Institutes of the Christian Religion, "Without knowledge of self there is no knowledge of God" and "Without knowledge of God there is no knowledge of self". In this scene, we see Peter give a great confession, but this great confession is of himself where he says, "for I am a **sinful** man." It's important to notice what kind of adjective Peter uses to describe the kind of man he is. Peter doesn't call himself righteous. Peter doesn't call himself great. Peter doesn't boast of his prayer life, ceremonialism, ritualism, alms giving, theological prowess, adherence to keeping the law, ceremonial hand-washing, going through John the Baptist's baptism, Sabbath observance, giving burnt offerings, or any of the like. No! The adjective Peter uses to describe himself is *hamartólos* which means "sinning," "sinful," "depraved," "detestable," "loss from falling short of what God approves," or "a blatant sinner." Peter saw who he truly was, a *hamartólos*. This is exactly the type of person that the Lord came to save. We see this in Luke 5:32 where Jesus says, "I have not come to call the righteous but hamartōlous to repentance." We see this again in Luke 15:7 where Jesus says this in the Parable of the Lost Sheep, "Just so, I tell you, there will be more joy in heaven over one hamartōlō who repents than over ninety-nine righteous person who need no repentance." We see this again in the Parable of the

Lost Coin where Jesus says this in Luke 15:10, "Just so, I tell you, there is joy before the angels of God over one hamartōlō who repents." Peter saw what kind of man he truly was, a *hamartólos.*

Fourth, we see that Peter is poor in spirit before the Lord Jesus Christ (Matthew 5:3). As we learned earlier, this is the individual who crouches, cowers, hides his face, and holds out his hand for help because he has absolutely nothing. To be poor in spirit is to beat your breast, turn your face away from heaven and say, "God be merciful to me the sinner." To be poor in spirit is to say what David said in Psalm 51:4, "Against you, you only, have I sinned and done what is evil in your sight." Martyn Lloyd-Jones has said this regarding being poor in spirit, "It means a complete absence of pride, a complete absence of self-assurance and of self-reliance. It means a consciousness that we are nothing in the presence of God. It is nothing, then, that we can produce; it is nothing that we can do in ourselves. It is just this tremendous awareness of our utter nothingness as we come face-to-face with God." J. C. Ryle has said this of poverty of spirit, "He means the humble, and lowly-minded, and self-abased; he means those who are deeply convinced of their own sinfulness in God's sight: these are people who are not 'wise in their own eyes and clever in their own sight ' (Isaiah 5:21). They are not 'rich ' and have not 'acquired wealth '; they do not fancy they ' do not need a thing'; they regard themselves as ' wretched, pitiful, poor, blind and naked ' (Revelation 3:17). Blessed are all such! Humility is the very first letter in the alphabet of Christianity. We must begin low, if we want to build high." Peter manifestly evidences poverty of spirit which is the beginning and foundation of the Christian life.

Fifth, we see the type of repentant heart that John the Baptist was proclaiming and calling for. John the Baptist says in Luke 3:5, "Every valley shall be filled in, every mountain and hill made low." When John said that *"every valley shall be filled in,"* he was stating that every sin shall be brought up and openly confessed. All the debase sins that one cherishes shall be raised up and elevated so that they may be brought low and humbled. He was saying that the sins that the people knew about in their lives needed to be confessed and rejected. He was saying that all the hidden sins in the valley of one's heart needed to be exposed. Likewise, John said that "every mountain and hill needed to be brought low." He's stating that every righteous act and that every self-exalting accomplishment must be brought low. There was no room for confidence in self-righteousness, self-importance, self-will, or self-desire. All the righteous accomplishments were to be brought low. There was no room for religious exaltation, only room for soul-searching repentance and humility. Here, we see Peter with no self-righteousness or self-exaltation, only an elevation of his sinfulness and humble bowing before the Messiah in reverence which describes the repentant heart that John the Baptist called for.

Sixth, we see that Peter sees himself as poor, blind, oppressed, and a prisoner (Luke 4:18). Peter saw his sinfulness which caused him to be poor in spirit. Peter was oppressed, or rather, broken by his sin. Peter saw himself as a prisoner of sin in that he was a man marked only by sinfulness. Therefore, we see that there is good news to be proclaimed to Peter as he is poor, blind, oppressed, and a prisoner. In fact, Luke makes a point to mark out Peter's acknowledgement of his sinfulness as this is exactly the type of person Isaiah 61:1 is proclaiming good news toward. Here, we see Peter poor in spirit, confessing he is marked by sin, and bowing down low before the Lord in reverence and worship. This is exactly the person who would receive the good news of the Lord's favor in Luke 4:18-19 and receive liberty, recovery of sight, and forgiveness.

Seventh, we see that Peter's eyes have been opened and he has a new relationship with sin. Prior to this account, we don't have any record of Peter's confession of his own sinfulness. However, this event marks a time when Peter saw his sin in a new light. Peter saw his sin for what it really was. Peter saw the vileness and ugliness of his own sin. Paul had a similar experience where he sees his sin in a brand-new light and gives this account in Romans 7:7-11, 13:

What then shall we say? That the law is sin? By no means! Yet if it had not been for the law, I would not have known sin. For I would not have known what it is to covet if the law had not said, "You shall not covet." But sin, seizing an opportunity through the commandment, produced in me all kinds of covetousness. For apart from the law, sin lies dead. I was once alive apart from the law, but when the commandment came, sin came alive and ***I died****. The very commandment that promised life proved to be* ***death to me.*** *For sin, seizing an opportunity through the commandment, deceived me and through it* ***killed me****. So the law is holy, and the commandment is holy and righteous and good. Did that which is good, then, bring death to me? By no means! It was sin,* ***producing death in me*** *through what is good, in order that sin might be shown to be sin, and through the commandment might become sinful beyond measure.*

We have an account of how Paul previously saw sin in his pre-conversion life, but then had a sudden illumination of his sin. So, what happened to Paul when he saw his sin as it truly was? Paul's sin killed him! We have four statements from Paul that when sin came alive, he died or was killed. Paul previously was alive. However, when he saw his sin as it truly was he "died" and it was "death" to him and it "killed" him and it "produced death" for him. It was as if sin came alive and plunged a knife in his heart and Paul felt every inch of the blade of sin kill him. His self-righteousness died. His pride died. His self-reliance died. This was a catastrophic and fatal heart wound. It's as if the law came to life and suddenly cut his throat slayed him. So, just as Paul experienced a new relationship with sin, so we see Peter experience his own sinfulness.

Eighth, we should see that Peter gives a title change for Jesus Christ. In verse 5, Peter calls Jesus "Master". However, in verse 8, he calls Jesus "Lord". Luke is intentional in bringing out this title change. It appears that Luke is using this title change to demonstrate Peter's acknowledgement of the Lord Jesus Christ. Although Peter had heard Jesus was the Christ, the Son of God, the Lamb of God who takes away the sin of the world, the Savior of the world, the Anointed One, seen Jesus drive out demons and heal many, this is the first time we see Peter call Jesus "Lord". Peter has come face to face with the Lord, God, and creator of the world. There is no other explanation behind such a catch of fish. Only the omniscient Lord of all creation would know that letting down a net at a given location would yield such a catch. Only the sovereign Lord of all creation could control creation in such a way to yield this catch of fish. Peter is bowed down at the knees of the omniscient and sovereign One who made the earth and all animals and who sustains the earth and all its creatures (Psalm 104). Peter is in the presence of the Creator and Sustainer of the world and Luke is very intentional to capture Peter calling Jesus "Lord" (John 1:1-14, Colossians 1:16-17).

Ninth, we should see that Peter sees Jesus as sinless. As we noted above, Calvin has said this about the knowledge of God and self, "Without knowledge of self there is no knowledge of God" and "Without knowledge of God there is no knowledge of self." Peter sees himself as sinful, but he sees Jesus Christ as sinless. When he tells Jesus to depart from him, this is an acknowledgement that he is in the presence of the holy, righteous, and sinless presence of the Lord Jesus Christ. Peter doesn't fall in front of John the Baptist and call him "Lord." Peter doesn't fall in front of Mary and call her "Lord." No, Peter falls before the Lord Jesus Christ. Luke is very careful to point out such broken and contrite hearts in his gospel account when sinners see themselves as they truly are and see the Lord Jesus Christ as He truly is. Luke records the sinful woman who wets Jesus' feet with her hair, kisses them, and pours perfume on them and then records that her sins are forgiven (Luke 7:36-50). Luke records the parable of the Pharisee and the Tax Collector where the tax collector stood at a distance, could not look up to heaven, and beat his breast in repentance and said, "God have mercy on me, the sinner." Luke is very careful in his gospel account to record those who have seen themselves as they really are and God and how He truly is and are humble, broken over sin and contrite in spirit (Isaiah 66:2). This is the broken-hearted one who is crushed in spirit because they see the Holy One as He truly is and see themselves as they truly are (Isaiah 57:12). The Old Testament is filled with the account of saints who were overcome with their sinfulness and overcome with the LORD's holiness and knew they were not deserving to be in the LORD's presence. Therefore, we see that Peter sees Jesus as sinless.

Luke 5:9 – *For he and all who were with him were astonished at the catch of fish that they had taken.*

As we noted above, this was a large catch of fish that required the help of several men to be able to bring in the catch. The word for "astonished" comes from thambos which means "astonished" "amazed and allied to terror or awe," or "dumbfounded." The fishermen had worked all night on this same body of water and had recovered no fish. It was unlikely that they would catch any fish in less favorable conditions. However, the catch they had brought in under these conditions would have caused such amazement.

Luke 5:10 – *and so also were James and John, sons of Zebedee, who were partners with Simon, and Jesus said to Simon, "Do not be afraid, from now on you will be catching men."*

James and John, who were also partners with Peter, would have helped bring in this large catch of fish. We see that James and John were also overcome and gripped with amazement.

Tenth, we should see that Peter is manifesting the fear of the Lord. Jesus says to Peter, "Do not be afraid, from now on you will be catching men." Here we see that Peter is manifesting the fear of the Lord. We read in Proverbs 9:10, "The fear of the LORD is the beginning of wisdom, and the knowledge of the Holy One is insight." Additionally, we see that Proverbs 1:7 says, "The fear of the LORD is the beginning of knowledge; fools despise wisdom and instruction." Peter is manifesting reverence in his heart toward the Lord Jesus Christ. Let's also notice that such reverence only comes about by a heart circumcision. In Deuteronomy 10:16, it says, "Circumcise therefore the foreskin of your heart, and be no longer stubborn" and in Deuteronomy 10:12, it describes what a circumcised heart will look like where it says, "And now, Israel, what does the LORD your God require of you, but to **fear the LORD your God**, to walk in all his ways, to love him, to serve the LORD your God with all you heart and with all your soul." We also see that this awesome fear of the LORD and heart circumcision is a heart circumcision that is performed by the LORD where it says this in Deuteronomy 30:6, "And the LORD your God will circumcise your heart and the heart of your offspring, so that you will love the LORD your God with all your heart and with all your soul, that you may live." Therefore, Peter is manifesting the fear of the Lord which is the result of a heart circumcision which is performed by the Holy Spirit.

Eleventh, we should see the gentleness of Jesus with Peter. As we learned earlier, Jesus explains in Matthew 12:20 how He will gently deal with sinners where He says, "a bruised reed he will not break, and a smoldering wick he will not quench." Matthew Barnes says this about how the Savior would deal with the bruised reeds, "A bruised, broken reed is an emblem of the poor and oppressed. It means that he would not oppress the feeble and poor, as victorious warriors and conquerors did. It is also an expressive emblem of the soul broken and contrite on account of sin; weeping and mourning for transgression. He will not break it;

that is, he will not be severe, unforgiving, and cruel. He will heal it, pardon it, and give it strength." Jesus doesn't destroy Peter by doubling down on Peter's sinfulness. Rather, Jesus confirms that Peter will be fishing for men. Luke captures this grace and mercy wondrously in the Parable of the Prodigal Son. God is the one who draws the lost sinner to Himself (Luke 15:17). God is the one who brings about repentance in the lost sinner (Luke 15:18–20). God is the one who sees the lost sinner a long way off and has compassion, runs after Him, and embraces him with kisses (Luke 15:20). God is the one who is ready to forgive all sins, give His righteousness, give His inheritance, give His full forgiveness and pardon, give everything to the lost sinner and throw a celebration (Luke 15:22–24). God is the one who celebrates and restores the broken relationship between God and man (Luke 15:32). Rather than destroy the broken, contrite, and poor in spirit sinner, the Lord and Savior offers lavish grace to be a part of His kingdom and ministry.

Twelfth, we should see that Peter will now be catching men. Jesus draws a definitive line in the sand when He says, "from now on." The word "now on" comes from the word *nun* and means, "even now," "now then," "now, in light of what has gone before," "henceforth," or "hereafter." It's as if Jesus is saying, "From this very point on, you will now be catching men." In Matthew 4:19 at the calling of the four disciples, Jesus says, "Follow me, and I will make you fishers of men." When Jesus says, "will make," he uses the future tense and indicative mood. This is simply stating that at some point, the disciples would become fishers of men. As we learn from Jesus' statement in Luke 5:10, from now on, Peter will be fishing for men. How does one catch men alive? Peter would now have firsthand experience of what it meant to be caught by the Lord. It would be to proclaim the gospel and to call for repentance and faith in Christ. Having been caught himself by the Lord, Peter would now know how to catch men. From this very point henceforth, Peter would fish for men and Luke is very deliberate to note this in his gospel.

Luke 5:11 – *And when they had brought their boats to land, they left everything and followed him.*

Thirteenth, we should see the response of faith from Peter. Peter and the rest of the disciples, including James, John, and Andrew left everything to follow Jesus. This was their response of faith in the Lord Jesus Christ. Fishing had been their occupation and means by which they earned a living. They had just received a catch of fish that could have supplied 12 to 36 years of income for them. They were in a position to either grow their fishing business or live a life of ease. However, rather than continue fishing, growing their fishing business, or living a life of ease, they left everything to follow the Lord Jesus Christ. This response was one of repentance, self-denial and cross bearing loyalty (Matthew 16:24). This was the response of faith in following the Lord as a self-denying and cross-bearing disciple or believer. Peter saw his sin, saw the sinless Christ, saw that Christ was greater than his occupation, saw that Christ was greater than him, saw the gentle and merciful Lamb of God and responded in submissive, humble, and repentant faith in Christ for the forgiveness of his sins.

Lastly, we should understand that this sudden change is brought on only by the regenerating work of the Holy Spirit. As we learned in John 3:1-10, regeneration is the sovereign monergistic work of God the Holy Spirit in giving spiritual life to spiritually dead and sinful man so that man is enabled to repent and respond in saving faith to Jesus Christ. If we remember back, Jesus says this about the regenerating work of the Holy Spirit in John 3:8, "The wind blows where it wishes, and you hear its sound, but you do not know where it comes from or where it goes. So it is with everyone who is born of the Spirit." Pastor

Randy Anderson of First Evangelical Free Church in Sioux Falls has said this regarding regeneration, "Where true regeneration takes place, there will be the immediate fruits of repentance and faith in Jesus Christ."

As we close this section, we can see the mountain of evidence pointing to Peter's new birth or conversion. The hope in writing this section is to show what true conversion looks like from a Biblical perspective. It is to demonstrate what true Biblical repentance looks like. It is to demonstrate what true Biblical saving faith looks like. It is to demonstrate what Biblical regeneration looks like. It is also to demonstrate that conversion and regeneration are not brought on by sacraments, rituals, ceremonies, law observance, or good works. Let us keep Peter's conversion account in mind as we continue through the rest of this book.

CHAPTER 4

Peter Hears Jesus Preach on the Narrow Gate and Narrow Way

Matthew 7:13 – *Enter through the narrow gate; for the gate is wide and the way is broad that leads to destruction, and there are many who enter through it.*

The Sermon on the Mount covers the character and attitudes of people who are in the kingdom of heaven, sets forth the true standard of the law which cannot be achieved by man, attacks superficial works and worship and contrasts them with true spiritual works and worship, calls for the priority and preeminence of the kingdom of heaven, and warns listeners to go through the narrow gate and enter the kingdom of heaven. Christ's masterful sermon attacked and corrected true righteousness that gave entrance into the kingdom of heaven (Matthew 5:20), explained the correct understanding of murder (Matthew 5:21–22), explained the correct understanding of adultery (Matthew 5:27–30), explained the correct understanding of divorce (Matthew 5:31-32), explained the correct understanding of speaking truthfully (Matthew 5:33-37), explained the correct understanding of retaliation (Matthew 5:38-42), explained the correct understanding of loving one's enemies (Matthew 5:43–48), explained true giving

(Matthew 6:1–4), explained true prayer (Matthew 6:5–15), explained true fasting (Matthew 6:16–18), explained the right and wrong priorities (Matthew 6:19–24), explained what to truly seek (Matthew 6:25–34), exposed hypocritical judging (Matthew 7:1-6), and more. Such an exposition of the law and righteousness should have brought the listeners to brokenness and poverty of spirit, to mourning over sin, and to desire the true righteousness that exceeded the righteousness of the Pharisees and brought them into the kingdom of heaven.

As Jesus concludes His Sermon on the Mount, He starts making black and white distinctions for His audience. He will state that there two gates (Matthew 7:13). He will state that there two ways (Matthew 7:13–14). He will state that there are two destinies (Matthew 7:13-14). He will state that it will be hard to find the narrow gate and enter it because of false prophets and false teachers (Matthew 7:15–20). He will state that there are going to be false disciples who will make it difficult to enter the narrow gate and that there is danger in making a profession of faith with no possession of saving faith (Matthew 7:21–23). Finally, Jesus states that there are two foundations and two ways to listen (Matthew 7:24–27). We will start in Matthew 7:13–14 to see Jesus' exhortation to enter through the narrow gate. This exposition should become blatantly obvious that sacramental conversion and salvation is eternities away from the Lord's call to enter through the narrow gate and come to a repentant faith in Him.

First, in verse 13, let's notice that Jesus is giving a command. Jesus is saying you must enter through the narrow gate. This entrance into the narrow gate is not passive. It's clear that we are saved by grace, through faith, in Christ (Ephesians 2:8–9). However, the free gift of grace by faith never operates outside of man's intellect, emotions, and volition. In fact, the word "enter" is written in the aorist tense imperative mood. The aorist imperative calls for a specific, definite, and decisive choice. It often expresses a note of urgency. The aorist imperative communicates a sense of getting something done, once for all, and swiftly. It's not enough to look at the gate, admire the gate, and think nice thoughts about the gate. No, you must enter through it! Isaiah captures this truth of the free gift of faith which has a volitional component in Isaiah 55:1, where he says, "Come, all you who are thirsty, come to the waters; and you who have no money, come, buy and eat! Come buy wine and milk without money and without cost." Notice that it's all free and costs nothing, but there is still the volitional component to come, buy, and eat. So, it is with the narrow gate. Entering the narrow gate is a command. There's nothing you can do to buy your way to get through the narrow gate but entering through the narrow gate always has an intellectual, emotional, and volitional component to it. Saving faith is never void of intellect, emotion, and volition.

Second, let's notice that entrance through the narrow gate is a struggle. In fact, in Luke 13:24, Jesus says, "Strive to enter through the narrow door; for many, I tell you, will seek to enter and will not be able." The word *strive* is translated from the original word *agónizomai*, which means "to struggle or to strive (as in an athletic contest or warfare)." Additionally, *agónizomai* is written in the present tense and imperative mood and "enter" is written in the aorist tense and infinitive mood. The aorist infinitive is calling for a simple, single momentary action. The present imperative is calling for an ongoing action. It's almost as if Jesus is saying, "Agonize to enter through the narrow door and don't stop agonizing until you enter through the narrow door." Also note in Luke 13:24 that many will seek to enter but will not be able. Entering this gate is not going to be easy. Entering through this gate will take effort. In fact, in Matthew 11:12, Jesus says these words, "And from the days of John the Baptist until now the kingdom of heaven has been treated violently, and violent men take it by force." Jesus isn't saying that you must be a violent person to enter. No, he's saying that entering the kingdom of heaven is a struggle and those that struggle violently are those that enter. Once again, this is not a works-based salvation. Jesus is indicating that entering the kingdom of heaven is far from a passive entrance. As we'll see later, the call to enter requires repentance, denial of self, death to self, and a loving submission and trust in Christ alone. These are the words of Christ Himself that proclaim that this entry will be agonizing, and we'll speak of this more later.

Third, let's note the definite article *the* narrow gate. It is a definite article and not an indefinite article of *a* or *an*. There is one narrow gate and that is Jesus Christ. In John 10:7, 9 Jesus says, "Truly, truly I say to you, I am the door of the sheep." And "I am the door; if anyone enters through Me, he will be saved, and will go in and out and find pasture." There is but one narrow gate. There is only one broad gate as well. The Lord Jesus Christ is the narrow gate!

Fourth, let's note that "the" gate is narrow. The word *narrow* is translated from the original word which is *stenos*. You hear the English word *stenosis* derived from this. It's important to note that the gate is narrow in that this is a gate that doesn't allow the passage of many people at one time. No, this gate needs to be entered individually. This gate needs to be sought after and entered by one person at a time. Note that Jesus is speaking to the people that this is a personal decision. He doesn't say, "You can enter based on someone else's merits. You can enter with your mom. You can enter with your dad. You can enter because of your last name." No, this gate must be entered by just you and purposefully. In fact, when Jesus says the gate is narrow, He is giving the idea that you will not run through it. You will not be able to take your self-righteousness, self-will, and cherished sin. Entering this gate will strip you of everything. We'll learn more about this in the gospel calls.

Fifth, let's note that we must enter this gate urgently because the broad gate and the broad road are connected which leads to destruction. Jesus is telling us that this is an urgent matter. You need to go through this narrow gate right now. Otherwise, you're headed towards hell and destruction. This is not a decision that you should wait on. As James 4:14 says, "Yet you do not know what your life will be like tomorrow. For you are just a vapor that appears for a little while, and then vanishes away." You must deal earnestly and urgently with God for your eternal future rides on entering this narrow gate.

Sixth, let's note that the gate is wide. *Wide* has been translated from the original word *platus*. The word *platus* means "to be broad like a street." The wide gate isn't necessarily just talking about the false religions of Islam, Buddhism, Taoism, Confucianism, Taoism, Shintoism, agnosticism, universalism, and any other "ism" religion that exists. No, this could also include the false Christs of the Jehovah Witnesses and the Mormons. Let's be even more specific. This wide gate also includes the false gospels of Roman Catholicism, which include faith plus works being needed for salvation. This wide gate also includes the false gospel of the Lutheran church, Eastern Orthodox Church, United Methodist Church, Anglican Church, United Church of Christ, or any other sacramental church, which says that water baptism saves.

Seventh, let's note that the wide gate gives way to the broad way. *Broad* is translated from the original word which is *euruchóros*. The word *euruchóros* means "broad, spacious, wide." This broad road talks to one's lifestyle or manner of walking. This broad road allows one to live their life any way they want. This broad road allows for antinomianism or antilaw. This broad road allows for spiritual apathy towards Christ. This broad road requires no cross carrying, no self-denial, no submission, no following of Christ. This broad road is broad because it is not confined to a submissive faith to follow Christ according to God's Word.

Eighth, let's note that the wide road gives way to destruction. Entering through the broad gate and walking the broad way leads to hell. This broad gate and broad road leads to the unquenchable fire (Matthew 3:12). This broad gate and wide road lead to an eternal destiny that will be worse than the burning sulfur which rained down on Sodom and Gomorrah (Genesis 19:24, Matthew 11:24). This broad gate and wide road will lead into outer darkness where there will be weeping and gnashing of teeth (Matthew 25:30). The broad gate and wide road will lead to the lake of fire (Revelation 20:14–15). The broad gate and wide road will lead to receiving eternal torment (Luke 12:47). The broad gate and wide road will lead to a fire that cannot be escaped (Luke 16:25–26).

Ninth, let's note that many enter through the wide gate. Jesus says that there are many that enter through the broad gate that leads to destruction (Matthew 7:13). The word *many* comes from the original word *polus*. *Polus* means "much, many, high in number, multitudinous, great in amount." This is a somber statement. In God's sovereign and omniscient wisdom, He has so determined that a vast multitude will go to hell. A large amount of humanity will suffer the wrath of God in hell. Multitudes will spend the rest of eternity burning in fire. There will be many that never repent. There will be many that never came in a saving way to Christ. I don't know if this point can be overemphasized. Does it not break your heart that many of your loved ones are headed toward eternal destruction? Does it not break your heart that they do not have Christ? Does it break your heart that many are self-deceived in false religion including false "Christian" churches? Do you have a heart for the lost like the Good Shepherd? Do you wish to seek to tell people how to enter through the narrow gate? Does it bother you when a false gospel is preached that leads people to hell?

Tenth, let's note that the road is narrow that leads to life. The word *narrow* comes from the original word *thlibó* which means "to press, afflict, or properly to rub together to constrict." It gives the idea that it's a road of affliction or persecution. Think of rubbing your index finger and your thumb together. This is the sense in which this word is used. It is tight. It is pressed together. It is narrow. The way is narrow because one's life is lived according to God's Word. God calls His saints to be holy. Not perfect, but holy and set apart. God has good works foreordained for His people (Ephesians 2:10). God's purpose is to have His saints stand out as a salt and light (Matthew 5:14). God desires His people to bear much fruit (John 15:8). God desires His people to be holy (1 Peter 1:16). God has removed the heart of stone from all those who have entered the narrow gate and given them a heart of flesh, a new spirit, and the Holy Spirit to be able to follow His statutes (Ezekiel 36:25–27). God will have written His law on the minds and hearts of all of those who enter the narrow gate. God will teach them to know Him so they can walk the narrow road (Hebrews 8:10–11). All those who enter the narrow gate, and thus enter into the New Covenant, will have fear of the Lord, and singleness of heart and action, so that they will never turn away from Him (Jeremiah 32:38–40).

Eleventh, note that there are few who find that narrow gate and narrow road. Jesus says, "But small is the gate and narrow the road that leads to life, and only a few find it." *Few* is translated from the original word which is *oligos*. *Oligos* means "few, little, or small." Jesus is not saying that heaven will be scarcely populated but is emphasizing that a great majority of the people will not find saving faith in Christ.

Twelfth, let's note that the narrow gate leads to the narrow road. In other words, when one is justified, he is placed on the narrow road. He does not enter the narrow gate, then go on the broad road, and then later decide to walk the narrow road. No, when someone enters the narrow gate, they are immediately placed on the narrow road. After justification, sanctification immediately follows. This speaks not to the perfection of one's walk as a Christian, but rather, an immediate change in their walk of life that will grow in conformance to God's Word and the image of His Son as Romans 8:29–30 says, "For those God foreknew he also predestined to be conformed to the image of his Son, that he might be the firstborn among many brothers and sisters. And those he predestined, he also called; those he called, he also justified; those he justified, he also glorified."

Thirteenth, let's note that the gate is hard to find. It's not only agonizing and difficult to go through, but on top of that, it's hard to find as Jesus says, "There are few who find it." As stated previously, the broad gate not only includes the false religions of the world, but also includes false Christianity. In just two verses, Jesus is warning all generations to be diligent to find the narrow gate, count the costs of walking the narrow road, and then agonize to enter through the narrow gate for few are those who find it. There are false teachers that will make it difficult to find and enter through the narrow gate (Matthew 7:15-20). There are false disciples that will make it difficult to find and enter through the narrow gate (Matthew 7:21-23). There is call to self-denial, cross-bearing, and faithful and loving submission and trust to Christ that will make it difficult to find and enter through the narrow gate (Matthew 16:24-26). Thus, Peter would have been very aware of this command to enter through the narrow gate and that there would be few that find it.

Chapter 5

Peter's Confession, the Church, the Crucifixion and Resurrection, and the Gospel Call to Take Up Your Cross

Matthew 16:24 – *Then Jesus told his disciples, "If anyone would come after me, let him deny himself and take up his cross and follow me."*

This chapter will cover some of the most well-known verses in the New Testament, and rightfully so. In this chapter we will see Peter's great confession, the first prophecy of the church, the prophecy of the crucifixion and resurrection, and the gospel call to carry one's cross. We will spend a fair amount of time in this chapter as it contains much on the person and work of Jesus, as well as Christ's gospel call.

Before we jump into the chapter, it would be helpful to understand where Christ is in His ministry. Jesus has healed a leper which demonstrates He is holy, innocent, undefiled, and separate from sinners in that He could touch and heal the worst of diseases in a defiled and ceremonially unclean leper, make the leper ceremonially clean, and yet remain undefiled (Luke 5:12-16). Jesus has healed a paralytic which demonstrates His authority to forgive sins (Luke 5:17-26). Jesus healed an invalid and called God His Father which was a claim that made Him equal with God (John 5:1-45). Jesus claimed that He is Lord of the Sabbath which is a claim to deity in that He is Lord over the entire Levitical system (Matthew 12:1-8). Jesus healed a man with a withered hand demonstrating his divine compassion and mercy (Matthew 12:15-21). Jesus has healed the centurion's servant (Matthew 8:5-13). Jesus has raised a widow's son from the dead demonstrating His authority to give life and resurrect the dead (Luke 7:11-17). Jesus has healed a blind and mute man demonstrating that Jesus' kingdom is separate, distinct, different, more powerful, and greater than the kingdom of Satan and demons (Matthew 12:22-28). Jesus has restored two demon possessed men (Matthew 8:28-34). Jesus has raised Jairus' daughter from the dead and healed a woman with a hemorrhage (Matthew 9:18-26). Jesus has healed a blind and mute man (Matthew 9:27-34). Jesus has performed the miracle of feeding five thousand which demonstrates His creative power, compassion, and sovereign provision (Matthew 14:13-21). Jesus has healed many of the sick of Gennesaret (Matthew 14:34-36). Jesus has claimed to be the Bread of Life (John 6:25-69). Jesus has healed the Syrophoenician woman (Matthew 15:21-28). Jesus has healed many by the Sea of Galilee (Matthew 15:29-31). Jesus has performed the miracle of feeding four thousand (Matthew 15:32-39). The Pharisees and Sadducees have demanded a great sign from heaven demonstrating their unbelief in Jesus (Matthew 16:1-4). Lastly, Jesus has warned the disciples to watch out and beware of the leaven or teaching of the Pharisees and Sadducees (Matthew 16:5-12). Therefore, as we enter this section, we see that Jesus has done many miracles and works to attest to His claims and teaching. We see that Jesus has told the disciples to leave the false teaching Pharisees alone (Matthew 15:14), the Pharisees remain in obstinate unbelief in Jesus (Matthew 16:1-4), and Jesus has warned His disciples to beware of the teaching of the Pharisees and Sadducees (Matthew 16:5-12).

This is the setting as we'll enter Matthew 16:13-17. In this section, we see a confession given by Peter of the person of the Lord Jesus Christ. In Matthew 16:18-20, we see that Christ is the head, possessor, and builder of the church. In Matthew 16:21-23, we see the work of Christ in His crucifixion and resurrection. In Matthew 16:24-26, we see the gospel call terms to come to Christ for salvation and follow Him in repentance and faith. With understanding this context, we will begin this chapter.

Peter's Confession - Matthew 16:13-17

Matthew 16:13 – *Now when Jesus came into the district of Caesarea Philippi, he asked his disciples, "Who do people say that the Son of Man is?"*

As we saw above, there was much teaching and many miracles that Jesus had performed. Everywhere He went, He was teaching the good news of salvation and was performing miracles and healing. The Pharisees had called Jesus "Beelzebul," the prince of demons (Matthew 12:22-32). Many of Jesus' disciples no longer walked with Him after Jesus claimed to be the Bread of Life and that they needed to feed on His flesh and drink His blood (John 6:22-71). Therefore, we see that the religious leaders were calling Jesus the prince of demons and Jesus was losing many disciples.

Jesus' question to His disciples gets at the very heart of the gospel. The person of the Lord Jesus Christ is at the very heart of the gospel. The gospel is concerned with the person and work of the Lord Jesus Christ. The gospel is concerned about God's Son, Jesus Christ. This gospel does not concern the prophet Muhammad of Islam. This gospel does not concern the false god,

Allah of Islam. This gospel does not concern Buddha. This gospel does not concern Sun Myung Moon. This gospel does not concern Mary Baker Eddy. This gospel does not concern Ron Hubbard. This gospel does not concern Joseph Smith. This gospel does not concern the false god, Vishnu of Hinduism. This gospel does not concern the false god, Brahman of Hinduism. No, this gospel is all about God's Son, Jesus Christ. Therefore, answering this question correctly is essential to the gospel.

Matthew 16:14 – *And they said, "Some say John the Baptist, others say Elijah, and others Jeremiah or one of the prophets."*

It was clear that many people thought Jesus was a man of God by stating they thought He was John the Baptist, or Elijah, or Jeremiah, or one of the prophets. This helps us understand that Jesus was a powerful teacher and preacher. John the Baptist was known for his bold proclamation, for his strong confrontation against sin, and for his unwavering message of repentance. John the Baptist was not a reed swaying in the wind (Matthew 11:7). Likewise, Elijah was a prophet who confronted Ahab and all the false prophets (1 Kings 18:1-40). In fact, king Ahab called Elijah the "troubler of Israel" (1 Kings 18:17). We also see that after the LORD sent fire down on the burnt offering, Elijah had all the false prophets seized and slaughtered (1 Kings 18:36-40). These prophets were bold and unwavering and so we see when the people made these claims of Jesus, we can know that Jesus was powerful in His preaching and teaching.

Matthew 16:15 – *He said to them, "But who do you say that I am?"*

Jesus wasn't interested in the answers of the people. Jesus wanted an answer from His disciples. After the disciples had seen much of the works of Christ and heard many of His claims, He wanted to know who they thought He was.

The disciples initially gave the claims of others and said, "Some say John the Baptist" which alone is an eternally fatal understanding. The disciples also made the claim of Jesus, "Some say Elijah" which alone is an eternally fatal understanding. The disciples also made the claim of Jesus, "Jeremiah or one of the prophets" which alone is an eternally fatal understanding. Napoleon said of Jesus, "I know men, and Jesus Christ is no mere man." True, but this statement alone is an eternally fatal understanding. Pilate said of Jesus, "He's a man without fault." True, but this statement alone is an eternally fatal understanding. Diderot said, "He's the unsurpassed." True, but this statement alone is an eternally fatal understanding. Strauss said, "He's the highest model of religion." True, but this statement alone is an eternally fatal understanding. John Stuart Mill, the philosopher, said, "He's the guide of humanity." True, but this statement alone is an eternally fatal understanding. Lecky said, "He's the highest pattern of virtue." True, but this statement alone is an eternally fatal understanding. Renan, the French atheist, said; "He's the greatest among the sons of men." True, but this statement alone is an eternally fatal understanding. Close is not good enough when understanding the person of Jesus Christ.

This is where a majority of cults will go wrong. They will have some flaw in their Christology that misunderstands the person of the Lord Jesus Christ and which will always lead to a false gospel. The Mormons will claim that Jesus is a spirit child like all mankind. This is a damnable heresy that will lead to a false gospel. The Jehovah's Witness will say that Jesus was the archangel Michael. This is a damnable heresy that will lead to a false gospel. Therefore, getting the answer of who Jesus is has eternal consequences.

Matthew 16:16 – *Simon Peter replied, "You are the Christ, the Son of the living God."*

Peter, the spokesmen of the disciples speaks up and gives the answer of the person of Jesus. Let's think back to what Peter had seen and heard. John had said this of Jesus in John 1:29, "The Lamb of God who takes away the sin of the world." John claimed that Jesus outranked him because Jesus was before him which spoke to Jesus' preeminence (John 1:30). John had claimed that Jesus was anointed with the Holy Spirit (John 1:32). John claimed that Jesus was the one who would baptize with the Holy Spirit (John 1:33). John testified that Jesus was the Son of God (John 1:34). Andrew claimed that Jesus was the Christ (John 1:41). Nathanael claimed that Jesus was the Son of God and King of Israel (John 1:49). Let's think about the beginning of the chapter to gain an understanding of all that Jesus had done and claimed. The crowds couldn't get the right answer and the Pharisees couldn't get the right answer. However, Peter gave the right answer.

Paul makes the same claim to Jesus' deity where he says this in Colossians 1:15, "He is the image of the invisible God, the firstborn of all creation" and, in Colossians 1:19, he also says, "For in Him all the fullness of God was pleased to dwell," and makes a similar statement in Colossians 2:9, "For in Him the whole fullness of deity dwells bodily." Likewise, the author of Hebrews says of Jesus, the Son of God, in Hebrews 1:3, "He is the radiance of the glory of God and the exact imprint of His nature, and he upholds the universe by the word of His power. After making purification for sins, He sat down at the right hand of the Majesty on high." Thus, we see Jesus as the Christ, the Son of the Living God.

We should also see that because Jesus is God He is also coequal and coeternal with God the Father and God the Holy Spirit. In John 5:17–18, after Jesus healed the invalid, Jesus makes a statement of being equal with the Father where it says, "But Jesus answered them, 'My Father is working until now, and I am working.' This was why the Jews were seeking all the more to kill Him, because not only was He breaking the Sabbath, but He was even calling God His own Father, making Himself equal with God." In John 10:30, Jesus makes another statement of being coequal with the Father where He says, "I and the Father are one." Jesus reiterates this same point later on but states it in another way where He says this about the work He is doing in John 10:38, "But if I do them, even though you do not believe me, believe the works, that you may know and understand that the Father is in me and I am in the Father." Jesus makes another claim later which shows His coequality with the Father in John 14:10, where He says, "Do you not believe that I am in the Father and the Father is in me? The words that I say to you I do not speak on my own authority, but the Father who dwells in Me does His works." The point is that Jesus, being God, is coequal and coeternal with the Father. Jesus is saying He is one in essence with Father. Additionally, we should see that Jesus is the only begotten Son of God (John 3:16). The word "only begotten" has been translated from monogenés which properly means "one-and-only," "one of a kind," literally "one of a class and the only of its kind." Jesus is the only one-of-a-kind Son of God. Jesus is not a created being. We can know that Jesus is not a created being as He is the Son of God and God is immutable and eternal. God cannot get better, for if He could get better, He would not be God. God can't get worse, because if He became worse, He would be less than God. Jesus is not a created being as God is eternal and God is immutable. God doesn't become more, and God doesn't become less. Additionally, another attribute of God is the aseity of God, or rather, God is self-sufficient and exists of and from Himself by His own self and self-will. John 1:4 captures the aseity of God and Jesus where it says, "In him was life, and the life was the light of men." This is simply stating that all created life came from Him because He is the source of all life, or rather, He is completely self-sufficient and self-existent in and of Himself and needs nothing. The one who is self-sufficient and self-existent in and of Himself cannot be created as He is eternal and is the origin and source of all life. Therefore, Jesus is the coeternal, co-equal, and only begotten Son of God.

Jesus is the Anointed One of God where He proclaims that He is the fulfillment of Isaiah's prophecy in Luke 4:18-19 when He says, "The Spirit of the Lord is upon me, because he has anointed me to proclaim good news to the poor. He has sent me to proclaim liberty to the captives and recovering of sight to the blind, to set at liberty those who are oppressed, to proclaim the year of the Lord's favor." He is the promised Messiah. He is the Prophet that was foretold of in Deuteronomy 18. He is the eternal King as Paul says in 1 Timothy 1:17, "To the King of the ages, immortal, invisible, the only God, be honor and glory forever and ever. Amen" and in 1 Timothy 6:15 where he also says, "he who is the blessed and only Sovereign, the King of kings and the Lord of lords." He is the eternal Savior as the angel declares in Luke 2:11, "For unto you is born this day in the city of David a Savior, who is Christ the Lord." He is the eternal High Priest as the author of Hebrews says in Hebrews 7:24, 26, "but he holds his priesthood permanently, because he continues forever... for it was indeed fitting that we should have such a high priest, holy, innocent, unstained, separated from sinners, and exalted above the heavens." He is the Creator and Sustainer of the universe (John 1:1-14, Hebrews 1:1-3, Colossians 1:16-17, 1 Corinthians 8:6). The person of Jesus is that He is the Christ, the promised Jewish Messiah, the only begotten Son of the Living God (John 3:16) which makes Him God and equal with God the Father and God the Holy Spirit. He is thus, truly God and truly man. Peter's confession of the Lord Jesus Christ carries the full weight, depth, and breadth of this reality.

Matthew 16:17 – And Jesus answered him, "*Blessed are you, Simon Bar-Jonah! For flesh and blood has not revealed this to you, but my Father who is in heaven.*"

We learned earlier that the word *blessed* comes from *Makarios* which means "happy," "blessed," or "to be envied." This word describes a believer in an enviable or fortunate position where they receive God's favor and grace. This is the kind of happiness that comes from receiving divine favor. So why would Peter be blessed? We clearly see that this revelation comes from the Father. This hearkens back to what Jesus told His disciples after towns had refused to repent and believe in Him where he says this in Matthew 11:27, "All things have been handed over to me by my Father, and so no one knows the Son except the Father, and no one knows the Father except the Son and anyone to whom the Son chooses to reveal him." Additionally, Peter would remember this statement from the Lord in the Lord's discourse on being the Bread of Life in John 6:44, "No one can come to me unless the Father who sent me draws him." Peter is ultimately blessed because the Father and the Son have chosen to reveal the true person of the Lord Jesus Christ to Peter. Peter is blessed because the Father has drawn Peter to His beloved, only begotten, one-of-a-kind Son with whom He is well pleased.

Peter Learns About the Church – Matthew 16:18-20

Matthew 16:18 – *And I tell you, you are Peter, and on this rock I will build my church, and the gates of hell shall not prevail against it.*

There is much debate and commentary written on this verse. I don't intend to bog down this section with commentary, but only provide the most relevant facts of this verse.

First, we see that the rock on which Christ's church will be built is Peter's confession. The *petra* or "huge mass or rock" that *Petros*, or Peter, which can be translated as "a stone," has just confessed is that Jesus is the Christ, the Son of the Living God. This is how Christ is going to build His church, which is based on the person and work of the Lord Jesus Christ. As we noted above, Jesus is the Jewish Messiah and Son of God who has been sent as the Lamb of God to take away the sins of the world (John 1:29). Thus, the church is built on the person and work of the Lord Jesus Christ. It is not built on Peter as Peter makes this abundantly clear in his epistle in 1 Peter 2:6 where he says, "For it stands in Scripture: 'Behold, I am laying in Zion a stone, a cornerstone chosen and precious, and whoever believes in him will not be put to shame.'" The word "cornerstone" comes from *akrogóniaios* which can mean "belonging to the extreme corner." The corner stone needed to have the correct angles so all the angles of the building would be symmetrical. The angle of the cornerstone would determine the angle of every other stone laid against it. Thus, the person and work of the Lord Jesus Christ is the cornerstone and very foundation of the church and whoever believes in Him will not be put to shame. Paul says it this way in Colossians 1:18, "And he is the head of the body, the church." Paul says the very same thing in Ephesians 1:22-23, "And he put all things under his feet and gave him as head over all things to the church, which is his body, the fullness of him who fills all in all." Therefore, the church is built on the confession of Peter that Jesus is the Christ, the Son of the Living God.

Second, we should see that the church is the assembly of all Christian believers. The word *ekklésia* is a compound word with ek meaning "out from and to" and *kaléō* meaning "to call." Properly, these are the people called out from the world and to God, the outcome being the Church. Of course, this word can be used to describe a building in today's terms, but in this context, the church are those who have been called out of the world and now belong to the Lord Jesus Christ.

Third, we should see that this church belongs to and is the possession of the Lord Jesus Christ. Jesus makes this abundantly clear when He says, "my church." This church does not belong to the pope. This church does not belong to a pastor. This church does not belong to a denomination. This church does not belong to an organization. No! This church belongs to and is owned by the Lord Jesus Christ. Peter emphasizes this in his epistle where he says this in 1 Peter 2:9, "But you are a chosen race, a royal priesthood, a holy nation, a people for his own possession, that you may proclaim the excellencies of him who called you out of darkness into his marvelous light. Once you were not a people, but now you are God's people; once you had not received mercy, but now you have received mercy." Thus, the church belongs to the Lord Jesus Christ.

Fourth, we should see that Christ's church will be built by Him. The word "build" comes from *oikodomeó* and it means "to erect a building." Notice that Christ is the one who builds the church. How does Christ build His church? He builds his church off of His person and work. The church is built off of the person of the Lord Jesus Christ and His propitiating, reconciling, expiating, ransoming, redeeming, regenerating, justifying, sanctifying, and glorifying work. The church is not built by contemporary music, skits, plays, bright lights, short services, short sermons, or any of the like. No! Christ will build His church off of the gospel which is all about the person and work of the Lord Jesus Christ. Peter says this of Christ building His church in 1 Peter 2:5, "you yourselves like living stones are being built up as a spiritual house, to be a holy priesthood, to offer spiritual sacrifices acceptable to God through Jesus Christ."

Fifth, we should see that death shall not overcome Christ's church. Jesus said in John 10:17-18, "The reason my Father loves me is that I lay down my life – only to take it up again. No one takes it from me, but I lay it down on my own accord. I have authority to lay it down and authority to take it up again. This command I received from my Father." When Christ died on the cross and then rose from the dead, it was proof positive that His salvific work was accepted by God. Christ's resurrection was God's apologetic on the sufficiency of Christ's substitutionary death on the cross for sinners. The resurrection was God's ultimate validation of Jesus' person and work on the cross. Christ's resurrection is also the apologetic of every believer in Christ that they will rise from the dead just as their Savior did as it says in 1 Corinthians 15:20-21, "But in fact Christ has been raised from the dead, the firstfruits of those who have fallen asleep. For as by a man came death, by a man has come also the resurrection of the dead." Lastly, Jesus gives a firm testimony on the resurrection life and security that believers have in Him in John 10:28, "I give them eternal life, and they shall never perish; no one will snatch them out of my hand." Thus, Christ's called out ones shall prevail over death.

Matthew 16:19 – *I will give you the keys of the kingdom of heaven, and whatever you bind on earth shall be bound in heaven, and whatever you loose on earth shall be loosed in heaven.*

Here we see that Jesus will give the keys of the kingdom of heaven to the church and the authority to bind and loose. Although this would appear to be a difficult statement to interpret, this verse can be understood by clearly articulating what some of the terms in the passage are.

First, we should understand what the "keys" are. Simply, a key is what can open or close a door. In this context, a key is what will open or close the kingdom of heaven. Another way of stating this is that the key will open the way into the kingdom of heaven, but the key can also be used to keep the kingdom of heaven closed.

Second, we should understand what the "kingdom of heaven" is. In this context, the kingdom of heaven is the "sphere of salvation" or "salvation" and is interchangeable with "the kingdom of God." There is a kingdom which means there is a King. Since it is the kingdom of heaven, God is King in heaven and is King over those who enter His kingdom. The individuals who have inherited eternal life and salvation are those who have entered the kingdom of heaven. Those who are outside of the kingdom of heaven are those who are unconverted and unregenerated.

Third, we should understand the terms "bind" and "loose" mean. The word "bind" comes from *deó* and it means "to tie," "to bind" and can also mean "to declare to be prohibited and unlawful." The word "loose" comes from *luó* and it means "to loose," "to release," "to dissolve." This word in this context, could also mean "to declare lawful." Thus, we see that when something is "bound," it is the same thing as saying that someone is not forgiven or bound in their sins. When something is "loosed," it is the same thing as saying someone has been loosed from their sins or forgiven.

Fourth, when we put all of these terms together, we see that Jesus will give the church the keys to open up the way into the kingdom of heaven and salvation, but these same keys will close the kingdom of heaven and deny salvation. Thus, the church will declare how to enter the kingdom of heaven and be "loosed" from sin and will also declare what would keep someone out of the kingdom of heaven and be "bound" in one's sin.

Fifth, we should understand that this should all be understood in context of the gospel. This is the gospel of the person and work of the Lord Jesus Christ and the response of repentance toward God and faith in the Lord Jesus Christ. As we mentioned above, having a correct understanding of the Lord Jesus Christ is eternally important. Having a correct understanding of the work of the Lord Jesus Christ is eternally important. Having a correct understanding of the subjective response of repentance toward God and faith in the Lord Jesus Christ is eternally important. This gospel determines whether sins are bound or loosed. This gospel determines whether one is inside the kingdom of heaven or outside the kingdom of heaven.

Matthew 16:20 – *Then he strictly charged the disciples to tell no one that he was the Christ.*

We'll learn the reason why Jesus told His disciples not to tell anyone that He was the Christ in Matthew 16:21-23. Essentially, the reason is that Jesus needed to explain the purpose and mission of the Messiah. As we'll see in the following section, the disciples needed much explanation on why the Messiah came and what was His purpose. It was not for economic, political, or military purposes. His purpose was to deal with sin as John the Baptist said, "Behold, the Lamb of God, who takes away the sin of the world!."

Peter Learns of the Crucifixion and Resurrection – Matthew 16:21-23

Matthew 16:21 – *From that time Jesus began to show his disciples that he must go to Jerusalem and suffer many things from the elders and chief priest and scribes, and be killed, and on the third day be raised.*

As we enter this section, we can see that Jesus is going to explain to His disciples that He must go to Jerusalem, suffer, be killed, and rise again on the third day. This is an excellent segue into understanding the fourth Servant song In Isaiah 52:13 – 53:12. In Peter's first epistle he references Isaiah 53:9, 53:7, 53:5, and 53:6 in 1 Peter 2:22-25. Although Peter quoted Isaiah 53 to explain how a Christian should look to Christ's example on how to suffer persecution, it demonstrates how Peter understood Isaiah 53 as being a prophecy of Christ's suffering. In fact, this Servant Song is referenced in John's gospel, Paul's epistle to the

Romans, Matthew's gospel, Luke's gospel, and the book of Acts. Therefore, this fourth Servant Song from Isaiah holds significance in the minds of the gospel writers, and it surely held significance to Peter. This Servant Song is the Old Testament gospel that prophesies Christ's arrival, life, rejection, trial, death, burial, resurrection, ascension, intercession, and exaltation. Therefore, when Jesus showed His disciples why He must go to Jerusalem, suffer, die, and rise again, we can see that the disciples and New Testament writers saw this as a prophetic and divine explanation of Christ's life, death, and resurrection. Not only this, but this Old Testament gospel explains the divine dilemma of how a holy God can be reconciled to sinful man. This is the gospel of divine accomplishment versus the works-based salvation in all other false religions and also in false Christianity. We will look at these verses to gain an understanding of what Christ was going to tell His disciples and how the disciples would have understood this passage of Scripture after Christ's exaltation (8) (9).

Isaiah 52:13 – *Behold, my servant shall act wisely; he shall be high and lifted up, and shall be exalted*

Here we see that Christ will act wisely and be highly exalted. But how would Christ act wisely? What would He accomplish? We see that Christ would act wisely by only doing the will of the Father (John 6:38). We see that Christ did only what He was shown from the Father (John 5:19). The Lord's bread was to do the will of His Father (John 4:34). When Christ was faced with drinking the full cup of wrath and asked that the cup be removed if possible, He submitted and bowed to the Father's will (Luke 22:42). Therefore, the Messiah would act wisely because He submitted Himself fully to the will of the Father.

We also see Christ would be exalted because of His victory and great redemptive act. Christ would accomplish the mission for which He was sent. In fact, Isaiah sees that Christ would be highly exalted where it says Christ will be, "high" and "lifted up," and "exalted." We see that Christ's praise crescendos in exaltation. It could even be said this way, "My servant will be highly exalted, exalted even higher, and exalted to the highest extent." Christ would be triumphant as the King of kings and Lord of Lords (Revelation 17:14, 19:14). At the end of Isaiah 53:12, we find out why Christ will be exalted to the highest and greatest extent possible. He will be exalted above all because, "he poured out his soul to death and was numbered with the transgressors; yet he bore the sin of many, and makes intercession for the transgressors."

Isaiah 52:14 – *As many were astonished at you – his appearance was so marred, beyond human semblance, and his form beyond that of the children of mankind*

This verse looks forward to and speaks of the physical beatings that Christ would receive. We see that during the unjust trials, Christ was spit upon in the face and struck with fists by the Sanhedrin (Matthew 26:68). In fact, the word for "struck" is *kolaphizó* and means "a blow from the fist" and it means to hit hard with the fist to make the blow sting and crush. It says that others "slapped" Jesus and this word comes from *rhapizó* which means to "strike with the palm of your hand." Thus, we see that at Jesus' trial, He was punched and slapped repeatedly. We also see that Jesus was flogged or scourged (Matthew 27:26). Matthew doesn't give the details of this scourging, but what this scourging typically entailed was a piece of wood that had leather thongs and in the end of the thongs were bits of sharpened metal. The victim would be tied to a post so the body could be stretched out. The victim would then be whipped over the body which would tear and pierce the flesh and would often expediate the crucifixion. We also see that soldiers would put a crown of thorns on Christ (Matthew 27:29). Since many blood vessels are close to the surface on the head, the head bleeds easily. Therefore, we can assume that there would have been profuse bleeding coming from Christ's head due to the crown of thorns piercing his skin. Additionally, we see that the guards took a rod and continued to strike Jesus in the face and spit on him (Matthew 27:30). So how was Jesus marred beyond recognition? He was repeatedly struck in the face, His flesh was torn, pierced, and flayed. He was continually struck in the face with rods, and His head was pierced by a crown of thorns. Therefore, His bodily figure would have been marred beyond recognition and His face would have been disfigured, swollen, and bloody beyond recognition.

Isaiah 52:15 – *so he will sprinkle many nations, and kings will shut their mouths because of him. For what they were not told, they will see, and what they have not heard, they will understand*

Because of the Messiah's salvific work He would offer forgiveness of sins for many nations. This word "sprinkle" carries with it the blood that is used in Levitical service for animal sacrifice. This sprinkling alludes to the forgiveness of sins. This once for all sacrifice would be given for the forgiveness of sins for people from every nation, tribe, and language (Revelation 7:9). Christ would be the atoning and propitiating sacrifice for the sins of many people.

Additionally, we see that kings would shut their mouths because of Christ. Kings of nations are regal and powerful. Kings of the world issue decrees. Kings of the world are honored by men. Kings of the nations are served by men. However, this King of kings and Lord of lords is not like the kings of the earth. This King did not come to be served, but to serve and give His life as a ransom for many (Mark 10:45). This Lord of lords was not born in the best of hospitals or palaces, but was born in a manger (Luke 2:7). This King of kings who created all things, stepped down into His creation and His own received Him not (John

1:11). This King who set apart the people of Israel for Himself and set apart the land of Israel for His people was crucified and condemned to death by His own people. This is why kings will shut their mouths. No king has ever been exalted so high and has purposefully condescended so low. There is no other king like this King who would lay down His life for His people (John 10:11). Therefore, kings would shut their mouth at the wonder and majesty of Christ the King.

Isaiah 53:1 – *Who has believed what he has heard from us? And to whom has the arm of the LORD been revealed?*

The prophet prophesies that this good news of salvation will not be believed by many. In Christ's ministry, there was widespread popularity because of His powerful preaching and wondrous miracles. However, there were very few true disciples and believers. In fact, in Luke 13:23 there was a man who rightly understood this truth about very few receiving eternal life where he said to the Lord, "Lord, will those who are saved be few?".

The "arm of the LORD" is often referred to as God working out salvation (Isaiah 59:1, Psalm 98:1). When the prophet asks, "to whom has the arm of the LORD been revealed?," he is asking, "to whom has God's salvation been revealed?" This speaks of the truth that very few would see the salvation that Christ brought. Christ's hometown of Nazareth rejected Him (Luke 4:16-30). Cities were rejecting Him (Matthew 11:20-24). The religious leaders claimed He cast out demons by Beelzebul and rejected Him (Matthew 12:24). Many disciples walked no longer with Him because of His teaching (John 6:66). The people heard but could not understand, they saw but could not perceive, they could not hear with their ears, they could not see with their eyes, and their heart could not understand (Matthew 13:14-15). Thus, it was true that the Lord's salvation was revealed to very few and few believed upon Him.

Isaiah 53:2 – *For he grew up before him like a young plant, and like a root out of dry ground; he had no form or majesty that we should look at him, and no beauty that we should desire him.*

Why did so many not believe in Christ? Here is the answer. The Lord came and grew up as a nobody. He was just simply a root coming out of parched ground. He had a contemptible beginning. His parents were lowly, unknown, and unimpressive. The story of His conception was not believable. The Lord grew up in Nazareth, and as Nathanael said in John 1:46, "Can any good thing come from Nazareth?". The Lord was the son of a carpenter (Mark 6:3). The Lord didn't come in pomp and circumstance. No, He had a humble and lowly entrance and upbringing. There was nothing from an earthly perspective that would have drawn people to Jesus Christ. He did not have the earthly splendor, regal, and riches that accompanied the kings of the earth.

Isaiah 53:3 – *He was despised and rejected by men, a man of sorrows and acquainted with grief; and as one from whom men hide their faces he was despised, and we esteemed him not.*

As we saw earlier, Christ was rejected by many people during His ministry. Towns, cities, and religious leaders rejected Him. Though He would go on teaching, preaching, and healing many, they would not believe His words or His works (John 10:38). Israel's prophesied Messiah was rejected by those He came to save.

He was well acquainted with sorrow and grief. He casted out demons in a primarily Gentile area and was rejected by the city (Matthew 8:28-34). Jesus would see the devastation of sin and weep over the death of loved ones (John 11:28-37). Jesus would weep over Jerusalem for rejecting Him (Luke 19:41-44). Thus, Jesus was a man of sorrows. He cared for people's illnesses, hunger, disease, afflictions, and sins, but His people did not accept Him as He really was, their Messiah.

Isaiah 53:4 – *Surely he has borne our griefs and carried our sorrows; yet we esteemed him stricken, smitten by God, and afflicted.*

The griefs and sorrows that the Lord took upon Himself are the griefs and sorrows that are the result of sin. This is the imagery of the scapegoat on the Day of Atonement. The High Priest would lay both hands on the head of the goat, confess all the wickedness, rebellion, and sin of the Israelites over the goat, and the goat would carry the sins to a remote place and be released into the wilderness (Leviticus 16). This would picture a scapegoat that was to come who would carry away the sins of His people. This is the picture of Jesus taking up the sins of His people and removing them, never to be remembered again. This is the forgiveness spoken of in Hebrews 8:12 where the Lord will be merciful toward His people's iniquities and remember their sins "ou mē" or "no not" more.

However, this is not what the people thought. The people thought Christ was stricken by God and afflicted. The leaders of Israel wanted to kill Jesus because they believed He was a blasphemer. They heard Him call God His Father and wanted to kill Him (John 5:17-18). When Jesus confirmed He was the Christ and the Son of God, the high priest tore his robe and charged Jesus with blasphemy (Matthew 26:63-68). The people were persuaded that Christ's crucifixion was just for His blasphemy. They believed Jesus was stricken, smitten, and afflicted by God. They could not see that He was going to the cross to forgive sins. Peter would eventually see this as Christ's expiating work on the cross, or forgiveness of sins as Peter would say this in 1 Peter 2:24, "He himself bore our sins in his body on the tree."

Isaiah 53:5 – *But he was pierced for our transgressions; he was crushed for our iniquities; upon him was the chastisement that brought us peace, and with his wounds we are healed.*

In this verse, we see both the doctrines of propitiation and reconciliation. "Propitiation" comes from *hilastérion* and can mean "a sin offering by which the wrath of a deity shall be appeased." This word carries with it the idea of appeasement or satisfaction. The reason there is satisfaction is because the full punishment has been delivered. Therefore, because the full punishment has been delivered, the one who has delivered the punishment has been appeased or satisfied.

The physical beatings were certainly part of Christ being a substitutionary propitiation for sin. He was certainly pierced with the crown of thorns (Matthew 27:29). He was certainly pierced when He was scourged (Matthew 27:26). He was certainly pierced when He was crucified (Matthew 27:35). Christ was certainly crushed and bruised when He was certainly struck and beaten (Matthew 26:67-68).

However, God the Father is the one who needed to be appeased and satisfied, not man. Therefore, it was God the Father who needed to crush His Son (Isaiah 53:5, 53:10). It was God the Father who needed to curse His Son (Galatians 3:13). It was God the Father who needed to forsake His Son (Matthew 27:46, Psalm 22:1). It was God the Father who needed to punish His Son (Romans 3:25). It was God the Father who needed to condemn His Son (Romans 8:3). It was God the Father who showed up in darkness at Calvary to crush, curse, forsake, punish, and condemn His Son (Luke 23:45, Matthew 27:45, Mark 15:33). On the cross, the Father treated His one and only Son like a condemned and cursed sinner. God the Father punished Him with the divine wrath that sinners deserve. On the cross, Jesus suffered the full wrath of God for all sinners who would ever believe. On the cross, the full omnipotent wrath of God toward sin was unleashed on the Lord Jesus Christ. This wrath of God toward sinners is only understood perfectly by God. Although sinners who reject Christ are suffering in hell, they are suffering for their own sins. However, Christ died for all the sins of all believers. If one could take the full fiery heat and weight of the sun, the stars, and the galaxies and place it on Christ to crush Him, this would not even come close to what Christ suffered on the cross. The eternal Son of God took the full omnipotent wrath of His Father.

This is the chastisement that brought peace. There is no expiation without propitiation. Peter certainly understood that God the Father was satisfied when He crushed His beloved Son. Peter knew of the darkness of Golgotha. Peter would have remembered the earthquake following Christ's death (Matthew 27:51). Peter would have known of the temple curtain being torn in two (Matthew 27:51, Mark 15:38, Luke 23:45). Just as Jesus was pierced for our transgressions, Peter would have known what it meant for Christ to be "crushed" for our iniquities. Peter speaks of Christ's propitiation and reconciliation as he references Isaiah 53:5 in 1 Peter 2:24 where he says, "By his wounds you have been healed."

Isaiah 53:6 – *All we like sheep have gone astray; we have turned – every one – to his own way; and the LORD has laid on him the iniquity of us all.*

Here, we see that all people are like sheep. Sheep are dumb and defenseless. Sheep wander into danger. Sheep are dirty. This is speaking of the absolute depravity of men. Men are dumb, defenseless, dirty, depraved, and are in need of being saved. As we mentioned above, this is talking of the substitutionary atonement or propitiation of Christ. God the Father imputed all unrighteous and sins of the elect on His Son and then punished His Son. Jesus said this in John 10:11 about His sheep, "I am the good shepherd. The good shepherd lays down his life for the sheep." Jesus reiterated this same point in John 10:14-15 where He says, "I am the good shepherd; I know my sheep and my sheep know me – just as the Father knows me and I know the Father – and I lay down my life for the sheep." This is exactly what Peter had in mind when he says this in 1 Peter 2:25, "For you were straying like sheep, but have now returned to the Shepherd and Overseer of your souls." Peter had in mind Christ's substitutionary propitiation that reconciled sinful men to holy God.

Isaiah 53:7 – *He was oppressed, and he was afflicted, yet he opened not his mouth; like a lamb that is led to the slaughter, and like a sheep that before its shearers is silent, so he opened not his mouth.*

This verse looks at Christ's silent submission. When Christ stood before the unjust trial of the Sanhedrin and Herod, He did not defend Himself or retaliate in wrath but rather, He stood silent (Matthew 26:57-68, 27:11-14, Luke 23:6-12). Although the accusations of Christ were false, the trials were unjust, the beatings were undeserved, and the mocking was sacrilegious, Jesus would not retaliate. Jesus was standing in the place of sinners. On the day of judgment, the books will be opened and everyone will be held accountable to God and every mouth will be silenced (Romans 3:19). Just as when the books are opened, the sinner is proved guilty, and the sinner is silenced and condemned to hell, so Jesus stood silent as one who was guilty and condemned, though no sin could be charged against Him (Matthew 26:60). Peter recalled this silent submission in 1 Peter 2:23 where he says this, "When they hurled their insults at him, he did not retaliate; when he suffered, he made no threats. Instead, he entrusted himself to him who judges justly."

Isaiah 53:8 – *By oppression and judgment he was taken away; and as for his generation, who considered that he was cut off out of the land of the living, stricken for the transgression of my people?*

This looks at the trials and sentencing of Christ. Christ was subject to unjust trials by the Jewish leaders. The trials allowed for false witnesses, false testimony, and no lawful retribution for false testimony (Matthew 26:57-68, Deuteronomy 19:16-21).

This also speaks of Christ dying suddenly when it says, "he was cut off out of the land of the living." This predicted Christ's sudden death. This predicted that Christ would not die an old man, but that His life would be cut off suddenly. It predicted that Christ would die suddenly for the transgressions of the LORD's people. Once again, this speaks of the substitutionary propitiation of Christ for the transgression of His people. Just as a burnt offering needed to be killed for the sins of the one sacrificing, so Christ needed to die for the transgression of His people. The Hebrew author saw this clearly in Hebrews 9:22 where he said, "without the shedding of blood there is no forgiveness of sins." In other words, sin requires death and where there is no sacrificial death, there is no forgiveness of sins. So, Christ needed to die for the sins of His people. Once again, Hebrews 9:26 talks about the sacrificial death where the author says, "But as it is, he has appeared once for all at the end of the ages to put away sin by the sacrifice of himself."

Isaiah 53:9 – *And they made his grave with the wicked and with a rich man in his death, although he had done no violence, and there was no deceit in his mouth.*

This verse undoubtedly talks about Christ's death and burial. Crucifixion was considered one of the most brutal and shameful modes of death. This foreshadowed Christ being killed and treated as a vile sinner. However, it also foresaw that Christ's grave would be with a rich man. This undoubtedly was fulfilled in Joseph of Arimathea who took Christ's body with Nicodemus, wrapped it with spices and linen, and then placed it in the new tomb where no one had ever been laid (John 19:38-42). We see Peter quote this verse again in his epistle where he says this in 1 Peter 2:22, "He committed no sin, and no deceit was found in his mouth." Undoubtedly, Peter would be able to look back to Isaiah 53:9 and attest to Jesus' sinless nature, testify that He was killed like a vile criminal and sinner, and confirm that Nicodemus and Joseph of Arimathea took the body of His Lord and buried Christ in a grave that was owned by a rich man.

Isaiah 53:10 – *Yet it was the will of the LORD to crush him; he has put him to grief; when his soul makes an offering for guilt, he shall see his offspring; he shall prolong his days; the will of the LORD shall prosper in his hand.*

Here, we see a prophecy of Christ's propitiation and resurrection. When it says, "it was the **will** of the LORD to crush him," this word "will" comes from *chaphets* and can also mean "to delight in" or to "be pleased." As we mentioned earlier, it delighted God the Father to crush, curse, condemn, punish, and forsake His Son. God is angry with sin. God hates sin. God sees sin as an abomination. God sees sin as wickedness. God sees sin as repulsive. God cannot look upon sin with favor. Because God hates sin and must punish sin, it delighted God the Father to take out His holy, righteous, and omnipotent wrath on His perfect, eternal, holy, sinless, and blameless Son, the Lord Jesus Christ. Therefore, God the Father was fully satisfied because all His omnipotent and righteous wrath was taken out on His Son who took the wrath of God for His all His sheep.

After Jesus had completed His substitutionary work for sinners, He uttered these words found in John 19:30, "It is finished." "It is finished," is translated from *tetelestai* which means "to end," "to bring to conclusion," "to accomplish," "to fulfill," or "to finish." Please note that Jesus didn't say, "I am finished." No! He said, "It is finished." His perfect propitiating and sin bearing substitutionary work was complete. Jesus paid the full price for sin. Jesus took the whole wrath of God. There is not one sin of God's people that was not punished at Calvary. There is not one sin of

God's people that the Father did not lay on His only begotten Son. God's justice was fully satisfied. In the secular sense, *tetelestai* was used to signify the full payment of a debt. The parchment on which the debt was recorded was stamped with the word *tetelestai* which meant the debt had been paid in full.

Charles Spurgeon has said of this word, "an ocean of meaning in a drop of language, a mere drop. It would need all the other words that ever were spoken, or ever can be spoken, to explain this one word. It is altogether immeasurable. It is high; I cannot attain to it. It is deep; I cannot fathom it. It is finished is the most charming note in all of Calvary's music. The fire has passed upon the Lamb. He has borne the whole wrath that was due to His people. This is the royal dish of the feast of love." A.W. Pink has said of *tetelestai*, "Eternity will be needed to make manifest all that *tetelestai* contains." A.C. Gaebelein has said of *tetelestai*, "Never before and never after was ever spoken one word which contains and means so much. It is the shout of the mighty Victor. And who can measure the depths of this one word!."

For those who have come to Jesus Christ in repentance and faith, they are no longer enemies of God. There is no more punishment for sin to those who are in Christ Jesus (Romans 8:1). There was one perfect sacrifice that was able to propitiate the righteous anger and wrath of God toward sin and this propitiating sacrifice is never to be repeated (Hebrews 9:25-27).

This verse also speaks of Christ's resurrection where it says, "he shall see his offspring." No one can see their offspring if they are dead. Only one who is alive would be able to see His offspring. Therefore, this verse captures Christ's resurrection. Peter preached this very resurrection in his first sermon on the day of Pentecost where he says this in Acts 2:31, "he foresaw and spoke about the resurrection of the Christ, that he was not abandoned to Hades, nor did his flesh see corruption." Although Peter would reference Psalm 16, Peter was being taught that there was going to be a resurrection of Christ.

Lastly, we see here that there is a promise of regeneration. The LORD would have many offspring because of Christ. Christ would carry out His salvific mission and bring many sons to glory and make them children of God (Hebrews 2:10, 1 John 3:1). Therefore, Christ's work would ensure that He would give new birth to all those for whom He laid down His life (John 3:3, 10:11).

Isaiah 53:11 – *Out of the anguish of his soul he shall see and be satisfied; by his knowledge shall the righteous one, my servant, make many to be accounted righteous, and he shall bear their iniquities.*

Because of Christ's substitutionary and vicarious suffering for sinners, we see that He would, "make many to be accounted righteous." Of course, this speaks of the doctrine of justification, or rather, the legal and forensic declaration that one is declared righteous before the throne of God based on the merit of the Lord Jesus Christ. All of one's unrighteous was put on the sinless Lord Jesus Christ and all of Christ's righteousness was imputed and credited to the unrighteous sinner. Christ's work would guarantee a right standing, right relationship, and reconciliation between holy God and sinful man. Peter would make this very statement of justification by faith at the Jerusalem Council where he would declare that one's heart was cleansed by faith and not by circumcision or the law of Moses (Acts 15:1-11). Justification was through faith in Christ and was by the grace of the Lord Jesus (Acts 15:8-11).

Isaiah 53:12 - *Therefore I will divide him a portion with the many, and he shall divide the spoil with the strong, because he poured out his soul to death and was numbered with the transgressors; yet he bore the sin of many, and makes intercession for the transgressors.*

Because Christ would give Himself as a substitutionary sacrifice for sinners, He would be exalted. This speaks of Christ's exaltation. Christ would secure the Father's inheritance for guilty sinners and all the Father has would be given to Christ and Christ would give all of this inheritance to those for whom He died.

So what is the spoil that the exalted Christ would give to the transgressors for whom He died? It means the sinner would be seated with Christ in the heavenlies with every spiritual blessing (Ephesians 1:3). It means the sinner is regenerated or born again by the Holy Spirit (John 3:1–10; 1 John 3:1; 1 Peter 1:3, 23; Titus 3:5; Ezekiel 11:19–20, 36:24–27; Jeremiah 24:7, 31:33–34, 32:38–40; Matthew 5:8). It means the sinner is forgiven all his past, present, and future sins (Psalm 103:12, Isaiah 1:18, Ephesians 1:7, John 1:29, Micah 7:19, Romans 8:33–34, Hebrews 8:12). It means the sinner is reconciled to God through Christ (2 Corinthians 5:19, Romans 5:10–11, Colossians 1:21–22). It means the sinner becomes a child of God (Romans 8:16, Matthew 5:9). It means the sinner possesses a right standing with God or justification before God (Romans 3:22–28). It means the sinner is adopted into the family of God (Ephesians 1:5). It means the sinner is raised up with Christ and seated in the heavenly realms (Ephesians 2:6). It means the sinner is made a coheir with Christ (Romans 8:17). It means the sinner receives Christ as their Great High Priest (Hebrews 4:14). It means the sinner receives God as their Heavenly Father (Romans 8:15). It means the sinner receives Christ as their brother (Hebrews 2:11–12). It means the sinner receives eternal life (John 17:3). It means the sinner receives the Holy Spirit (Galatians 3:2, 14; Ephesians 1:13; 1 Corinthians 12:13; 2 Corinthians 1:21–22). It means the sinner's salvation is eternally secure (John 6:37–40, 10:28–29, 17:1–26; Romans 8:31–38). It means the sinner's sins were all punished in Christ on the cross (2 Corinthians 5:21; Romans 3:25, 5:19; Galatians 3:13, 2:20; John 10:11, 19:30; Hebrews 9:25–29, Colossians 2:13–15; Isaiah 53:1–12). It means the sinner has the guarantee that Christ will bring them to be with Him forever in heaven (John 14:1–3, 17:24; Hebrews 11:6; Revelation 21:1–7, 22:1–5). It means the sinner will reign forever with God (Revelation 22:5). It means the sinner will not be touched by the second death (Revelation 2:11). It means the sinner will have a resurrected and glorified body (1 Corinthians 15:12–58). It means the sinner now has the mind of Christ (1 Corinthians 2:16). It means the sinner inherits the kingdom of heaven (Matthew 5:3). It means the sinner is comforted by God (Matthew 5:4). It means the sinner inherits everything the Father possesses (Matthew 5:5). It means the sinner is filled with righteousness (Matthew 5:6). It means the sinner is given mercy and pardon for sin (Matthew 5:7). It means the sinner will receive a joyful welcome into Christ's kingdom (Matthew 25:21). It means the sinner will be rewarded by the Lord Jesus Christ (Matthew 25:23). It means the sinner has confidence before God in judgment (Matthew 25:31–40). It means the sinner will worship God in spirit and in truth (John 4:24). It means the sinner will worship the Lord in heaven for all eternity (Revelation 7:9–17). It means the sinner is part of the Bride of Christ (Revelation 22:17).

As we close this section, we can see why Peter would quote this Servant Song in his first epistle. Isaiah 52:13-53:12 predicts the life, death, and resurrection of Christ. This Servant Song predicted Christ's life (Isaiah 53:1-2), Christ's expiation (Isaiah 53:4), Christ's propitiation (Isaiah 53:5, 10), Christ's silent suffering and mistrials (Isaiah 53:7-8), Christ's death (Isaiah 53:8), Christ's burial (Isaiah 53:9), Christ's sinlessness (Isaiah 53:9), Christ's resurrection (Isaiah 53:11), Christ's work of justification (Isaiah 53:11), Christ's exaltation (Isaiah 53:12), and Christ's intercession (Isaiah 53:12). So, when Peter quotes Isaiah 53 four times in his epistle regarding Christ's sinlessness (1 Peter 2:22), Christ's silent suffering (1 Peter 2:23), Christ's expiation and propitiation (1 Peter 2:24), and Christ's reconciliation (1 Peter

2:25), we can assume with confidence that at some point, Christ explained His suffering, death and resurrection using Isaiah 53. On this very day, Peter would begin to learn why Christ needed to suffer, be killed, and be raised. On this very day, Christ was explaining His person and His work.

Peter Learns Christ and His Church will be in Conflict with Satan

Matthew 16:22-23 - *And Peter took him aside and began to rebuke him, saying, "Far be it from you, Lord! This shall never happen to you." But he turned and said to Peter, "Get behind me, Satan! You are a hindrance to me. For you are not setting your mind on the things of God, but on the things of man."*

We clearly see that Peter did not fully comprehend the reason Jesus needed to suffer, die, and rise again. This is why Jesus strictly warned the disciples to not let anyone know He was the Christ. The Jews did not understand that Christ needed to deal with sin. Although Jesus' rebuke seems harsh, it was necessary. The disciples needed to understand the work of the Lord Jesus Christ. They needed to be taught that Jesus needed to be a sinless, spotless, and sacrificial Lamb that would undergo the wrath of God for sinful men to forgive, redeem, ransom, justify, sanctify, and glorify those for whom He would die. Peter's rebuke of the Lord was met with an equally forceful rebuke from the Lord. Such a thought from Peter was counter to Christ's redemptive work. Such a comment was not heavenly minded, but was satanically motivated. Therefore, we see that Christ's church would be in a conflict with Satan. Satan, the enemy of God, would constantly be at war with Christ and His church. Therefore, Peter would learn an important lesson that Satan would be opposed to Christ's person, Christ's work, Christ's church, and God's Word. Peter would give this warning and command regarding the devil in 1 Peter 5:8-9 where he says, "Be sober-minded; be watchful. Your adversary the devil prowls around like a roaring lion, seeking someone to devour. Resist him, firm in your faith, knowing that the same kinds of suffering are being experienced by your brotherhood throughout the world." Therefore, let us understand what Peter would have understood of Satan.

In the Bible, Satan is called the devil (Matthew 4:1), Lucifer (Isaiah 14:12), Beelzebul (Matthew 12:24), Belial (2 Corinthians 6:15), the evil one (Matthew 13:19), the tempter (Matthew 4:3), the ruler of this world (John 14:30), the god of this age (2 Corinthians 4:4), the prince of the power of the air (Ephesians 2:2), the accuser of the brethren (Revelations 12:10), the old serpent (Revelation 12:9), the great dragon (Revelation 12:9), the roaring lion (1 Peter 5:8), Apollyon (Revelation 9:11), the father of lies (John 8:44), the antichrist (1 John 4:3), the ruler of the demons (Matthew 9:34), an angel of light (2 Corinthians 11:14), and more. The names that have been given to the devil rightly characterize who he is.

The name *devil* comes from *diabolos* which means "slanderous" or "falsely accusing." Properly, this is "a false accuser who unjustly criticizes to hurt, malign, and sever a relationship." It can also mean "one who makes charges that bring down and destroy." This characteristic is most prominent in how the devil slanders God's Word. He tempted Eve to believe that God's faithfulness, omniscience, kindness, and character could not be trusted (Genesis 3:1–19). The devil speaks slanderously about God's Word and tries to get man to doubt the reality of the divine standard, doubt God, doubt God's character, doubt God's work, doubt God's love, and doubt God's ability. The devil is a twister, corrupter, and perverter of Scripture (2 Peter 3:16, Matthew 4:1–11). The devil speaks slanderously about the truth of God's Word to bring about the destruction of souls.

The name *Satan* comes *Satanas* and this word means "adversary." The devil is also called the *antichrist* which comes from *antichristos* which means "one who puts himself in the place of Christ" or "against Christ." It is used to describe an opponent of Christ. Both *Satan* and *antichrist* are fitting names for the devil as he is the adversary of God. The devil will oppose everything concerning God. The devil opposes God's standard for male and female (Genesis 1:27) by saying that women can be men and men can be women. The devil opposes God's standard for marriage between a man and a woman (Matthew 19:4–6) by saying that women can marry women and men can marry men. The devil opposes God's standard for murder (Matthew 5:21–22) by saying that women have the right over their body to murder unborn children. The devil opposes God's standard for adultery (Matthew 5:27–28) by saying that adultery is only committing a physical act and that pornography is not adultery. The devil opposes God's standard for righteousness (Matthew 5:20, 48) by saying that ceremonies and sacraments can save someone or give God's righteousness and saving grace. The devil opposes God's Word by causing men to misinterpret Scripture (Luke 11:52). The devil is opposed to everything that is righteous.

The devil is also called *the evil one* which comes from *ponéros* which means "evil," "bad," or "wicked." It is derived from *pónos* which means "pain or laborious labor." Properly, it emphasizes the inevitable agonies and misery that always go with evil. It is used to describe not only evil in nature, but what is viciously evil in its influence and what is actively harmful. This denotes someone who is not content in being corrupt themselves, but also seeking to corrupt others and draw them into the same destruction.

What is deeply ominous about this title is that this is the title given to the devil in the parable of the Sower where the devil is the evil one who continually snatches away the salvific Word and message from one's heart (Matthew 13:19, Luke 8:11–12). The devil is actively and willfully set on propagating evil by fighting

God and His Word to damn men's souls (Matthew 13:19, Luke 8:12).

The devil is also called *Beelzebub* which means "lord of the flies" or "lord of filth." *Baal* was an ancient pagan word for "lord" and *Zebub* or *Zebul* is translated to "flies." The Ekronites worshipped Beelzebub who was the god of flies as noted in 2 Kings 1:16. Additionally, the word *Zebel* could also be used which meant "dung." Essentially, *Beelzebel* means the "lord of the dung." Over the centuries, this title was used to refer to Satan. This would be a very appropriate title for Satan to essentially say that the devil is lord over everything that is filthy, dirty, worthless, and rotten. Additionally, the name *Belial* is a term which refers to the devil as "the utterly worthless one." Beelzebub, Beelzebel, and Belial all capture the very character of the devil which is that he is utterly worthless because he is the lord over everything filthy, dirty, worthless, and rotten, which is opposed to the Lord.

The title *ruler of this world* is the title Jesus gives to the devil in John 14:30. A similar title that Paul would give the devil was the *prince of the power of the air* (Ephesians 2:2) and the *god of this age* (2 Corinthians 4:4). This is to say that the devil is "the ruler of everything unholy and sinful in the world." The apostle John would describe the devil's rulership this way in 1 John 2:16, "For all that is in the world—the desires of the flesh and the desires of the eyes and pride of life—is not from the Father but is from the world." Paul would describe the devil's rulership this way in Ephesians 2:1–2, "And you were dead in the trespasses and sins in which you once walked, following the course of this world, following the prince of the power of the air, the spirit that is now at work in the sons of disobedience." Paul, John, and Jesus would say that Satan's rulership is one where he proudly and wickedly rules over sexual immorality, impurity, sensuality, idolatry, sorcery, enmity, strife, jealously, fits of anger, rivalries, dissensions, divisions, envy, drunkenness, orgies, adultery, homosexuality, stealing, greediness, revelry, evil thoughts, false witness, slander, crude joking, filthiness, foolish talking, and covetousness (Galatians 5:19–21, 1 Corinthians 6:9–10, Matthew 15:19, Ephesians 5:3–5).

Satan loves pornography. Satan loves homosexual marriage. Satan loves the LGBTQ movement. Satan loves gender fluidity. Satan loves witchcraft. Satan loves murder in the name of religion. Satan loves abortion. Satan loves every kind of theft. Satan loves vandalism. Satan loves materialism. Satan loves dirty jokes. Satan loves when men treat football as more important than church. Satan loves when parents treat their child's sports as more important than the Bible. Satan loves selfishness. Satan loves self-righteousness. Satan loves short tempers. Satan loves corrupt politics. Satan loves the atheist state of North Korea. Satan loves when people follow politics rather than Christ. Satan loves divorce. Satan loves broken homes. Satan loves alcoholism. Satan loves fentanyl addiction. Satan loves smartphone addiction. Satan loves abusive parents. Satan loves rebellious children. Satan loves little white lies. Satan loves every evil thing. Paul gave an admonition in Philippians 4:8 on what the Christian should think about where he says, "Finally, brothers, whatever is true, whatever is honorable, whatever is just, whatever is pure, whatever is lovely, whatever is commendable, if there is any excellence, if there is anything worthy of praise, think about these things." Let us note that Satan hates and opposes all things that are true, honorable, just, pure, lovely, commendable, and excellent.

The devil is also called *an angel of light* by Paul in 2 Corinthians 11:14, where Paul says, "For even Satan disguises himself as an angel of light. So it is no surprise if his servants, also, disguise themselves as servants of righteousness." It is true that Satan is the god of all false religion which includes Hinduism, Buddhism, Taoism, Shintoism, Islam, Judaism, Sikhism, Confucianism, Zoroastrianism, and more. Not only is Satan an angel of light in false religion, he's also an angel of light in false Christianity. Jesus says this about false Christianity in Matthew 24:23–24, "Then if anyone says to you, 'Look, here is the Christ!' or 'There he is!' do not believe it. For false christs and false prophets will arise and perform great signs and wonders, so as to lead astray, if possible, even the elect." Jesus warned that there were going to be false messiahs and false prophets. Likewise, Paul gave a similar statement about false prophets and a false Christianity in 2 Corinthians 11:4, "For if someone comes and proclaims another Jesus than the one we proclaimed, or if you receive a different spirit from the one you received, or if you accept a different gospel from the one you accepted, you put up with it readily enough." Paul warned of false teachers that would proclaim a different Jesus and a different or false gospel.

Satan is the angel of light in Mormonism which teaches Jesus was a spirit child of the heavenly father and heavenly mother. Satan is the angel of light in the Jehovah's Witnesses which teach that Jesus was the archangel Michael before the creation of the world. Satan is the angel of light in the Lutheran, Roman Catholic, Eastern Orthodox, Greek Orthodox, and Anglican churches that teach regeneration, conversion, and salvation through water baptism. Satan is the angel of light in the Unitarian Universal church that teaches that Jesus does not send people to hell. Satan is the angel of light in the Christian Science church which teaches that Mary Baker Eddy's writings are equivalent to the Bible. Satan is the angel of light in Oneness Pentecostalism that denies the Trinity. Satan is the angel of light that teaches purgatory, salvation is by faith plus works, transubstantiation, easy believism with no repentance, anti-Trinitarian doctrine, the prosperity gospel, salvation by ceremonies and sacraments, baptismal regeneration, abhorrent Christology, and more. The *angel of light* title is a proper title of Satan who propagates every abhorrent and heretical form of false religion and false Christianity to oppose Christ and damn men's souls (1 Timothy 4:1–2).

Satan is called the *father of lies* by Jesus in John 8:44. Satan is a master liar. He is a manipulator of the truth. He is skilled in mixing truth with error (Matthew 4:1–11). He is masterful in covering a damning lie with enough truth to make it believable. He is the deceiver of the whole world (Revelation 12:9). He is clever in his falsehood. He is the father of lies and, when he speaks, he speaks out of his own character. The many names of the devil define his character and works.

When Peter is calling his listeners to resist the devil, he is giving a command to stand one's ground against Satan by standing firm on the Word of God by obeying it. To resist the devil is to make a stand against everything he propagates and instigates. Peter would have learned a significant lesson on this day that Satan would be opposed to Christ, Christ's church, Christ's gospel, and God's Word.

Peter Hears the Cross Carrying Gospel Call to Follow Christ – Matthew 16:24-26

Matthew 16:24—*Then Jesus said to his disciples, "If anyone wants to come after me, he must deny himself, take up his cross, and follow me.*

Mark 8:34—*And he summoned the crowd together with His disciples, and said to them, "If anyone wants to come after me, he must deny himself, take up his cross, and follow me.*

Luke 9:23—*And he was saying to them all, "If anyone wants to come after me, he must deny himself, take up his cross daily, and follow me."*

As we enter this section, we are going to see the Lord issue a gospel call to follow Him in saving faith. Christ has explained that the church would be built off of Him, the church would be given the keys of the kingdom of heaven, that He needed to die and rise again, and that He and His church would be in conflict with Satan. He will now turn and issue a gospel call. This gospel call determines whether you save your soul or lose your soul. This gospel call determines whether your sins are bound or loosed. This gospel call determines whether you are inside or outside the kingdom of heaven. This gospel call explains how to pass through the narrow gate. Therefore, this gospel call is of critical importance to understand.

Jesus never hid His cost of what it meant to be one of His disciples or what it meant to be a believer in Him. The crowd that had gathered with Jesus were made up of true disciples who had left everything to follow Him (Matthew 4:19). There was one of Jesus' twelve disciples that followed Him but was unregenerate and unconverted, Judas (John 6:70). There were people in the crowd who were amazed at His teaching but were uncommitted (Luke 4:32). There were people that followed Him because of His miracles but were uncommitted (John 6:2) There were people that followed Him because He provided food for them but were uncommitted (John 6:26–27). The crowd that followed Jesus was mixed with the committed, the curious, and the counterfeit. The crowd that followed Jesus was mixed with the faithful, the feigned, and the false. The crowd that followed Jesus was mixed with the sincere, the skeptical, and the pseudo.

The crowd and religious leaders were faced with making a decision on Jesus based on His claims and the works He was doing (John 5:36). However, there were always obstacles that came along with following Jesus. Jesus' teaching caused many of His disciples to depart from Him (John 6:66). Jesus' message to religious Jews that they were poor, blind, prisoners, and oppressed caused them to want to kill Him (Luke 4:19–29). Jesus' healing on the Sabbath caused the religious leaders to want to kill Him (Mark 3:6). Jesus' claim to deity caused people and religious leaders to stumble (Luke 5:21–25). Jesus' claim to be one with God the Father caused the Jewish leaders to want to kill Him (John 5:16–18). Jesus casting out demons into pigs caused great fear in an entire city and they asked Him to leave (Luke 8:37).

There was always a decision to be made on how to respond to the person and work of the Lord Jesus Christ.

First, notice that Christ's invitation to follow Him is for everyone. Christ's call to follow Him in a salvific way was and is open to everyone. Christ would turn to both His disciples and to the crowd when He issued the call. Jesus didn't hide this invitation in the fine print. Jesus didn't whisper this call. Jesus didn't issue this call to only a select few. No, Jesus Christ invited all people everywhere to follow Him. To the committed followers, this was a reminder of the call they answered and an exhortation to follow Him with deep commitment. For those that were unconvinced, undecided, and opposed, this served as a clarion call to come to and follow Christ in a salvific way. This invitation rang out to the crowds 2,000 years ago and the invitation remains open to all people everywhere today.

Second, notice that the one who issues the call also defines the terms of how He will be followed. Mankind can only follow Jesus Christ on His terms. There are no escape clauses. There is no bargaining with the terms. There is no negotiating with the terms. Jesus is the one who defines the terms on what it means to be His disciple, to be a believer, to be His slave. Jesus is the one who defines how to enter the Narrow Gate (Matthew 7:13–14). Jesus is the one who defines how to enter the kingdom of God (Mark 1:15). Jesus is the one who defines how to enter the kingdom of heaven (Matthew 4:17). This is the call that the Lord Jesus Christ has put forth. You will either accept this call or deny this call. You can embrace the call or ignore the call, but how you respond to this call determines all eternity for you. How you respond to this call determines whether you lose your soul or keep your soul.

Third, notice that Jesus knew that all types of people would desire to come to Him in a salvific way. The word *wants* comes from *theló* which means to "wish," "desire," "intend," or "to be willing." *Theló* carries with it the desire, wish, or intention to follow a course of action. Jesus knew that the religious Jew, the down-and-out prostitute, the despised tax collector, the desperate leper, the half-breed Samaritan, the detested Gentile, the desolate paralytic, the religious teacher, the religious leader, and others would desire to receive salvation from Him. Likewise, even today, Jesus knows that the religious Catholic bishop, the religious Lutheran, the religious Eastern Orthodox churchgoer, the opioid addict, the porn addict, the self-righteous professing Christian, the practicing homosexual, the crooked businessman, the moral but lost grandparent, and many other people would be desiring salvation through Him. Jesus wasn't looking for a large number of disciples. Jesus was looking for the quality of the disciple. Additionally, the word "to come" is written in the aorist tense and infinitive mood. This is calling for a simple, single momentary action. Another way of saying this would be to say, "If anyone would desire to come to me once and for all, let him deny himself, take up his cross, and follow me." For all those desiring to come after Him in a salvific way, Jesus wanted everyone to be crystal clear on what it meant to be a believer, a disciple, and a follower of Him. Jesus didn't want people to be self-deceived. Jesus didn't want people to be misguided followers of Him. Therefore, for all people who would seek to be followers of His and even those that would reject, He issued this call.

Fourth, notice that the first command He gives to the crowd is to *"deny himself"* which is given in the aorist tense and imperative mood. The word *deny* comes from the original word *aparneomai. Aparneomai* is a compound word with *apó* mean "from" and *arnéomai* meaning "deny." The prefix *apó* intensifies *arnéomai* and the word *aparneomai* means to "deny," "disown," "repudiate," or "disregard." Properly, *aparneomai* means "to strongly deny." It means "to utterly deny that which was originally refused." It is important to note that this verb is in *aorist tense and imperative mood* which simply means that it is "a command that signifies and calls for a one-time activity or the completion of an activity." Unlike a *verb,* which is a *present imperative,* meaning the action is commanded to be followed in the present tense, the *aorist imperative* calls for the completion of the action. Therefore, we can know that Jesus is calling for a decisive self-denial for anyone that would desire to be His disciple.

Jesus used this word, *aparnéomai,* when prophesying Peter's denial of Him. Peter's first denial of Jesus was in front of a servant girl who said to Peter in Matthew 26:69, "You too were with Jesus the Galilean," and Peter responded to her in Matthew 26:70, "I do not know what you are talking about." Peter's second denial took place with another slave woman who saw Peter and said to him in Matthew 26:71, "This man was with Jesus of Nazareth," and Peter took an oath and responded in Matthew 26:72 by saying, "I do not know the man." Peter's third denial came when he was approached by some where they said in Matthew 26:73, "You really are one of them as well, since even the way you talk gives you away," and Peter cursed and swore and said to them in Matthew 26:74, "I do not know the man!"

So, what does it mean when Jesus called for self-denial? In Jesus' ministry, He was very clear on what was included with self-denial. Jesus would call for a denial of self-righteousness (Luke 18:9–14). Jesus called for a self-denial of works-righteousness salvation (Matthew 5:20). Jesus called for a self-denial of the love of money (Matthew 6:24). Jesus called for a self-denial of false religion (Matthew 15:12–14). Jesus called for a self-denial of following the world and the deceitfulness of wealth (Matthew 13:22). Jesus called for a denial of loving the world (John 15:19). Jesus called for the self-denial of living for worldly comfort (Luke 9:57–58). Jesus called for the self-denial of other relationships taking preeminence over Him (Luke 14:26, Matthew 10:34–38). Jesus called for a self-denial of running one's own life (Luke 14:26). Jesus called for a self-denial and repentance of one's sin. Jesus' call to deny oneself is a radical call of repentance, submission, and faith in Him. Just as Peter said, "I do not know the man," so all true believers in Christ are called to say the same thing to our sinful, self-righteous, self-willed, and self-absorbed way of life. This is a call to be done living for yourself. It was a call to stop being the lord of your life. Jesus is calling you to deny the unholy trinity of me, myself, and I. This is a call to repent of your sins, say goodbye to your worldly desires and pride, say goodbye to self-will, self-sufficiency, self-wishes, and self-righteousness in exchange for the Lord Jesus Christ's yoke, His will, and His rule over your life. Jesus called for a submission unto Him by saying goodbye to one's life.

Let's also note that it is a self-denial that encompasses the whole of one's person which includes one's mind, one's heart, one's will, one's soul, and one's body. There is not one single element of one's person that is not included in "deny himself" or "deny yourself." In Hebrew, the heart is the center of one's being. It is not merely the home of one's affections, but also the seat of the will and moral purpose. The condition of one's heart determined one's influence. In Proverbs 4:23, it says this regarding the heart, "Watch over your heart with all diligence, for from it flow the springs of life." Jesus warned that true defilement came from the heart in Matthew 15:18–19, where He said, "But the things that come out of the mouth come from the heart, and those things defile the person. For out of the heart come evil thoughts, murders, acts of adultery, other immoral sexual acts, thefts, false testimonies, and slanderous statements." The denying of oneself was to deny the whole of oneself. In fact, Jesus clarifies this in Matthew 16:25–26, where He says, "For whoever wants to save his **life** will lose it; but whoever loses his **life** for my sake will find it. For what good will it do a person if he gains the whole world, but forfeits his **soul**? Or what will a person give in exchange for his **soul**?" The words *life* and *soul* come from the original word *psuché*. *Psuché* can mean "the human soul," "the soul as the seat of affections and will," "the self," "a human person," "an individual," or a "life." It is a person's distinct identity. Kenneth S. Wuest says this of *psuché* which is, "that part of man which wills, and thinks, and feels, or in other words, to the will power, the reason, and the emotions, to the personality with all his activities, hopes and aspirations." Jesus was calling for the whole of one's body and soul to be submitted to Him. No longer would one's personal knowledge and wisdom be the driving force, but rather, it would be substituted for the knowledge and wisdom of the Lord Jesus Christ. Christ is not calling for sinless erfection. May it never be! What Christ is calling for is the renunciation, denunciation, and repudiation of one's life. Jesus is calling for commitment, submission, devotion, dedication, faithfulness, fidelity, and loyalty of one's life unto Him. It is a self-denial that will not learn, think, and act apart from God's Word but will learn, think, and act on sin, salvation, the Bible, theology, the church, living, marriage, money, family, job, eternity, and everything else according to God's Word. William Macdonald says this on self-denial, "There are 'No-No's' in that school which we must learn to renounce." In other words, the self-denying Christian must learn to say "yes" and not "no" to Jesus' commands.

Fifth, notice that there is a second command which is to "*take up a cross*." The word *take up* is also written in the *aorist imperative*, simply meaning that it is "a command that signifies and calls for a one-time activity or the completion of an activity." This is a command to make a final decision to not only deny yourself, but to also die to yourself. Notice that this is not cross-wearing, it is cross-bearing. Bearing a cross 2,000 years ago had a very specific meaning. *Bearing a cross* meant strapping an instrument of death on your back. It was a walk of death that included disgrace, shame, pain, and persecution. Disgrace was guaranteed. Shame was promised. Pain was a certainty. Persecution was inevitable. Jesus was calling for a self-denying, cross-bearing, Christ-identifying walk where a person would so identify with Him that they would do so even to the point of death. Notice in Luke's account that Christ says this cross-bearing would be daily.

A cross-bearing death to self was to be the walk and manner of one's life. Cross-bearing was not glorious. In fact, the Jews would have been very familiar with this picture as the Proconsul Varus crucified 2,000 Jews who besieged Sabinus and made an example of them and their insurrection.

Crucifixion to the point of death on the cross could take from six hours to several days and could be due to the aftereffects of compulsory scourging, maiming, hemorrhage, and dehydration causing hypovolemic shock. Death could also be precipitated by cardiac arrest. The Roman guards would not leave the site until the victim was dead. They could kill the victim by breaking the victim's legs, stabbing the heart or chest with spears, or building a fire at the foot of the cross to asphyxiate the victim. This statement by Jesus would have been shocking. As we noted earlier, just as one was to deny the unholy trinity of me, myself, and I, they were also called to repent and die to worldly desires, die to pride, die to self-will, die to self-sufficiency, die to self-wishes, and die to self-righteousness. They were to live for Christ's yoke, Christ's will, and Christ's rule over their life. This is a step of self-humiliation. This is a step of self-renunciation. Taking up one's cross is to die to self and surrender and submit to the King of heaven, the Lord Jesus Christ.

Sixth, notice Jesus' third command which is to *"follow me."* The word *follow* comes from *akoloutheó* which means "to follow the one who precedes," "to join one as an attendant," or "to accompany one." Properly, this means "to be in the same way with." It carries the idea of cleaving steadfastly to one and to conform wholly to that one's example in living and, if need be, in dying also. It is a strong word that gives the idea that the one following is not following begrudgingly but is willfully following step for step with Christ. The one following isn't resentfully following, but rather, is seeking to follow Christ wholeheartedly. The self-denying, cross-bearing follower is conforming their mind to that of Christ to mimic Christ in thought, word, deed, and intent.

Let's also notice that unlike the previous two commands which were in the aorist imperative, this command is in the present imperative. The *present imperative* signifies that it is a command that is to be continually followed. Jesus is defining the call to submissive saving faith. It is to make the conclusive decision to deny yourself, die to yourself, and to follow Christ wherever He goes as a self-denying, cross-bearing follower. You cannot follow Christ without denying yourself. You cannot follow Christ without taking up your own cross. You cannot change Christ's terms. You cannot wipe away these verses. You cannot bargain with the Way, the Truth, and the Life (John 14:6). Heaven and earth will pass away, but Christ's Word will not pass away Matthew 5:18, 1 Peter 1:24–25).

Jesus gave several examples where following Him was connected with hearing and doing. Jesus was very clear on the importance of submissive listening and following. Jesus explained that His sheep would be those that listened and followed Him where He says this in John 10:3–4, "To him the gate keeper opens. The sheep **hear** his voice, and he calls his own sheep by name and leads them out. When he was brought out all his own, he goes before them, and the sheep **follow** him, for they know his voice."

Likewise, Jesus made a similar statement about a grain of wheat needing to die before it bore fruit, that one must lose one's life to save it, and that His servants would be faithful followers of Him where He says this in John 12:24–26, "Truly, truly, I say to you, unless a grain of wheat falls into the earth and dies, it remains alone; but if it dies, it bears much fruit. Whoever loves his life loses it, and whoever hates his life in this world will keep it for eternal life. If anyone serves me, he must **follow** me; and where I am, there my servant will be also; if anyone serves me, the Father will honor him." Jesus would go on to say that those who hear His words and does them is a wise man whereas those who hear His Word and don't act upon them are foolish (Matthew 7:24–27). Jesus would pronounce that those who hear His Word and keep it are those who are blessed where He says this in Luke 11:28, "Blessed rather are those who **hear** the word of God and **keep it**!" When Jesus was calling all people to follow Him in a salvific way, it was a call to submissive, self-denying, cross-bearing, obedient faith. When Jesus stops, His sheep would stop. When Jesus would turn left, His sheep would turn left. Jesus' sheep would learn to think of prayer according to Jesus (Matthew 6:5–15, Luke 18:1–18). Jesus' sheep would learn to think of sin according to Jesus (Matthew 5:21–22, 27–30). Jesus' sheep would learn how to think about His teaching (John 8:31). Jesus' sheep would learn how to live in a fallen world (Matthew 5:13–16). Jesus' sheep would learn how to think of Him (Matthew 12:8, 16:16; Luke 24:46–47; John 6:35, 48, 51; 8:12, 58; 9:5; 10:7, 9, 11, 14; 11:25; 15:1). Jesus' sheep would learn to think of marriage according to Him (Matthew 19:1–10). Jesus' sheep would learn to think of handling persecution according to Him (Matthew 10:16–25). Jesus' sheep would learn how to forgive according to Him (Matthew 18:21–35). This is all to say that Jesus was calling for a self-denying, submissive faith in Him that would willingly follow Him wherever He went.

Another way to describe a self-denying, cross-bearing follower of Christ can be understood through how the writers of the New Testament identified themselves. Many of the New Testament writers identified themselves as a *doulos* or slave. The title of being a slave has negative connotations now, but that title doesn't bear that stigma when it comes to being a slave of Christ in the New Testament. A *doulos* in the New Testament and, as used by Peter and Paul, was one who willingly committed himself to serve a master he loves and respects. The *doulos* had no life of his own, no will of his own, no purpose of his own, and no plan of his own. All things were subject to his master. Every thought, breath, and effort were subject to the will of his master. The *doulos* was one who was absolutely surrendered and totally devoted to his master. The existence of the *doulos* was for the will and purpose of his master and nothing else.

Paul referred to himself as a slave or *doulos* of Christ (Romans 1:1, Philippians 1:1, Titus 1:1). Paul referred to Timothy as a *doulos* of Christ (Philippians 1:1). James referred to himself as a *doulos* of Christ even though he was half-brother to Jesus (James 1:1). Peter referred to himself as a *doulos* of Christ (2 Peter 2:1). Jude referred to himself as a *doulos* of Christ even though he was half-brother to Jesus (Jude 1:1). John referred to himself as a *doulos* of Christ (Revelation 1:1). Jesus referred to a true believer that did His will as His faithful *doulos* (Matthew 25:21). Jesus said that those who were a true *doulos* of His would do the things He commanded (Luke 17:10). Jesus told the Jewish leaders that there was a *doulos* to sin, but if the Son sets one free, they would be free indeed, or rather, a child of God (John 8:34–42).

Conversely, the one who claimed allegiance to Christ but never did His work was a wicked and lazy *doulos* (Matthew 25:26). The one who claimed allegiance to Christ but never denied self, bore a cross, and followed Him was self-deceived and Jesus says this of them in Matthew 7:21–23, "Not everyone who says to me, 'Lord, Lord' will enter the kingdom of heaven, but the one who does the will of my Father who is in heaven will enter. Many will say to me on that day, 'Lord, Lord, did we not prophesy in your name, and in your name cast out demons, and in your name perform many miracles?' And then I will declare to them, 'I never knew you; leave me, you who practice lawlessness.'" Even though many people would and will do works in Christ's name, He claims that they were never saved, regenerated, or converted into His kingdom. The word "never" comes from *oudepote* with *oude* meaning "not" and *pote* meaning "at one time or other." Essentially, when Jesus says, "I never knew you," He is saying that there was never a point in time that He ever savingly knew those who claimed allegiance to Him.

Please note that the true believer has no rights. The true believer has no vote. Jesus becomes the exclusive Lord of the believer's life. Jesus is not following the believer. Jesus is not the copilot of the true believer's life. Jesus is not sitting in the back seat and following where you go. No, at salvation, the believer denies self, dies to self, and takes the leap of saving faith to follow Christ. The believer does not know where the Lord will lead, but the believer will obediently and submissively follow the Lord regardless of where He leads them. The world, the flesh, family, friends, and one's own understanding are not being followed. The Lord Jesus Christ is the one being followed. Charles Spurgeon has said this of this call to salvation, "There are no crown-wearers in heaven that were not cross-bearers here below."

Matthew 16:25—*For whoever wants to save his life will lose it; but whoever loses his life for my sake will find it.*

Mark 8:35—*For whoever wants to save his life will lose it, but whoever loses his life for my sake and the gospel's will save it.*

Luke 9:24—*For whoever wants to save his life will lose it, but whoever loses his life for my sake, this is the one who will save it.*

Jesus will now give his listeners the ultimate paradox. The paradox is that if you would hold on to your life, you will lose it. If you hold on to your priorities, hold on to your own purpose, hold on to your personal agenda, hold on to false religion, and continue to be lord of your life, then you will lose your life eternally. However, if you will lose your life for the sake of the Lord Jesus Christ and the gospel, you will save it. This is the paradox. You must lose your life to gain it. You must die to live. It is important to notice that the word *life* is translated from *psuché* which can also be translated as the "soul." As we learned earlier, the soul is the home of one's affections and the seat of the will and moral purpose. Is the Lord Jesus Christ worth denying yourself, dying to yourself, and following Him or is there more worth in remaining the lord over your life? There must be a crucifixion before there is a resurrection. You cannot serve two masters as you will ultimately love one and hate the other (Matthew 6:24). You are either with Jesus or you are against Him (Luke 11:23). You either gather with Jesus or you scatter (Matthew 12:30). There are no fence straddlers. There are only those for Christ and those opposed to Christ.

Notice that the one who loses his life, or rather soul, for Christ's sake and the gospel will save it. Whoever denies the self, takes up their cross, and decides to follow the biblical Jesus will find their life, or rather, eternal life. Eternal life is not just speaking of the quantity of life, meaning eternality. It is also speaking of a new quality of life. The word *eternal* comes from *aiónios* and means "age-long" or "unending." *Aiónios* certainly has in mind the quantity of time, but it also carries with it the quality of a particular age. It can mean the unique reality of God's life in the soul of a man or God's life at work in the believer. Thus, believers who have eternal life are those who experience the quality of God's life now as a present possession. To have eternal life is to have a brand-new quality of life. This means that the believer will have abundant life (John 10:10). This means they will have new life (John 3:3). This means they will have a new quality of life (John 3:16). This means that Christians will now be swimming upstream rather than floating downstream with the world and false religion. The Christian will have lost their life to gain it. What once was up is now down. The world's way is now seen as the wrong way and Christ's way is the only way. This is the paradox of losing your life to find it in Christ and the foolishness of holding on to one's life, but ultimately losing it eternally.

Matthew 16:26—*For what will it profit a man if he gains the whole world and forfeits his soul? Or what shall a man give in return for his soul?*

Mark 8:36–37—*For what does it profit a man to gain the whole world and forfeit his soul? For what can a man give in return for his soul?*

Luke 9:25—*For what does it profit a man if he gains the whole world and loses or forfeits himself?*

Jesus is calling for everyone to do a spiritual accounting assessment. Since there are two options that will account for one's spiritual destiny, this decision will require the utmost diligence. In other words, do a hypothetical spiritual equation. If you could have all the money in the world, become king over every nation, own all the land, own every possession, and control the whole world system, what good would this be if you lose your soul and go to hell? If you could gain the approval of all mankind but not have the approval of God, what would you have gained? If you could gain everything the world has to offer for a finite period of time, but ultimately lose your soul and go to hell for all eternity which is a place of God's full wrath and is a place of blackest darkness (Jude 13, Matthew 22:13), filled with furious and concentrated fire everywhere (Matthew 13:42), where there is weeping and anger against God for the unrepentant Christ-rejecting and Christ-neglecting sinners (Matthew 8:12), where they will spend all eternity paying for every sin they've ever committed with no hope of escape (Luke 16:26) and only the expectation of excruciating torments to their body, soul, and spirit (Matthew 10:28) and an undying conscience that will haunt them day and night, forever and ever, with no reprieve (Luke 16:25); what have you gained? If you get to be lord of your life for a few years, but lose it forever, what have you profited? The fact of the matter is that you'll never own the whole world. You'll never control the world system. Jesus asks an impossible hypothetical question to his audience. You'll never be king over every nation. You'll never own everything in the world, but even if you could, what have you profited if you eternally forfeit your soul? Only a fool would hang on to creation and forsake the Creator. Only a fool would serve money rather than the Master. Only a fool would serve immorality rather than Immanuel. Only a fool would serve sexual licentiousness rather than the Sovereign Lord. Only a fool would serve a job rather than Jesus. Only a fool would serve the self rather than the Savior. Only a fool would serve a false Christianity rather than follow Christ. Only a fool would serve "me" rather than the Messiah.

Not only is a spiritual accounting necessary, but there is also an assessment that needs to be done on one's own soul. Jesus asks, "What shall a man give in return for his soul?" In other words, what could possibly be more valuable than one's own soul? The obvious answer is that there is absolutely nothing that could be more valuable than one's own soul, nor is there anything on earth that can be given in exchange for one's soul. This is clearly a call to saving faith. Jesus declares that the eternity of one's soul is at stake. What can a man give in exchange for his soul? The answer is nothing. The soul is the most valuable thing that any person has. The life and soul of an individual is what Jesus is calling for. This is one of the clearest calls to saving faith in Christ. There are several ways one could paraphrase these verses:

- If anyone would come to Me and desire salvation, let him deny himself, let him die to himself, and follow Me daily. For what would it profit a man if he kept his life, but lost his soul?
- If anyone would come to Me and desire to enter the kingdom of heaven, let him repudiate himself, let him mortify himself, and follow Me wherever I go. For if you maintain your position as lord of your life, you will lose it, but if you lose your life for My sake and the gospel, you will save your soul.

These verses are some of the clearest verses on Christ's call to a submissive and obedient faith in Him. We should see that this is clearly a gospel call to saving faith as the response of the individual to Jesus determines whether they lose their soul or save their soul.

So how is one to respond to the person and work of the Lord Jesus Christ, save their soul, enter the kingdom of heaven, enter through the narrow gate, be loosed from their sin, and not forfeit their soul? Deny yourself, take up your cross, and follow the Lord Jesus Christ!

CHAPTER 6

Peter Hears the Gospel Call for Preeminent Loving Faith Toward the Lord Jesus Christ

Luke 14:26 – *If anyone comes to me and does not hate his own father and mother and wife and children and brothers and sisters, yes, and even his own life, he cannot be my disciple.*

As we approach Luke 14:25–33, we find that Jesus was in His Perean and Judean ministry and Jesus had just finished giving a parable about a great banquet. In the parable of the Great Banquet, a man prepares a banquet and issues an invitation or a *kaleó* which is a summons or an invitation. The man throwing the banquet has his slaves go and issue the invitation (Luke 14:16–17). The preinvited guests were Israel (Luke 14:17). However, the preinvited guests made excuses that they could not attend because they were preoccupied with land (Luke 14:18), possessions (Luke 14:19), and relationships (Luke 14:20). The preinvited guests were not truly interested in the good news of Jesus Christ, salvation, and eternal life. These people demonstrated that they possessed the hearts that were more interested in the cares of the world and the deceitfulness of riches (Matthew 13:23). The man was angry at the preinvited guests and ordered that the slave go and issue the call of the great banquet to everyone else in the city such as the poor, the crippled, the blind, and the lame which would refer to the spiritually destitute in Israel (Matthew 5:3–12, Luke 14:21–22). Finally, the master tells his servant to go into the highways and hedges and compel everyone else to come to his banquet. The people that are invited who are from the highways and hedges are the Gentiles (Luke 14:23). Thus, we see that Jews and Gentiles would be invited to the great banquet. Additionally, the man tells the slave to "compel people to come in." The word *compel* comes from *anagkazó* which means "to compel or constrain while doing so with urgency and a pressing need." It is a strong word and conveys the idea of pressure being applied to bring about an immediate action or decision. This is where we will pick up Luke 14:25–33. Jesus has just given the parable of the Great Banquet and laid out the tragedy of not responding to the invitation to the great banquet. This is where we'll pick up Jesus' gospel invitation for a preeminent loving faith in Him.

Luke 14:25—*Now great crowds accompanied him, and he turned and said to them*

As we noted in the previous chapter, there were many reasons why people would follow Jesus as they were interested in His teaching, miracles, physical provisions, and more. Jesus would now turn to the large crowd and would declare the cost that was required to follow Him. This invitation called for supreme loyalty and love toward the Lord Jesus Christ. It is important to note that Jesus turned to the great crowds when He issued this call. This was a call that needed to be heard by those in the crowd who were the committed, the curious, and the counterfeit. It needed to be heard by those that were the faithful, the feigned, and the false. The call needed to be issued to the sincere, the skeptical, and the pseudo. Those that were true disciples would be reminded of the cost they committed to when they entered the kingdom of God and the commitment which was needed to follow the Lord. Those that were false disciples or uncommitted needed to be reminded of the cost of entry into the kingdom of God. Even today, all faithful servants of Christ are called to issue this call regardless of church membership or church attendance. The size of the crowd is not what was important, what was important was the message and accepting the invitation to follow the Lord Jesus Christ.

Luke 14:26—*"If anyone comes to me and does not hate his own father and mother and wife and children and brothers and sisters, yes and even his own life, he cannot be my disciple."*

First, let's notice that this invitation is open to everyone. As we saw earlier in the parable of the Great Banquet, the invitation goes out to everyone. The invitation is for male and female, Jew and Gentile, barbarian and Scythian, circumcised and uncircumcised, slaves and the free, kings and servants, the wise and the unlearned, the poor and the rich, the religious and the unreligious. The New Testament is a marvelous record of the Lord Jesus Christ saving women (Luke 8:43–48), saving the ceremonially unclean (Luke 5:12–16), saving the paralyzed (Luke 5:17–26), saving despised tax collectors (Luke 5:27–32), saving prostitutes (Matthew 21:31), saving Roman Gentiles (Matthew 8:5–13), saving hardened false teachers such as Paul (Philippians 3:5–9), saving Samaritans (John 4:39–42), saving business owners (Acts 16:11–15), saving physicians (Colossians 4:14), saving pagan worshippers (1 Thessalonians 1:8–10), saving slaves (1 Corinthians 7:21), saving married couples (Acts 18), and more. The invitation is a generous call to all people to come to Christ for salvation.

Second, we should see that Christ is inviting everyone to know who He is which includes His person and His work. When coming to Christ, it is important to know who Jesus is. No one can be saved by a false Jesus. You could put your faith in an anchor but grasping on to an anchor for salvation will drown you, it will not save you. The object of one's faith needs to be the biblical Jesus Christ. Jesus is the Jewish Messiah and Son of the Living God (Matthew 16:16). Jesus is God and He is coequal and coeternal with God the Father and God the Holy Spirit (John 5:17–18; 10:30, 38; 14:10). Jesus is the eternal, Only Begotten, one-of-a-kind, Son of God (John 3:16). Jesus is the Anointed One of God (Luke 4:18–19). Jesus is the Savior of the world (Luke 2:11). Jesus is the Creator and Sustainer of the Universe (John 1:1–14). Jesus is the Son of David (Matthew 1:1–16, Luke 3:23–38). Jesus was born of a virgin (Matthew 1:23). Jesus was the Word made flesh (John 1:14). Jesus was physically born into this world as a man (Matthew 1:25). Jesus is, thus, truly God and truly man.

Not only must we know the person of Jesus, but we must also understand His work. Jesus' work is central to the gospel. Jesus lived a sinless life (Matthew 26:59–60) and fulfilled all righteousness found in the law and prophets (Matthew 5:17–20, Luke 24:44–46). He declared Himself to be the Christ (Matthew 16:16), the Only Begotten Son of the Living God through His teaching (John 3:16, Matthew 22:41–46), which was attested to by His miracles and display of divine power (John 10:37–38). Jesus offered Himself as a spotless and blameless sacrifice for sin (John 1:29) to propitiate the righteous anger of God by taking all the sins of God's people (John 10:11) and, thus, the full wrath of God that was due to man (Matthew 26:39, 27:45–46; Luke 22:44). His sacrifice propitiated the righteous anger of God and reconciled and brought peace from man to God and God to man (Matthew 27:51–53, John 19:30). His substitutionary sacrifice and death also redeemed sinful man to Holy God by forgiving man's sin and imputing Christ's righteousness to man (1

Corinthians 5:21, Isaiah 53:1–12). Jesus was resurrected from the dead on the third day by His own power (John 10:18), by God the Father (Galatians 1:1), and by God the Holy Spirit (Romans 8:11), which affirmed His person, His teachings, and salvific work for sinners (Romans 4:25). He ascended to the right hand of the Father (Luke 24:51) and is empowered with all authority to bring about the plan of salvation for all His people (Matthew 28:18) by causing them to be born again (John 3:1–10) and justified by His grace (John 3:16, 18, 36). He will also return to bring all His own to heaven with Him (John 6:37–40, 14:1–3) to be glorified (John 17:24) while also judging and condemning Satan, demons, and sinful man (Matthew 25:31–46, Revelation 20:7–15). This is the true person and work of Jesus. When coming to Christ for salvation, the person and work of the Lord Jesus Christ should be known and comprehended. Jesus is not calling us to decide without getting to know Him or His work. Just as we would take time to get to know someone before we decide to make a marriage commitment, Jesus invites us to get to know Him. Jesus is inviting us to learn about Him and seek Him through the Scriptures. This is no blind date. This is no quick commitment. Jesus gives the invitation to know His person and work and then commands and demands an answer.

Third, notice that the one issuing the call sets the terms. As we learned earlier in the previous chapter, Jesus is the one who sets the terms for what it means to come to Him for salvation. There is no escape clause. There is no redlining and modifying the terms. There is no negotiating with the one who sets the terms. The terms to come to and follow Jesus in a salvific way are His own terms. As we'll see in this call, there is no redemption without repentance. There is no salvation without submission. There is no salvation without sacrifice. There is no crown without bearing a cross. There is no heaven without holiness. There is no forgiveness without faith. The invitation rings out to everyone, and the call must be answered according to the Lord Jesus

Christ's terms. Heaven and earth will pass away, but God's Word will endure forever (Matthew 24:35).

Fourth, we should see that Jesus is calling for one's preeminent loving faith toward Him. Jesus' invitation would most likely be shocking to the crowd who was following Him. The fact that Jesus made a statement of someone hating rather than loving would have most certainly caught the crowd's attention. Although Jesus used the word *hate,* He was not calling for His disciples to turn on those they loved and have an evil disposition toward them. In fact, the Lord explained that we should love our enemies and pray for those who persecute us (Matthew 5:43). The Lord stated that the second greatest commandment was to love your neighbor as yourself (Matthew 22:39). The Lord upheld the fourth commandment when He indicted the Pharisees for cancelling, voiding, and disregarding the fourth commandment to withhold money that could be used to help one's parents (Mark 7:9–13). Therefore, we can see that Christians are called to love and pray for one's enemies, love our neighbor as ourselves, and honor one's parents.

When Jesus was calling for hate, He was showing contrast or preference. The Lord used this same method of showing contrast or preference in Matthew 6:24, where He says, "No one can serve two masters, for either he will hate the one and love the other, or he will be devoted to the one and despise the other. You cannot serve God and money." As in Jesus' example of serving both God and money, Jesus is simply saying that both God and money cannot have the same top priority as you will ultimately love one more than the other. If one loves money, they will hate God. To be devoted to money is to despise God. Matthew 10:37 helps us understand what Christ is saying where He says, "The one who loves father or mother more than me is not worthy of me; and the one who loves son or daughter more than me is not worthy of me." Jesus is purposefully creating extremes. He is pitting the affections of one's most loved ones against their affections to Him.

It is important to note that He doesn't start with friends, employers, or acquaintances. No, Jesus starts with those who are in your closest concentric circle. If you are a mother, Jesus is calling for your preeminent love and trust over your children. If you are a daughter, Jesus is calling for your preeminent love and trust over your mother. If you are a happily married husband, Jesus is calling for your preeminent love and trust over your wife. Jesus purposefully starts with the people that mean the most to you. Christ is calling for your preeminent allegiance, love, trust, and affection. Notice that in Matthew 10:37 if one has greater love and affection for anyone other than Him, He states that they are unworthy of Him. The word *worthy* comes from the original word *axios* and means "worthy," "worthy of," or "deserving." Properly, *axios* is the "assessment in keeping with how something weighs in on God's balance scale of truth."

Fifth, we should see that the one who is loving one's father, mother, wife, children, brothers, sisters, or anyone else more than the Lord Jesus Christ cannot be His disciple. The word *disciple* comes from the word *mathétés* which is "a learner, a disciple or a pupil." It was typical in Jewish culture for rabbis to be followed and have students or disciples. The disciples of rabbis would follow the rabbi to learn from him. This word *disciple* has been used earlier in the gospels and included followers who were curious, counterfeit, and committed. However, in this gospel call, Jesus raises the bar, refining and sharpening the definition of what it means to be a true disciple of His. Therefore, we see that this is an evangelistic call on what it means to come to and follow Him in a salvific way or to be a true disciple of the Lord Jesus Christ. What is most shocking is Jesus' statement at the end of verse 26. If anyone comes to Him in a salvific way and has a relationship and love that is over Him, He says, "He cannot be my disciple." Please note that Jesus doesn't say, "He may be able to be my disciple." No, Jesus says that such a person cannot be His disciple. *May* is a word of permission. *Cannot* is a word of ability.

For those that find a loving relationship greater than Jesus, they cannot be His disciple. We could paraphrase this condition several ways to emphasize this point:

- If anyone comes to Me for salvation but loves his father, mother, wife children, brothers, or sisters more than me, he is not worthy to be My disciple.
- If anyone comes to Me and desires to enter the kingdom of God but loves his father, mother, wife, children, brothers, or sisters more than Me, He hates Me and cannot be My disciple.
- If anyone comes to Me and desires eternal life but loves his father, mother, wife, children, brothers, or sisters more than Me, he despises Me and is not worthy of Me.
- If anyone comes to Me and desires to enter through the narrow gate, but loves his father, mother, wife, children, brothers, or sisters more than Me, he is not able and is unworthy to be My disciple.

This is all to say that at salvation Jesus becomes the sum and substance of one's life. Jesus is the priority and everything else becomes the periphery. This is to say that a person who has decided to follow Christ will live a life that loves Jesus to the extent that, by comparison, it appears as hate toward others. This is to say that the true disciple of Christ cares more about what Christ thinks than their most cherished loved ones. The disciple of Christ will still love all those in his close concentric circle, but it will become clear to those in the close concentric circle that the true disciple's allegiance, loyalty, and love are given to the Lord Jesus Christ.

Sixth, we should see that one who is loving his own life more than Christ cannot be His disciple. It is as if Jesus is just pushing down His foot on the accelerator. If there was ever a chance to lighten His terms of discipleship, it would seem appropriate to do so now. However, Jesus only intensifies His call. Not only does

Jesus call for hating one's father, mother, wife, brothers, sisters, and children, He now calls for one to hate their own life. In fact, the word *life* comes from the original word *psuché*. As we learned earlier, *psuché* can mean "the human soul," "the soul as the seat of affections and will," "the self," or "a human person, an individual." Jesus certainly isn't calling for self-mutilation, suicide, or anything of the sort. So, what does it mean when one hates their own life or hates their own soul?

Once again, Jesus is purposefully creating extremes. He is pitting the affections of one's own life and soul against their affections to Him. Jesus says it this way in John 12:25 regarding hating one's life, "Whoever loves his life loses it, and whoever hates his life in the world will keep it for eternal life." This could easily be translated to say, "Whoever loves his soul loses it, and whoever hates his soul in the world will keep it for eternal life." As we noted earlier, the one who hates His own soul and forsakes it for the sake of Jesus is the one who saves it. You could simply love your own soul and be the lord of your own life but, in the end, you lose it for all eternity. This is a call to absolute devotion and love to the Lord Jesus Christ. It is not only hard to love Jesus above one's most loved ones, but now Jesus is calling for one's love and devotion to Him to be greater than the love for one's own life. This call demands a spiritual evaluation of one's life and whether one's personal interests, personal hobbies, personal sins, personal ambitions, and personal pursuits will take precedence, priority, and preeminence over Christ. It is a call to assess whether one loves their own lordship over their life or loves Christ preeminently. To *love Christ preeminently* is to say that Jesus' direction for your life is the driving force and not your own pursuits. The Lord Jesus Christ may choose to give His true disciples abundance and great wealth. However, He may also call for one to give everything, perhaps one's own life, for the sake of Him and His gospel.

Jesus reiterates this very same message in Matthew 10:39, where He says, "Whoever finds his life will lose it, and whoever loses his life for my sake will find it." To love one's own life over Christ is to despise Christ. To love one's own life over Christ is to hate Christ. The one who loves their own life over Christ will never deny themselves, pick up their cross, and come after Christ because they love their life too much to deny themselves. To love one's life over Christ is to worship the unholy trinity of me, myself, and I. We could paraphrase Christ's call to hate one's own life this way:

- If anyone comes to Me for salvation but loves being the lord of his life more than Me is not worthy to be My disciple.
- If anyone comes to Me and desires to enter the kingdom of God but loves his life more than Me and will not deny himself shows his hate for Me and cannot be My disciple.
- If anyone comes to Me and desires eternal life but loves his life more than Me, despises Me and is not worthy of Me.
- If anyone comes to Me and desires to enter through the narrow gate but loves his own soul and selfish desires more than Me is not able and is unworthy to be My disciple.

To come to Christ and not hate oneself or give Christ one's preeminent love is actually self-love that will not repent of sins, will not say goodbye to worldly desires, will not say goodbye to pride, will not say goodbye to self-will, will not say goodbye to self-righteousness, will not self-deny, and will not take Christ's yoke and learn from Him. To love the unholy trinity of me, myself, and I is to hate the Lord Jesus Christ. Once again, these are absolute terms. Christ will not take second place. Christ the Creator will not share preeminent love and loyalty with anything or anyone else for He is a jealous God (Exodus 34:14).

Luke 14:27—*Whoever does not carry his own cross and come after me cannot be my disciple*

Seventh, we should see that the one who does not pick up his own cross, or rather, die to himself and come after Christ, cannot be His disciple. So, not only does Jesus call for the preeminent love over every other relation, including the love of one's own life, Christ now calls for His true disciples to carry their own cross. As we learned earlier, to take up one's cross is a command to make a final decision to not only deny yourself and hate yourself, but to also die to yourself. Notice that this is not cross-wearing, it is cross-bearing. Bearing a cross 2,000 years ago had a very specific meaning. Bearing a cross meant strapping an instrument of death on your back. It was a walk of death that included disgrace, shame, pain, and persecution. Disgrace was guaranteed. Shame was promised. Pain was a certainty. Persecution was inevitable. Jesus was calling for a self-denying, self-hating, cross-bearing, Christ-identifying walk where a person would so identify with Him that they would do so even to the point of death. Notice in Luke's account that Christ says this cross-bearing would be daily (Luke 9:23). A cross-bearing death to self was to be the walk and manner of one's life. Cross-bearing was not glorious.

To come after Christ is the same thing as following Him (Matthew 16:24, Mark 8:34, Luke 9:23). To come after Christ is to listen to the Good Shepherd and follow Him (John 10:3–4). To come after Christ is to hear His words and practice them (Matthew 7:24–27, Luke 6:46–49). To come after Christ is to hear His words and keep them (Luke 11:28). To come after Christ is to listen to His commands and obey them (John 14:23, 15:10). To come after Christ is to be a *doulos* of Christ, which is where the *doulos* has no life of his own, no will of his own, no purpose of his own, and no plan of his own. All things are subject to his master. Every thought, breath, and effort are subject to the will of his master. The existence of the d*oulos* was for the will and purpose of his master and nothing else. To come after Christ is to follow Christ with a submissive, self-denying, obedient, loving, and repentant faith.

This statement by Jesus would have been shocking. Just as one was to deny themselves, they were also called to repent and die to worldly desires, die to pride, die to self-will, die to self-sufficiency, die to self-wishes, die to self-righteousness, and die to themselves. They were to live for Christ's yoke, Christ's will, and Christ's rule over their life. This is a step of self-humiliation. This is a step of self-renunciation. Taking up one's cross is to die to self and surrender to the King of heaven, the Lord Jesus Christ. Is it possible to be a true disciple and follow after Christ without a faith that is submissive and obedient and that gives preeminent love to the Lord? Jesus does not think so. In fact, Jesus knows it is not possible where He says such a person "cannot be my disciple." To put it another way, Jesus said it this way in Matthew 10:38, "And whoever does not take his cross and follow me is not worthy of me."

Eighth, we should see that Jesus is making a claim to deity or to be God. There is nothing or no one in all creation that should have this kind of love and devotion other than God. As we recalled earlier, the greatest commandment by Jesus is the Shema and He reiterated this when asked what the greatest commandment is (Mark 12:28–34, 22:34–39). The Shema is found in Deuteronomy 6:4–5 and reads, "Hear, O Israel: The LORD our God, the LORD is one. You shall love the LORD your God with all your heart and with all your soul and with all your might." For Jesus Christ to turn to the crowd and call the crowd to love Him more than anyone else was a claim to deity and the people should have known this.

Ninth, Jesus spoke of this kind of love and inexpressible joy in coming to Him in saving faith in two parables. In Matthew 13:44–46, there are two parables: the Hidden Treasure and the Pearl. In Matthew 13:44, He says, "The kingdom of heaven is like treasure hidden in a field. When a man found it, he hid it again, and then in his joy went and sold all he had and bought the field." This is speaking of a man who finds Jesus Christ, the forgiveness of sins, eternal life, and reconciliation and a relationship with the Living God. The man is filled with joy inexpressible and sells everything to buy the field. This more specifically talks about the joy and price people are willing to pay to enter the kingdom of God. This is the most valuable possession in the world that is worth the cost of a personal cross, denying yourself, and submitting, and trusting in Christ. In Matthew 13:45–46, Jesus says, "Again, the kingdom of heaven is like a merchant looking for fine pearls. When he found one of great value, he went away and sold everything he had and bought it." There are differences in each parable, but the underlying theme is that those who have found the forgiveness of sins, Jesus Christ, and eternal life will pay the price because what they have found is so much more valuable than anything else in this life.

Luke 14:28–30—*For which of you, desiring to build a tower, does not first sit down and count the cost, whether he has enough to complete it? Otherwise, when he has laid a foundation and is not able to finish, all who see it begin to mock him, saying, 'This man began to build and was not able to finish.'*

Tenth, we should see that Jesus is calling people to count the cost to follow Him. He has laid down His terms for being His disciple. He is calling everyone to stop and consider the cost. He does not want a quick decision. He does not want to coerce anyone. He is not guaranteeing what will happen in the next five, ten, or twenty years. He is simply stating that you will need to carefully consider whether you're willing to commit to Him. In an ultimate shame and honor society, such as the Jewish culture, they would have understood this parable. They would know that it would be foolish to start to build a building without first determining whether they could finish. The one who had not carefully counted the costs and decided to build without considering the costs would ultimately face great shame. Is it worth losing your life to gain Jesus? Is hating your own soul, denying yourself, dying to yourself, taking up your own cross, and following Jesus worth it? Christ is calling for a serious spiritual assessment. Can you really and truly relate to Paul where he says in Acts 20:24, "But I do not account my life of any value nor as precious to myself, if only I may finish my course and the ministry that I received from the Lord Jesus, to testify to the gospel of the grace of God"? Can you truly relate to Paul in Philippians 3:7–9, where he says, "But whatever gain I had, I counted as loss for the sake of Christ. Indeed, I count everything as loss because of the surpassing worth of knowing Christ Jesus my Lord. For his sake I have suffered the loss of all things and count them as rubbish, in order that I may gain Christ and be found in him, not having a righteousness of my own that comes from the law, but that which comes through faith in Christ, the righteousness from God that depends on faith"? All those who have been justified by faith can relate to such self-denying, self-hating, cross-bearing faith in Christ.

Luke 14:31–32—*Or what king, going out to encounter another king in war, will not sit down and deliberate whether he is able with ten thousand to meet him who comes against him with twenty thousand? And if not, while the other is yet a great way off, he sends a delegation and asks for terms of peace.*

Eleventh, we should see that the King will return one day, and He will not be coming as the Suffering Servant, but as the conquering King. This King will come to judge and wage war (Revelation 19:11). This King will come with His armies (Revelation 19:14). This King will strike down nations with His Word (Revelation 19:15). This King will tread upon His enemies with the wrath of God (Revelation 19:15). This King will kill and destroy His enemies (Revelation 19:21). This King will come with a wrath so horrible that people will cry for mountains and rocks to fall on them rather than suffer the wrath of the Lamb (Revelation 6:16–17). This is the King that is coming, and He has made terms of peace. Jesus is saying that the king with 10,000 men should see that he is outnumbered and outmatched against the King with 20,000 men. This King will either say, "Well done, good and faithful slave" or "Bring them here and slaughter them before Me." This King will either say, "Enter into the joy of your master" or "Cast that worthless servant into outer darkness. In that place there will be weeping and gnashing of teeth." The King will either say, "Come, you who are blessed by my Father, inherit the kingdom prepared for you from the foundation of the world" or "Depart from Me, you cursed, into the eternal fire prepared for the devil and his angels." The King will either say, "Well done, good and faithful slave" or "Cut him in pieces and put him with the unfaithful." This King will either say, "Well done, good and faithful servant" or "You wicked and slothful slave, I never knew you, depart from Me you worker of lawlessness."

Jesus is stating that the king with 10,000 men should request terms of peace from the King with 20,000 men. Psalm 2 pictures this beautifully where the nations are seen raging against the LORD and against the One enthroned in heaven. At the end of Psalm 2, in verse 12, the psalmist says this, "Kiss the Son, lest he be angry, and you perish in the way, for his wrath is quickly kindled. Blessed are all who take refuge in him." Psalm 2:12 is a picture of someone coming to the throne and submitting to the LORD. The psalmist is picturing a dignitary receiving the humble kiss of an inferior submitting and pledging allegiance. In this very same way, the Lord Jesus Christ has given an invitation to submit to Him. The great banquet invitation has been issued. The terms of this invitation have been defined by the King of heaven for all mankind. You don't want to meet this King without agreeing to His terms of repentance and faith. You don't want to meet this King if you've created your own terms of peace. You don't want to meet this King relying on water baptism, confirmation, giving money to church, church membership, taking the Lord's Supper, good works, or any of the like for salvation. There is time to come to terms with this King for He is a good, gracious, kind, compassionate, forgiving, loving, and merciful King. If you come to this King on His terms of faith, He will forgive your sins and give you His righteousness. The transaction will be swift and instantaneous. This gracious King says, "Come now, let us reason together, though your sins are like scarlet, they shall be as white as snow; though they are red like crimson, they shall become like wool." (Isaiah 1:18). Come to this King and accept His invitation for you will find rest for your soul (Matthew 11:28–30) and grace in your time of need (Hebrews 4:16). Come to this King and receive His invitation into the kingdom of God and He will remember your sins no more (Hebrews 8:12).

Luke 14:33—*So therefore, any one of you who does not renounce all that he has cannot be my disciple.*

Twelfth, we should see that those who do not renounce all they have cannot be Christ's disciple. *Renounce* comes from the original word *apotassó* which means to "withdraw from," "renounce," or "send away." Properly, *apotassó* means "to say goodbye and depart from or to bid farewell, forsake, or send away." When Jesus calls for the renouncing of all one's possessions, He is now talking about possessions. As mentioned above, He may not ask you to give up everything, but you must be willing to give up everything if He calls you. In fact, in this life, He may give you an abundance or more than you need. However, He may require everything of you. Regardless of what He decides, are you willing to give up everything for Him? Therefore, Jesus Christ is calling you to become an owner of nothing and a steward of everything.

Thus, we see that Christ is asking for total allegiance and trust with your personal relationships, personal life, and possessions. This is the invitation to the great banquet. This is a gospel call for a submissive, preeminent loving faith in the Lord Jesus Christ and a relationship with Him. As in the parable of the Great Banquet, Christ called for an evaluation if you will lovingly submit to and trust in Him above land (Luke 14:18), possessions (Luke 14:19), and relationships (Luke 14:20).

1 Peter 1:8-9 – *Though you have not seen him, you love him. Though you do not now see him, you believe in him and rejoice with joy that is inexpressible and filled with glory, obtaining the outcome of your faith, the salvation of your souls*

So did Peter understand this gospel call of preeminent loving faith toward the Lord Jesus Christ? He certainly saw a rich young ruler who could not see his own sin, could not depart from his great wealth, could not hate his own life, could not renounce all that he had, and could not preeminently love the Lord Jesus Christ through faith (Matthew 19:16-26, Mark 10:17-27, Luke 18:18-27). After the rich young ruler departed, Jesus said this in Luke 18:24-25, "How hard it is for the rich to enter the kingdom of God! Indeed, it is easier for a camel to go through the eye of a needle than for someone who is rich to enter the kingdom of God." Those who heard asked, "who then can be saved" and Jesus replied, "What is impossible with man is possible with God." (Luke 18:26-27). Peter would tell the Lord that they had left everything to follow Him (Luke 18:28). The Lord would explain to Peter that those who left everything for His sake and the gospel would receive a hundredfold in this time and in the world to come (Mark 10:29-30). Thus, we see that Peter would know that such a call to leave everything to follow Christ was impossible. Peter understood that this response of faith was impossible with man, but not with God. So how would Peter understand anyone could respond to this kind of call?

We're able to get the answer in 1 Peter 1:3 where he says, "Blessed be the God and Father of our Lord Jesus Christ! According to his great mercy, he has caused us to be **born again** to a living hope through the resurrection of Jesus Christ from the dead." Peter would know that only by the regenerating work of God the Holy Spirit who is sent by the Father through the Son, could someone come to this kind of faith in the Lord Jesus Christ. Peter would also know that being born again is a work of God the Holy Spirit who works through the Word of God where he says this in 1 Peter 1:23, "since you have been **born again**, not of perishable seed but of imperishable, **through the living and abiding word of God**". Not only this, but Peter would know that being born again is a work of God the Holy Spirit who works through gospel Word where he says this in 1 Peter 1:25, "And this word is the **good news** that was preached to you." Therefore, Peter would know that through hearing the gospel of Jesus Christ, God the Holy Spirit works through this gospel Word to cause one to be born again (1 Peter 1:3, 1:23, 1:25).

He goes on to say this about their faith in 1 Peter 1:8, "Though you have not seen him, **you love him**. Though you do not now see him, you believe in him and rejoice with joy that is inexpressible and filled with glory." This kind of "love" that Peter is speaking about comes from the word *agapaó* which can mean "the love of reason, esteem," "to prefer to love," or "a discriminating affection which involves choice and selection." John Macarthur has said this of *agapaó* that it, "expresses the purest, noblest form of love, which is volitionally driven, not motivated by superficial appearance, emotional attraction, or sentimental worship." Kenneth Wuest describes this love as follows, "Agape is a love that impels one to sacrifice one's self for the benefit of the object loved... (it) speaks of a love which is awakened by a sense of value in the object loved, an apprehension of its preciousness." This type of love is also described as a love that denies self for the benefit of the object loved. So, when Peter noted that his readers love Christ, he goes on to explain the end result of such an *agapaó* toward the Lord Jesus Christ that has joy inexpressible and filled with glory. The result of such a preeminent loving faith toward Christ Jesus the Lord is the salvation of one's soul.

Chapter 7

Peter's Sermon on Pentecost and Gospel Call

Acts 2:38 – *And Peter said to them, "Repent and be baptized every one of you in the name of Jesus Christ for the forgiveness of your sins, and you will receive the gift of the Holy Spirit."*

As we enter this chapter, there is much that has taken place which we have not covered. For the purposes of this book, we will not be able to cover this, but we see the Lord has been crucified, died, buried, resurrected, and ascended. We also know that there are some significant events with Peter which includes the upper room discourse, Peter's denial of Christ, Peter witnessing the empty tomb, Jesus showing himself to Peter and the other disciples, Peter being recommissioned after the great catch of fish, Peter and the other disciples hearing the great commission, and more.

We will jump forward to the day of Pentecost where Peter delivers a gospel message to the Jewish audience. We'll notice that Peter's gospel message will include an indictment and conviction of sin and a warning of impending judgment. He will preach about the person of Jesus in that He is Lord and Christ.

He will proclaim the work of Christ which includes His death on the cross, His resurrection, His ascension, and His present enthronement. Peter will affirm the doctrine of the Trinity. Peter will also proclaim the promise of forgiveness and then deliver a gospel call of repentance and faith in the Lord Jesus Christ. As we go through this sermon, we will see several points that are important to highlight in Peter's message.

Before we get into the text of interest, Acts 2:14-41, we will skim over what has happened. When the Holy Spirit came, God-fearing Jews heard the loud, violent blowing sound and then found that everyone along with the apostles were speaking in tongues, or known languages, and declaring the wonders of God. Those who heard this were amazed, astonished, and perplexed by what this meant. On the other hand, there were others that mocked the apostles and other believers, claiming that they were full of wine or drunk. This is where we'll pick up Peter's first sermon.

Acts 2:14–15—*But Peter, standing with the eleven, lifted up his voice and addressed them: "Men of Judea and all who dwell in Jerusalem, let this be known to you, and give ear to my words. For these people are not drunk, as you suppose, since it is only the third hour of the day."*

First, let's notice that Peter lifts up his voice to everyone. Peter is about to deliver the good news of Jesus Christ which is why he'll lift his voice and demand the attention of his audience. It is quite possible that the crowd would be hostile. Just fifty days prior to Pentecost, Christ had been put to death. Christ had been sentenced to crucifixion by a Jewish mistrial, undergone a Roman mistrial, and He was betrayed by a Jewish population that had once cried hosanna to the Son of David. This same crowd ended up screaming for Christ's execution (Luke 23:21). Peter's audience may have included Pharisees and other Jewish leaders, and it may have also included the Jewish crowds that pled for the execution of Christ. Notice that Peter is addressing the "men of Judea and all who dwell in Jerusalem." Peter, now filled with the Holy Spirit and, who about fifty days earlier, had been afraid of a servant girl, was now going to testify for Christ.

Second, notice the confidence that Peter has in his message. Peter tells his audience to "let it be known" and "give heed" to his spoken words. Peter is giving a sure spoken testimony of the Lord Jesus Christ. Peter is acting like a herald and a preacher. He has news to deliver that will determine life or death, heaven or hell, commendation from the Lord or condemnation from the Lord, reconciliation with God or renunciation from God. Peter is going to give a message that will explain how to enter the narrow gate, how to enter the kingdom of heaven, and how to enter the kingdom of God. Peter will stand with the apostles and, likewise, the apostles will stand with Peter. Peter's testimony about Christ could have landed him with the same fate as Christ. Announcing Jesus as Lord and Christ could have drawn the same ire that Christ received from the Pharisees. However, it didn't matter to Peter. Peter rebukes the crowd, tells them that they aren't drunk as it's 9 am, and gives the explanation of what is happening.

Acts 2:16–21—*But this is what was uttered through the prophet Joel: "'And in the last days it shall be, God declares, that I will pour out my Spirit on all flesh, and your sons and your daughters shall prophesy, and your young men shall see visions, and your old men shall dream dreams; even on my male servants and female servants in those days I will pour out my Spirit, and they shall prophesy. And I will show wonders in the heavens above and signs on the earth below, blood, and fire, and vapor of smoke; the sun shall be turned to darkness and the moon to blood, before the day of the Lord comes, the great and magnificent day. And it shall come to pass that everyone who calls upon the name of the Lord shall be saved.'"*

Third, Peter explains that what has happened is a prophecy fulfilled that was spoken of by the prophet Joel. Joel's prophecy had indicated that the pouring out of the Spirit would occur before God would bring judgment on the world. The judgment day was and is known as the "Day of the LORD." Therefore, Peter quotes Scripture and declares that prophecy of pouring out His Spirit has been fulfilled.

Fourth, let's notice that the day of the LORD would be a day of great dread. This day was portrayed as a day of darkness and gloom (Joel 2:2). This is a day of clouds and blackness (Joel 2:2). This is a day where an army of strength comes which has never been seen (Joel 2:2). This is a day where fire devours and consumes everything in its way (Joel 2:3). This is a day the army comes in strength and for war and causes nations to tremble (Joel 2:4–5). This is a day where the army destroys its opponents with ease (Joel 2:6–9). This is a day the earth shakes (Joel 2:10). This is a day the heavens tremble (Joel 2:10). This is a day the stars fail (Joel 2:10). This is a day the LORD is captain of the hosts (Joel 2:11). This is a day the LORD's armies cannot be counted (Joel 2:11). This is a day which is dreadful (Joel 2:11).

Fifth, let's note that the Day of the LORD would also be a day of deliverance. Joel says of this day, "And everyone who calls on the name of the LORD will be saved." This means that all those that call on the name of the LORD shall be saved. This also means that those who do not call on the name of the LORD will be judged. Thus, the Jews knew that the Day of the LORD was a day that would be filled with both deliverance and judgment. Peter will give a concise answer on whose name to call upon for salvation in verse 36 where he says, "Let all the house of Israel therefore know for certain that God has made him both Lord and Christ, this Jesus whom you crucified."

Sixth, the Jews would know that the Day of the LORD was imminent. Not only would the Jews have known about the Day of the LORD, but they would also have believed that this prophecy would indicate that the Day of the LORD would be coming soon as the prophet Joel said this would happen in the "last days." Since the Spirit of the LORD had been poured out on all flesh, they would have known that they were in the last days. Therefore, they knew they were in the last days and would have believed the day of the LORD was at hand or drawing near.

Seventh, the people would know that the Holy Spirit had not been poured out on them. The people would know that the apostles and those with the apostles had the gift of the Holy Spirit because they were the ones who were prophesying the wonders of God and speaking in other known languages. This would lead them to the conclusion that the Spirit had not been poured out on them as they were not in possession of this same gift. According to the prophecy of Joel, they would be under divine judgment, and all the terror of the Day of the LORD would be theirs to experience in a judgment/non-deliverance way.

Eighth, the people would have begun to understand the baptism with the Holy Spirit and the baptism of fire that John the Baptist preached about. John the Baptist reiterated that the Messiah was the one who would baptize with the Holy Spirit where he says this in Luke 3:16, "John answered them all, 'I baptize you with water. But one who is more powerful than I will come, the straps of whose sandals I am not worthy to untie. He will baptize you with the Holy Spirit and fire.'" The Jews that Peter was addressing could have made the connection that either the Spirit would be poured out on them by Christ (i.e., baptized with the Holy Spirit) or they would be baptized with fire and experience the Day of the LORD (i.e., judgment). They would have also realized that this outpouring of the Holy Spirit was not done by man as John was consistently pointing to Christ as the baptizer with the Holy Spirit (salvation) and fire (condemnation and judgment).

Ninth, let's notice that the prophet Joel confirms who baptizes with the Holy Spirit. In Joel 2:28–29, notice that God says, "I will pour out my Spirit on all flesh" and "I will pour out my Spirit in those days and they will prophesy." Notice the "I" statement. It is God who pours out His Spirit. It is not man who pours out the Spirit. The Jews would have known that this outpouring of the Holy Spirit was not something that men did, but God. Joel's understanding of who baptizes with the Holy Spirit would have agreed with Matthew, Mark, Luke, the apostle John, John the Baptist, Peter, Paul, and Jesus.

Likewise, Peter's understanding of the baptism with the Holy Spirit would confirm exactly what Jesus taught His disciples.

- The baptism of the Holy Spirit could not come until Jesus had ascended and been glorified. (John 7:39)
- Jesus would ask the Father for the Holy Spirit to be given. (John 14:16)
- The Holy Spirit would be given from the Father to the Son. (John 15:26; Luke 11:13 24:49)
- The Holy Spirit would be given from the Father in the Son's name. (John 14:26)
- Jesus would send the Holy Spirit. (John 16:7)
- The Holy Spirit would be given to those who believe in Christ. (John 7:39)
- The baptism with the Holy Spirit would be a salvific work of God (John 7:37-39)

Acts 2:22—*Men of Israel, hear these words: Jesus of Nazareth, a man attested to you by God with mighty works and wonders and signs that God did through him in your midst, as you yourselves know*

Tenth, let's notice that Peter brings the audience's attention to the person and work of the Lord Jesus Christ. Peter announces that Jesus of Nazareth was a man attested to the people by God with mighty works and wonders and signs that God did through Christ. The word "*attested*" comes from *apodeiknumi* in the original language. *Apodeiknumi* means to "demonstrate," "set forth," "show by proof" or properly "demonstrating that something is what it "'claims to be'". Peter is saying that Jesus' claims should have been no surprise based off of His teaching and works. This statement by Peter would draw the people back to the mighty demonstrations of Christ's divine power, signs, and works. You could almost hear Peter say the following:

"Did you not hear or see when Jesus turned water into wine (John 2:1–11)? Did you not hear or see when Jesus healed the royal official's son in Capernaum who was close to death (John 4:43–54)? Did you not hear or see when Jesus healed the man who was possessed by a demon (Luke 4:31–37)? Did you not hear or see when Jesus healed Peter's mother (Luke 4:38–41)? Did you not hear or see when Jesus healed the man with leprosy (Luke 5:12–16)? Did you not hear or see when men lowered the paralytic through the roof and Jesus healed him (Luke 5:17–26)? Did you not hear or see when Jesus healed the man who was an invalid for thirty-eight years at the Bethesda pool (John 5:1–47)? Did you not hear or see when Jesus healed the man with the shriveled hand (Matthew 12:9–14)? Did you not hear or see how Jesus healed all of those from Judea, Jerusalem, and from the coastal region around Tyre and Sidon who came to hear Him and be healed of their diseases (Luke 6:17–19)? Did you not hear or see when Jesus healed the Centurion's servant (Luke 7:1–10)? Did you not hear or see when Jesus raised the widow's son from the dead (Luke 7:11–17)? Did you not hear or see when Jesus healed the demon possessed in Gadarenes and sent the demons into pigs (Luke 8:26–39)? Did you not hear or see when Jesus healed Jairus' daughter from the dead (Luke 8:40–56)? Did you not hear or see when Jesus healed two blind men (Matthew 9:27–31)? Did you not hear or see when Jesus healed the mute demon-possessed man (Matthew 9:32–34)? Did you not hear or see when Jesus fed five thousand (Luke 9:10–17)? Did you not hear or see when Jesus was in Gennesaret that all the people from that region carried the sick to Him and all who touched even the edge of His cloak were healed (Mark 6:53–56)? Did you not hear or see when Jesus healed the Syrophoenician woman's daughter from demon possession (Mark 7:24–30)? Did you not hear or see when Jesus went through Sidon, down to the Sea of Galilee and into the region of the Decapolis, that Jesus healed a deaf and mute man (Mark 7:31–37)? Did you not hear or see when Jesus fed the four thousand (Mark 8:1–9)? Did you not hear or see when Jesus healed the boy with the impure spirit (Matthew 17:14–21)? Did you not hear or see when Jesus healed the crippled woman on the Sabbath (Mark 13:10–17)? Did you not hear or see when Jesus healed the man born blind (John 9:1–41)? Did you not hear or see when Jesus healed the ten lepers (Luke 17:12–19)? Did you not hear or see when Jesus healed blind Bartimaeus (Matthew 20:29–34)? Did you not see the sky going black during the crucifixion of Christ (Luke 23:44)? Did you not feel the earth shake, see rocks split, and hear of the curtain leading into the Most Holy Place being torn when Christ died (Matthew 27:51)?"

Peter is stating that there was more than enough evidence demonstrated which would lead the Jews to understand that Jesus was the Christ sent by God. These works and signs demonstrated that Jesus was the Lamb of God who takes away the sin of the world (John 1:29), the Bread of Life (John 6:35), the Light of the world (John 8:12), the Door (John 10:7), the Good Shepherd (John 10:11), the Resurrection and the Life (John 11:25), the Way, the Truth, and the Life (John 14:6), the True Vine (John 15:1), I Am (John 8:58), the Lord of the Sabbath (Matthew 12:8), the Anointed One (Luke 4:18), the Son of God (John 5:17-18), and more. Peter is saying to the Jewish audience this day that Jesus' teaching and His works were so divine and obvious that they demonstrated that Jesus was who He claimed to be.

Acts 2:23–24—*This Jesus, delivered up according to the definite plan and foreknowledge of God, you crucified and killed by the hands of lawless men. God raised him up, loosing the pangs of death, because it was not possible for him to be held by it.*

Eleventh, Peter testifies that the crucifixion was the part of the sovereign and omniscient plan of God. This salvific plan of God was determined in eternity past. God the Father foreordained this plan that the Jews would kill Jesus. Christ's death didn't happen by accident. God the Father didn't look into the future and see that His Son would be betrayed and then try to find a way to deal with it. No, God the Father is omniscient and, when Christ was served up to be crucified for the sins of His people, everything was going exactly to the Father's plan. The cross was always part of the plan to reconcile sinners to God. God chose His sheep before the foundation of the world (Ephesians 1:4), and also selected His Christ who was the Lamb that would take away their sins (Revelation 13:8).

Twelfth, let's notice that Peter indicts the audience for murdering God's Christ and delivering the sinless One to lawless men. The trials that were performed were unjust and full of false testimony (Matthew 26:60). Jesus would stand trial before Annas, Caiaphas, the Sanhedrin, Pontius Pilate, Herod, and again before Pilate. Pilate said, "I find no guilt in this man." The false witnesses could not find guilt in Jesus. Jesus was delivered up to be crucified on false charges. Not only this, they wanted to crucify and kill Jesus who was sinless but release a sinful murderer, Barabbas (Luke 23:18-19). Not only did they desire to have a murderer released, but they also demanded that Christ be crucified although Pilate continued to state that he had found no guilt in Jesus (Luke 23:22-23). Not only this, but the people also said this in Matthew 27:25, "His blood be on us and on our children!". The people didn't want justice. They wanted to kill the sinless Messiah and release a sinful murderer. They didn't just want Christ's blood on their hands, they demanded that their children be held responsible for their actions as well. Thus, Peter is indicting each and every one of them as Christ killers. Peter is indicting them of killing God's foreknown, pre-destined, sovereignly selected Messiah. Although the sovereign plan of God was to have Jesus killed and crucified, this did not neglect human responsibility. Peter is charging them with the murder of their own Messiah. Peter is charging them with murdering the Christ, the Suffering Servant.

Thirteenth, let's notice that God rose Jesus from the dead which was an affirmation of Christ's work. Paul says this about the resurrection of Jesus in Romans 4:25, "who was delivered up for our trespasses and raised for our justification." When Christ died on the cross and then rose from the dead, it was proof positive that His salvific work was accepted by God. Christ's resurrection was God's apologetic on the sufficiency of Christ's substitutionary death on the cross for sinners. The resurrection was God's ultimate validation of Jesus' person and work on the cross. If Jesus were sinful, He would have remained in the grave. However, God the Father raised His beloved Son because He accepted Christ's work on the cross on behalf of sinners. Therefore, Peter exalts the resurrection of Christ and God raising Him from the dead.

Acts 2:25–28—*For David says concerning him, "'I saw the Lord always before me, for he is at my right hand that I may not be shaken; therefore my heart was glad, and my tongue rejoiced; my flesh also will dwell in hope. For you will not abandon my soul to Hades, or let your Holy One see corruption. You have made known to me the paths of life; you will make me full of gladness with your presence."*

Peter will now quote David from Psalm 16. As we learn from Peter, Psalm 16:8–11 is written by David. However, the one speaking in these verses is Jesus Christ. When you read the "I," "me," and "my" in this section, this is Jesus speaking.

Fourteenth, we should see that Christ's resurrection was foretold through David. When Jesus says, "I saw the Lord always before me, for he is at my right hand that I may not be shaken; therefore my heart was glad, and my tongue rejoiced; my flesh also will dwell in hope," this is a prophecy where Jesus is speaking with confidence that He always sees His Father and is always doing His will. As we learned earlier, but especially in reviewing Isaiah 53, Jesus' life was lived in total submission to His Father (John 5:19). This speaks to Jesus' confidence in the Father's plan. Jesus saw the task ahead and said, "Not my will but your will be done" (Luke 22:42). Jesus knew the crown of thorns, the mocking, the beating, the flogging, the crucifixion, and more were all awaiting Him but what troubled His heart to the point of death was facing the wrath of God for the sins of His people (Mark 14:34). However, Jesus saw the Lord before Him and was not shaken. Jesus did not do His will but fulfilled His Father's will. Jesus was not shaken from completing His work and fulfilling David's prophecy.

Fifteenth, Jesus had unwavering belief in His Father glorifying Him and His work. David would go on to say, "For you will not abandon my soul to Hades, or let your Holy One see corruption. You have made known to me the paths of life; you will make me full of gladness with your presence." If the Son had failed in His mission to live a perfect and sinless life, the Son would stay in the ground and be counted as a sinner. However, since the Son's work was perfect and sinless, Jesus was certain that His Father would glorify Him, raise Him from the dead, and He would be glorified in heaven (John 17:5). The resurrection speaks to Christ's victory over sin, death, and the devil. Jesus was not a victim at Calvary, He was a victor. Jesus was not defeated at Calvary, but dominant. Upon the cross, Jesus did not say "I am finished," but "It is finished." The Father resurrecting His Son was His approval of Christ's work and speaks to the perfect completion of Christ's work.

Acts 2:29–33—*"Brothers, I may say to you with confidence about the patriarch David that he both died and was buried, and his tomb is with us to this day. Being therefore a prophet, and knowing that God has sworn with an oath to him that he would set one of his descendants on his throne, he foresaw and spoke about the resurrection of the Christ, that he was not abandoned to Hades, nor did his flesh see corruption. This Jesus God raised up, and of that we all are witnesses. Being therefore exalted at the right hand of God, and having received from the Father the promise of the Holy Spirit, he has poured out this that you yourselves are seeing and hearing."*

Sixteenth, Peter is explaining that God's oath to David has been fulfilled and that the descendant from David, Christ, had established a kingdom where He would reign forever. Peter further exposits Psalm 16 and explains that David had died, was buried, but had not been resurrected. However, David was a prophet and knew that God swore an oath to him that his house, throne, and kingdom would last forever (2 Samuel 7:8–16, 27–29). Therefore, we can know that Peter's claim is that Jesus is the Son of David and His kingdom is one that will last forever.

Seventeenth, we see Peter and the apostles were eyewitnesses to the resurrection. Peter states that they were all witnesses of this resurrection (Acts 2:32, John 20:1-10, 20:19-23, 21:1-25). Peter and the disciples were not grave robbers (Matthew 28:11-15), they were eyewitnesses. Thus, when Peter testified that they were eyewitnesses of Jesus' resurrection, he was testifying that they had seen, heard, touched, and ate with the resurrected Jesus Christ.

Eighteenth, we see that Peter believes in the Trinity which is God the Father, God the Son, and God the Holy Spirit. We see this in Acts 2:33 where Peter makes reference to Christ being exalted at the right hand of God the Father and God the Father giving the Son the promise of the Holy Spirit. Peter wasn't an anti-Trinitarian heretic. Peter didn't believe in modalism and that

God just manifests Himself as three different persons. No! Peter believed in the Triune God.

Nineteenth, we see that Jesus was exalted. The question is, "Why was Jesus exalted?." Let's think back to what we learned about in the fourth Servant Song. We learned that Christ would be "high" and "lifted up" and "exalted" and we learned why He would be exalted in Isaiah 53:12 where it says, "Therefore I will divide him a portion with the many, and he shall divide the spoil with the strong, because he poured out his soul to death and was numbered with the transgressors; yet he bore the sin of many, and makes intercession for the transgressors." Christ was exalted because of His intercessory and substitutionary atonement for sinners. This is why Christ was glorified by His Father (John 17:5).

The twentieth point we should see is that Christ has been given all authority. When it says that Christ was exalted to the right hand of God, this means that He was given equal honor and authority as the Father. Therefore, when it says that Jesus was exalted to the right hand of God, this means He was given all authority in heaven and on earth (Matthew 28:18). This means that Jesus has all authority to grant forgiveness. This means that Jesus has all authority to carry out the plan of salvation. This means that Jesus has all authority to grant repentance. This means that Jesus has all authority to grant saving faith. This means that Jesus has all authority to grant regeneration. This means that Jesus has all authority over the devil. This means that Jesus has all authority over men. This means that Jesus has all authority to judge the living. This means that Jesus has all authority to judge the dead. This means that Jesus has all authority to destroy both body and soul in hell. This means that Jesus has all authority over creation. This means that Jesus has all authority period, paragraph, end of story.

The twenty-first point we should see is that Christ has received the promised Holy Spirit from the Father and has poured out the Spirit which is what the people were seeing and hearing. It's important to think back on what Jesus had promised to His disciples. Jesus had told them that He was going to go away and send the promised Holy Spirit (John 16:7). Jesus also said that those who believed in Him would receive the promised Holy Spirit (John 7:38–39). Here, Peter once again explains that Jesus is the one who baptizes with the Holy Spirit. Jesus' work was complete, and He had received the Holy Spirit from the Father which He had poured out. Once again, Matthew, Mark, Luke, the apostle John, John the Baptist, the prophet Joel, Jesus, Paul, and Peter all had the same understanding of who baptizes with the Holy Spirit and pours out the Holy Spirit, the Lord Jesus Christ (Luke 24:49, John 7:37-39, 14:15-17, 14:26, 15:26, 16:7).

Acts 2:34–36—*For David did not ascend into the heavens, but he himself says, "'The Lord said to my Lord, 'Sit at my right hand, until I make your enemies your footstool."' Let all the house of Israel therefore know for certain that God has made him both Lord and Christ, this Jesus whom you crucified.*

The twenty-third point we should see is that Jesus is both Lord and Christ. Peter notes that David never ascended into heaven but knew that the LORD would give all authority to someone. That someone is Jesus Christ. In the original language, it could also be translated, "YAHWEH said to my Adonai." This was a messianic passage of Scripture where it was prophesied by David that YAHWEH would give authority and power to David's Lord. In verse 36, Peter solves the mystery of who the Lord is. He says in verse 36, "Let all the house of Israel therefore know for certain that God has made him both Lord and Christ, this Jesus whom you crucified." What a statement! In Acts 2:21, Peter says that all who call on the name of the LORD will be saved and, in Acts 2:36, he says that the name that must be called on to be saved is Jesus who is both Lord and Christ.

The twenty-fourth point we should see is that those who are not baptized by the Holy Spirit are enemies of YAHWEH and His Christ. Those who are not baptized by the Holy Spirit are at warfare with YAHWEH and His Messiah. Thus, Peter is telling the crowd that they are enemies of YAHWEH. Peter is telling the crowd that Christ, who they crucified, possessed all authority and they were His enemy. Peter said this about the certainty of judgment for the ungodly in 1 Peter 4:5, "but they will give account to him who is ready to judge the living and the dead." When Peter is telling them YAHWEH has made Jesus both Lord and Christ and He will make His enemies a footstool, this is not only another indictment of their crucifixion of Christ, it's also a promise of divine judgment. The Christ who they were trying to get rid of, is the Christ who they are going to have to give an account to. They will either give an account as an enemy, or as a reconciled child of God in Christ.

The twenty-fifth point we should see is that Jesus is an eternal priest. The verse that has been quoted is Psalm 110:1. In Psalm 110:4 the LORD says this regarding the Lord, "You are a priest forever after the order of Melchizedek." Therefore, we see that if the Jewish crowd was paying attention, this was also a statement that Jesus was a priest in the order of Melchizedek. We won't fully explore the implications of what this means, but it demonstrates that Jesus is the Great High Priest, eternal High Priest, and preeminent High Priest. He is better because He's eternal, He has a better sacrifice, He offers a better covenant, and He enters a better temple.

Acts 2:37—*Now when they heard this they were cut to the heart, and said to Peter and the rest of the apostles, "Brothers, what shall we do?"*

The twenty-sixth point that we should see is that Peter's preaching, his exposition of Scripture, his demonstration of Jesus as Lord and Christ, his indictment of sin, and the promise of judgment brought conviction of sin. The Jewish audience was stunned. Peter had proved through Scripture that Jesus was the Christ, that they were in the last days, that the Spirit was not poured out on them, that Jesus was equal in power and status to God by being seated at the right hand of God, and that the enemies of the Lord Jesus were going to be Christ's footstool. The people could have also harkened back to John the Baptist's warning of Jesus being the Christ and His winnowing fork was in His hand separating the wheat from the chaff and the chaff would be burned with unquenchable fire. The people could have also remembered John the Baptist warning of the Christ having an ax in His hand and the ax being at the root of the tree ready to chop down the tree and throw it in the fire. If the Jewish audience had followed along, they knew they were subject to divine judgment. They knew they were enemies of YAHWEH and His Christ.

When it says the people were cut to the heart, this denotes a very strong reaction by the crowd. It's as if the veil had been taken away and they saw the atrocity that they had committed against God's Messiah. Peter's message of sin and judgment had plowed their hearts. Peter's preaching elicited the reality of sin, hell, and judgment. Peter's preaching brought down their spiritual pride and self-righteousness and elevated their sin.

This soul-searching preaching caused this cut to the heart. In fact, they interrupted Peter's sermon to ask what they must do. Peter was not yet done giving his speech when the people interrupted Peter's message. The people asked how they could be made right with God. They couldn't take another word from Peter, so they needed to stop Him and ask for the terms of peace with God. They saw themselves as enemies of God. No wonder they cried out in the middle of his sermon to ask for the terms of peace with God. They were opened and laid bare before the One to whom they were to give an account (Hebrews 4:13).

Acts 2:38—*And Peter said to them, "Repent and be baptized every one of you in the name of Jesus Christ for the forgiveness of your sins, and you will receive the gift of the Holy Spirit."*

The twenty-seventh point we should see is that Peter called them to a self-denying and cross-bearing faith in the Lord Jesus Christ. This was a call to repentance and faith. This is the same gospel call that the Lord Jesus gave (Matthew 16:24-26, Mark 8:34-37, Luke 9:23-26, 14:25-33, John 12:24-26). This was the call to "deny yourself, take up your cross, and follow Him." This was a gospel call that would determine whether you save your soul or lose your soul, whether you are forgiven your sins or remain bound in your sins, whether you enter the narrow gate or remain outside the narrow gate.

Peter tells them to repent and be baptized. Many would point to this passage and say that baptism gives the forgiveness of sins, but this is not what Peter is saying. Peter is saying that since the Jews killed Jesus the Lord and Messiah, they must perform a complete 180 degree turn. Peter is saying that since they rejected Jesus as Lord and Christ, they must now repent, surrender, and trust Jesus as their Lord and Christ. Peter is telling them to abandon Judaism for Christ. Peter is telling them to stop following the Pharisees and Sadducees. Peter is telling them to be completely identified and submitted to Jesus. The Jews would know that identifying with Jesus would potentially mean accepting the same fate the religious community and leaders gave to Jesus. This is no small repentance. This is a complete abandonment of the Jewish system. This is surrender to Jesus as the Lord and Messiah. This is willingness to pay the price for being associated with Jesus. This is hating your father, mother, wife, children, brothers, sisters, and even your own life for Christ (Luke 14:26). The Pharisees had already determined that Jesus was not the true Messiah so any such allegiance to Jesus Christ would be tantamount to worshipping a false god and was worthy of death (Deuteronomy 13:6-15).

There was a cost in Judaism for going and serving other gods. Since the Pharisees, Sadducees, and religious leaders of that day did not see Jesus as the Christ or believe Jesus' claim to deity, they surely saw Him as a false god even after the resurrection. Anyone that would follow Jesus Christ would be subject to the same treatment as Jesus which could include crucifixion or stoning. It's also important to remember that many of the Jews saw Jesus as a heretic as He claimed to be equal with God, claimed God as His Father, and claimed to be "I AM" (John 8:58).

Peter tells them to be baptized in the name of Jesus Christ for the forgiveness of sins. There are many sacramentalists who look to this passage and say that baptism is what gives forgiveness of sins, but Peter is not claiming that the baptism is what gives forgiveness. In fact, Peter understood John baptized with water, but Jesus would baptize with the Holy Spirit. Peter had seen enough ceremonial baptisms and ceremonial external washings (Matthew 15:1-20). Peter was taught by Christ that a person wasn't defiled by not performing a ceremonial washing with water and eating with unwashed hands. Peter was taught by the Lord that a person was defiled by what came out of their heart (Matthew 15:16-20). Peter saw the widespread ceremonial hand washings, ritual purifications, and baptisms, and would have been familiar with the Pharisaic external washings with water. Peter was not claiming that an external washing is what gave forgiveness of sins.

Peter is calling for a public declaration and commitment to Jesus as Lord and Christ as evidenced by being baptized in the name of Jesus Christ. Just as Jesus identified with sinners at His baptism, so Peter was calling the audience to identify Jesus as their Lord and Christ. Peter has just proven that Jesus is the Messiah and the Jewish people are guilty of killing Him. Peter is commanding them to be public disciples and followers of Christ.

He is calling them to abandon Judaism, to count their sacrifices as nothing, to count their circumcision as nothing, to count their righteous acts as nothing, and to trust in Christ completely and totally for salvation as evidenced by a public baptism in the name of Jesus Christ even if it costs them their life. This was an extreme repentance and call to faith in Jesus Christ for the Jewish community.

Peter's preaching was meant to bring them to poverty in spirit (Matthew 5:3). It was to shatter their self-righteousness, to bring low the hills of self-exaltation, to elevate the sin, and to bring the crowd to the place where they would call on the name of the Lord for salvation and ask for pardon of sin.

We can clearly see Peter's understanding of Christ's evangelistic call to faith. This was a radical repentance. This was submission to Christ the King. This was the radical call to deny yourself, take up your cross, and follow Jesus Christ (Matthew 16:24). This was a call to hate your own life (Luke 14:26). This was a call to love Christ preeminently by faith (Luke 14:25-33). We see that the Lord had taught Peter how to fish for men (Luke 5:10-11). We see that Peter preached sin, judgment, hell, the person and work of Christ, the promise of forgiveness, and then he proclaimed the gospel call of repentance toward God and faith in the Lord Jesus Christ. Peter had been well taught by the Lord.

The Jewish audience would need to so identify with Jesus that they would deny themselves, take up their cross, and follow Him. This is what Peter was really commanding them to do. The people knew it and knew the consequences of such a decision. Peter is calling the Jews to Christ exactly how Jesus called people. Peter is telling them to count the costs and decide whether they will publicly declare Jesus as Lord and Christ even if it costs them their family and relationships, their personal ambitions, their personal sins, and their personal belongings. Peter is telling them to come all the way and publicly declare Jesus as Lord and Christ. Peter is calling them to see Christ as the only way to be made right with

God. This was a call to surrender and trust in Jesus. This is what Peter was speaking of when he said, "Repent and be baptized every one of you in the name of Jesus Christ for the forgiveness of your sins, and you will receive the gift of the Holy Spirit."

Let's remember that it wasn't the baptism that gave forgiveness of sins, it was faith in Christ Jesus the Lord. Jesus makes this abundantly clear in John 7:38-39 where He says, "Whoever believes in me, as the Scripture has said, 'Out of his heart will flow rivers of living water.' Now this he said about the Spirit, who **those who believe in him were to receive**, for as yet, the Spirit had not been given, because Jesus was not yet glorified." Those who would come to faith in Christ would receive the Holy Spirit.

Although it was costly to come to Christ for salvation, those who would put their faith in Christ would receive a gift much more precious than all creation. Those that repent and trust Christ shall never be disappointed. Let's also note that all those that will give their life for Christ and the gospel must count the cost. It is costly to follow Jesus, but it is more costly not to follow Him. Peter was faithful in his call to bring people to Christ.

What a tragedy to wrongly interpret this verse, twist it, and manipulate it to justify water baptism giving the forgiveness of sins. What utter blindness to twist this verse and teach baptismal regeneration.

Acts 2:39 – *For the promise is for you and for your children and for all who are far off, everyone whom the Lord our God calls to himself.*

The twenty-eighth point we should see is that Peter will demonstrate the lavish grace of God. On the day the Lord was crucified, the people were calling for Christ's crucifixion (Matthew 27:22). What is most astonishing is that they desired His death so vehemently that they were accepting of the consequences of this decision where they said this in Matthew 27:25, "His blood be on us and on our children." They were willing to accept the penalty for crucifying Jesus and even have this penalty be given to their children.

However, when Peter says that the gift of forgiveness through Jesus Christ is available for them and for their children, this is a statement of epic grace. Christ Jesus is willing to forgive them for crucifying Him. Christ Jesus is willing to offer this same forgiveness to their children if their children would embrace Him through faith. Christ Jesus is willing to forgive and be at peace with them. Not only this, but this promise of forgiveness and receiving the Holy Spirit is also for those who are far off. This includes all those in the future who were not even born. This includes Gentiles. What a shocking statement of grace. What a shocking statement of the Lord's willingness to be reconciled to man. What a shocking statement of love. What a shocking statement to know that the vilest of sins can be forgiven. All praise to this King who calls out a wretched and sinful people for Himself and makes trophies of grace out of the worst of sinners!

Acts 2:40-41 – *And with many other words he bore witness and continued to exhort them, saying, "Save yourselves from this crooked generation." So those who received his word were baptized, and there were added that day about three thousand souls.*

The last point we should see is Peter's evangelistic zeal. Peter's sermon wasn't done. It says with many words he "bore witness." This word "bore witness" comes from *diamarturomai* which means to "give solemn evidence" and "thoroughly bear witness." This word carries with it a witnessing done with a high level of self-involvement or personal interest. Additionally, it says that Peter was "exhorting." The word for exhorting comes from *parakaleó* which can mean to "summon," "beseech," or "admonish." This word has with it the idea of pleading, imploring, begging, and persuading someone to seek that which pleases

God. Peter continued to give sound Scriptural evidence combined with a heart's desire to see the people be reconciled with God. His desire was for the people to be forgiven and to accept Jesus for who He really is, Lord, God, and Christ. Peter was not reserved in voice; he raised his voice. Peter was not indifferent, he was impassioned. Peter was not casual, he was commanding. Peter was not soft, he was Spirit filled. Peter was not boring and tired, he was burning with truth. In fact, when Peter called them to repent, this command is written in the aorist tense and imperative mood. As we noted earlier the aorist imperative calls for a specific, definite, and decisive choice. It often expresses a note of urgency. The aorist imperative communicates a sense of getting something done, once for all, and swiftly. Peter was calling them, urging them, pleading with them, and persuading them to be reconciled to God through Christ. For men to stand in a pulpit today with no passion, with no zeal, with no earnestness, with no urging, and with no pleading, is an absolute disgrace and the furthest thing from evangelistic preaching in the New Testament. Lastly, notice that who received the gospel were those who were baptized. It wasn't the baptism that gave the Holy Spirit. It was believing the gospel and responding in faith which gave the gift Holy Spirit. Apodechomai means to "receive," "welcome," "embrace," "welcomingly receive," or "receive with gladness." Those that gladly received, believed, and embraced the gospel in faith were those who were saved from the crooked and perverse generation.

As we close this chapter, we should be inspired by Peter's preaching. We should be inspired by this masterful sermon which exposed sin, warned of judgment, exalted the person and work of the Jesus, and called for repentance and faith in the Lord Jesus Christ. Peter's theology on conversion is manifestly present in his first sermon on the day of Pentecost. It was to give the bad news of sin, death, and judgment, give the good news of Jesus Christ's person and work, and then issue a gospel call of repentance toward God and faith in the Lord Jesus Christ for the forgiveness of sins. Just as Peter did on the day of Pentecost, so we also must preach in such a way to exalt the person and work of Christ. Preach to convict men of their sin, of impending judgment, and the horror of dying in their sins. Preach Christ as the only way of salvation. Be faithful to give the gospel call as Jesus and Peter did. Never compromise from proclaiming the gospel call to come to Christ for salvation:

Deny yourself, take up your cross, follow Christ. Repent and believe the good news of Jesus Christ.

Chapter 8

Peter's Sermon in Solomon's Colonnade and Gospel Call

Acts 3:19 – *Repent therefore, and turn back, that your sins may be blotted out*

In this chapter we will examine Peter's message that he delivers to the crowd of people after he heals the lame beggar. In this message from Peter, we'll see an indictment of sins, a warning of judgment, the promise of the forgiveness of sins, a demonstration that Jesus was the Christ prophesied from the Old Testament, a demonstration that the Old Testament prophets foretold that Christ would suffer which pointed to Christ's propitiating and expiating work, a gospel call of repentance and faith, and a demonstration that Jesus was the fulfillment of the Abrahamic Covenant and the means by which all nations would be blessed.

To get a running start into the text of interest, Acts 3:11-26, we will briefly go over what has happened. Peter and John have gone up to the temple and come across a lame man who is asking for alms and who is 40 years old (Acts 3:1-3, 4:22). Peter commands the man's attention, tells the man they do not have silver or gold to give the man, then commands the man to get up and walk in the name of Jesus Christ of Nazareth, and takes him by the hand to raise him up (Acts 3:6-7). The man is healed, begins praising God, and many are filled with wonder and amazement (Acts 3:9-10).

Acts 3:11-12 – *While he clung to Peter and John, all the people, utterly astounded, ran together to them in the portico called Solomon's. And when Peter saw it he addressed the people: "Men of Israel, why do you wonder at this, or why do you stare at us, as though by our own power or piety we have made him walk?*

First, let's notice that Peter uses this opportunity to preach the good news of Jesus Christ. The man who had been healed is holding fast to Peter and John as the crowds are rushing toward them in amazement. Peter will capitalize on this moment and address the crowd to explain the miracle that has just taken place. Peter will make the most of the opportunity. Notice that Peter immediately shifts the focus away from him and John. Notice that he explains that this miracle was not performed based on his own power or based on his godliness. Peter is going to point the crowd to the origin and the means by which the lame beggar was healed. However, before he does that, he is going to give a heart-piercing indictment to the crowd. As we noted earlier in the book, John Calvin in the Institutes of the Christian Religion has made these two statements, "Without knowledge of self there is no knowledge of God" and "Without knowledge of God there is no knowledge of self." Peter is going to give them a scathing reality of who they really are and proclaim who Jesus is.

Acts 3:13 – *The God of Abraham, the God of Isaac, and the God of Jacob, the God of our fathers, glorified his servant Jesus, whom you delivered over and denied in the presence of Pilate, when he had decided to release him.*

Second, let's notice that Peter emphasizes that Jesus is the chosen and glorified servant of YAHWEH. When Peter is proclaiming that the God of Abraham, Isaac, Jacob, and their fathers has glorified Jesus, Peter is stating that Jesus is the glorified servant of the God of the Old Testament. Essentially, Jesus was not some rebel leading an insurrection against Judaism. No, God the Father had chosen Jesus to be His Lord and Christ.

Third, we'll see that Peter indicts the crowd for their sinful depravity in that even a Roman governor saw Jesus was innocent. When Jesus was brought to Pilate, Pilate asked Jesus if He was the king of the Jews (John 18:33). Jesus would claim that His kingdom was not of this world and that He came to bear witness to the truth (John 18:34-37). Pilate then went outside and told the Jews this in John 18:38, "I find no guilt in him." After Jesus was sent back from Herod, Pilate told the chief priests and rulers of the people this in Luke 23:13-14, "You brought me this man as one who was misleading the people. And after examining him before you, behold, I did not find this man guilty of any of your charges against him." Pilate would have Jesus flogged and present Jesus again and gave the following testimony in John 19:4, "Take him yourselves and crucify him, for I find no guilt in him." One last time, Jesus would be presented and Pilate would give his final verdict on the sinless nature of Christ where he said in John 19:6, "Take him yourselves and crucify him, for I find no guilt in him." Thus, we see that Peter is testifying that even a Gentile Roman governor testified to the Jews of Jesus' innocence four times.

Acts 3:14 – *But you denied the Holy and Righteous One, and asked for a murderer to be granted to you*

Fourth, we should see that Peter indicts the crowd for rejecting their Messiah. The word *arneomai* means to "deny," "disown," "repudiate," or "disregard." The Jews didn't just deny Jesus, they demanded that he be put to death and crucified. Pilate found no guilt in him and there was absolutely no charge that could be brought against Christ's entire life in the unjust trials. Peter is indicting them for spiritual blindness and hardness of heart because they could not see Jesus as He really was, God's sinless Messiah.

Fifth, we see Peter testify to Jesus' sinless nature. Peter would say this about Jesus in 1 Peter 2:22, "He committed no sin, neither was deceit found in his mouth." Jesus was and is the Holy and Righteous One. Jesus was and is the Christ and Son of the Living God, the Lamb of God who takes away the sin of the world, the Anointed One, and more. The testimony and works of Jesus were overwhelming to point them to Christ (John 10:37-38). Likewise, the absolute absence of sin was overwhelming evidence that Jesus was the Christ. The people denied the truth telling, wonder working, sinless Servant of Jehovah.

Sixth, we see that Peter indicts the crowd for releasing a murderer rather than the Messiah. We see the Jews wanted to release Barabbas who was a robber and who was thrown in prison for an insurrection and for murder (John 18:40, Luke 23:19). Not only this, the Jews cried out for Christ's death where they said, "Away with him, away with him, crucify him!" (John 19:15). Additionally, the Jews gave a reply to Pilate as Pilate presented Jesus as their King and they replied back in John 19:15 by saying, "We have no king but Caesar." This claim by the Jews was absolutely outrageous. In Psalm 10:16 it says, "The LORD is king forever; the nations have vanished from his land." Therefore, for the Jews to say they had no king but Caesar was to deny YAHWEH as their true King. Thus, Peter is indicting them for demanding the release of a robber and for rejection of the Righteous One.

Acts 3:15 – *And you killed the Author of life, whom God raised from the dead. To this we are witnesses.*

Sixth, we see Peter indict the crowd for murdering the Messiah. Rather than toning down his message, he continues to lay on the charges. We can get an idea of how much zeal, passion, and intensity there was to kill Christ where it says this in Luke 23:23, "But they were urgent, demanding with loud cries that he should be crucified. And their voices prevailed." The original word for "urgent" comes from *epikeimai* and means "to press hard" or "be insistent." The crowd wasn't just suggesting that Jesus be crucified. No, they insisted upon it. Additionally, the original word for "demanding" comes from *aiteó* and can mean "request," "petition," or "call for." The crowd was insistent, pressing hard, and demanding that Christ be killed. Additionally, we see that their voices prevailed. The word for "prevailed" comes from *katischuó* and means to "prevail against," "overpower," or "get the upper hand." Thus, we see that the crowd relentlessly pressed hard and zealously demanded for Jesus' crucifixion and they did so with overpowering voices. Peter is bringing them right back to Good Friday to show them how zealous, demanding, and insistent they were to kill the Author of Life.

Seventh, let's notice that Peter is claiming that Jesus is God the Creator by stating that Jesus is the Author of life. The word "author" comes from *archégos*. It is a compound word with *arxḗ* meaning "the first" and *ágō* meaning "to lead." Properly *archégos* means "originator," "author," "founder," "prince," "leader." It carries with it the idea of a person who is the originator or founder. We have a very clear picture of who David views is the author of life in Psalm 139:13-16 where he says, "For you created my inmost being; you knit me together in my mother's womb. I praise you because I am fearfully and wonderfully made; your works are wonderful, I know that full well. My frame was not hidden from you when I was made in the secret place, when I was woven together in the depths of the earth. Your eyes saw my unformed body; all the days ordained for me were written in your book before one of them came to be." So, who is the Author of life?

This would be God. Who created all mankind? This would be God (Genesis 1:26-27). Who is the author of the new birth? This would be God (John 3:1-10). Thus, Peter is claiming that Jesus is God the Creator.

Eighth, let's see that God raised Jesus from the dead. Jesus was resurrected from the dead on the third day by His own power (John 10:18), by God the Father (Galatians 1:1) and God the Holy Spirit (Romans 8:11), which affirmed His person, His teachings, and salvific work for sinners (Romans 4:25). The Triune God raised Jesus from the dead. As we noted in the previous chapter, the resurrection was God's ultimate validation of Christ's salvific work for sinners.

Ninth, Peter states that they are witnesses of Christ's death and resurrection. Peter states that they were all witnesses of this resurrection (Acts 2:32, John 20:1-10, 20:19-23, 21:1-25). Peter and the disciples were not grave robbers (Matthew 28:11-15), they were eyewitnesses. Thus, when Peter testified that they were eyewitnesses of Jesus' resurrection, he was testifying that they had seen, heard, touched, and ate with the resurrected Jesus Christ. The word for "eyewitnesses" is *martus* which is where we get the word "martyr." *Martus* is a "martyr" or "witness." Peter didn't have a second-hand account of Christ's death and resurrection. Peter had the first-hand account of Christ's suffering, death, and resurrection.

Acts 3:16 – *And his name – by faith in his name – has made this man strong whom you see and know, and the faith that is through Jesus has given the man this perfect health in the presence of you all.*

Tenth, we should see that the lame man was healed by the power of Jesus of Nazareth. Peter will explain that the miraculous healing power came through Jesus Christ. There is much controversy around the word of faith movement, name it and claim it theology, and heretical and fraudulent "faith healers." This miracle was instantaneous and complete unlike what is done in fraudulent faith healing ministries. It wasn't staged. Peter wasn't healing a headache, lower back pain, a muscle strain, or any of the like. No, through the power of Jesus, this man who could not walk was suddenly able to walk again.

Eleventh, we should see that the beggar demonstrated faith in Jesus Christ. In this portion of Scripture, it would be most appropriate to focus on the object of the man's faith rather than the outcome of the man's faith. This lame man sat at the temple gate on a daily basis (Acts 3:2). This small detail would suggest that the man would have been aware of the news behind the person and work of Jesus Christ as news about Jesus spread everywhere and Jesus' ministry was well known and public (Acts 26:26). Therefore, it would not be a stretch to suggest that when the man put his faith in Jesus, he was knowledgeable of the person and work of Jesus. Peter simply acknowledges this man's faith in the person and work of Jesus. Thus, Peter's testimony gives every indication that the lame man was made well both physically and spiritually by faith in Jesus.

Acts 3:17 – *And now, brothers, I know that you acted in ignorance, as did also your rulers*

Eleventh, we see that Peter acknowledges that the crowd acted in ignorance, but yet this did not justify their actions. Peter will now address the Jewish crowd as brothers as they are all Israelites and testify that they acted ignorantly. The word for "ignorance" is *agnoia* which can mean "without mind," "without knowledge," or "ignorance." It is true that the crowd acted in ignorance. Jesus was attested to them by God in that He did mighty works, wonders, and signs (Acts 2:22). It was inexcusable for them to crucify Jesus as God had demonstrated that Jesus was who He claimed to be by His teaching and works. The rulers were also at fault and acted with ignorance. Everyone was indicted in this message. Peter's message held everyone accountable for their sins. We'll see that although the both the rulers and the crowd acted foolishly and ignorantly, Peter will proclaim that there is a way to have their sins forgiven (Acts 3:19).

Acts 3:18 – *But what God foretold by the mouth of all the prophets, that his Christ would suffer, he thus fulfilled*

Twelfth, we should see that Christ's suffering fulfilled the Old Testament prophecies of a suffering Messiah. Peter is saying that Scripture is sufficient to demonstrate that God's Messiah would need to suffer for the sins of His people. So where would we find such prophecies about the Messiah suffering? We can easily demonstrate that many of the prophets foresaw this suffering Christ.

- Moses wrote in Genesis 3:15 that the woman's promised Seed would bruise the head of the serpent and the serpent would bruise the heel of the Seed which was fulfilled on Calvary (Mark 15:16-40, Matthew 26:57-27:50, Luke 22:47-23:49, John 18:1-19:30).
- The Psalmist wrote that Christ would be betrayed by a friend in Psalm 41:9, 55:12-14 and was fulfilled in John 13:18, 21.
- Zechariah wrote that Christ would be sold for thirty pieces of silver in Zechariah 11:12 and was fulfilled in Matthew 26:15.
- Zechariah wrote that Christ would be given for the price of a potter's field in Zechariah 11:13 and was fulfilled in Matthew 27:7.
- The Psalmist, David, wrote that Christ would suffer intensely in Psalm 22:14-15 and was fulfilled in Luke 22:42, 44.

- Isaiah wrote that Christ would suffer for others (Isaiah 53:4-12) and was fulfilled in all the gospel accounts of Christ's betrayal, unjust trials, beatings, and crucifixion.
- Isaiah promised Christ would be patient and silent under suffering in Isaiah 53:7 and was fulfilled in Matthew 26:63, 27:12-14.
- Micah wrote Christ would be struck on the cheek in Micah 5:1 and was fulfilled in Matthew 27:30.
- Isaiah wrote Christ's appearance would be marred beyond human likeness in Isaiah 52:14, 53:3 and was fulfilled in the gospel accounts which recorded Christ being physically beaten, flogged, and crucified.
- Isaiah wrote that Christ would be spit upon and flogged in Isaiah 50:6 and was fulfilled in Mark 14:65 and John 19:1.
- The Psalmist, David, wrote that Christ's hands and feet would be pierced in Psalm 22:16 and was fulfilled in John 19;18, 20:25.
- The Psalmist, David, wrote that Christ would be mocked in Psalm 22:7-8 and was fulfilled in Matthew 27:39-44.
- The Psalmist, David wrote that Christ's garments would be divided and lots cast for His clothing in Psalm 22:18 and was fulfilled in Matthew 27:35.
- Zechariah wrote that Christ would be pierced in Zechariah 12:10 and was fulfilled in John 19:34, 37.

There are more verses from the Old Testament prophets where God foretells that God's Christ would suffer. Thus, Peter is drawing his audience back to the Old Testament and demonstrating that God's Christ needed to suffer, but most importantly, God's Christ needed to suffer as a substitutionary sacrifice for the sins of His people. Peter would write this about Christ's suffering for sinners in 1 Peter 3:18, "For Christ also suffered once for sins, the righteous for the unrighteous, that he might bring us to God".

Thirteenth, Peter is highlighting the importance of Christ's work. Most specifically, Peter is bringing attention to Christ being punished for the sins of His people which would ultimately bring expiation or forgiveness. Peter speaks of this propitiation and expiation when he quotes Isaiah 53 in 1 Peter 2:24, "He himself bore our sins in his body on the tree, that we might die to sin and live to righteousness. By his wounds you have been healed." God the Father is the one who needed to be appeased and satisfied, not man. It was God whose righteous wrath against sin needed to be satisfied. Therefore, it was God the Father who needed to crush His Son (Isaiah 53:5, 53:10). It was God the Father who needed to curse His Son (Galatians 3:13). It was God the Father who needed to forsake His Son (Matthew 27:46, Psalm 22:1). It was God the Father who needed to punish His Son (Romans 3:25). It was God the Father who needed to condemn His Son (Romans 8:3). It was God the Father who showed up in darkness at Calvary to crush, curse, forsake, punish, and condemn His Son and cause Him to suffer (Luke 23:45, Matthew 27:45, Mark 15:33). The substitutionary work of Christ on behalf of sinners was essential in Peter's explanation of the gospel. Christ's work of suffering and substitution was and is important to explain expiation and propitiation.

Acts 3:19-21 – *Repent therefore, and turn back, that your sins may be blotted out, that times of refreshing may come from the presence of the Lord, and that he may send the Christ appointed for you, Jesus, whom heaven must receive until the time for restoring all the things about which God spoke by the mouth of his holy prophets long ago.*

Fourteenth, let's see that Peter is calling for repentance. It's important to note that Peter isn't suggesting repentance. Peter isn't recommending repentance. Peter isn't proposing repentance. No! Peter is commanding repentance. In fact, the word "repentance" and "turn back" are written in the aorist tense and imperative mood. As we've mentioned earlier, the aorist imperative calls for a specific, definite, and decisive choice. It often expresses a note of urgency. The aorist imperative communicates a sense of getting something done, once for all, and swiftly. This call to repentance carries with it the full force of John the Baptist's message of repentance as well as the Lord Jesus Christ. This message of repentance carries with it the elevating and acknowledgment of sin, the turning away from sin and to God, bringing down self-righteousness, bringing down self-will, poverty of spirit for sinning against God, mourning over sinning against God, a changing of the mind, a turning of the heart, a denial of self, and a dying of self. John preached repentance (Matthew 3:3-10, Luke 3:3-17). Jesus preached repentance (Mark 1:15, Matthew 4:17, 11:20-24, Luke 13:3, 5, 15:5, 7, 10). Jesus, before He ascended back to heaven said this regarding repentance in Luke 24:46-47, "Thus it is written, that the Christ should suffer and on the third day rise from the dead, and that **repentance for the forgiveness of sins** should be proclaimed in his name to all nations, beginning from Jerusalem." Therefore, Peter is proclaiming this same message of repentance for the forgiveness of sins in Jesus Christ's name.

If we recall the ground work that has been laid thus far, we can recall that repentance is a gift from God and radical change in mind (Acts 5:31, 11:18, 2 Timothy 2:25) where the sinner understands his sin against God and is thus, poor in spirit (Matthew 5:3, Luke 18:9-14), has godly sorrow and mourns over his sin against God (Matthew 5:4, 2 Corinthians 7:10), and turns away from his sin and sinful former way of life (Ephesians 4:22) and toward God for righteousness and salvation (Matthew 5:5-6, Luke 3:3-17, Acts 17:30, 20:21, 1 Thessalonians 1:9). Saving faith is a gift from God (Ephesians 2:8-9) where a sinner has knowledge of Jesus' person and work where a sinner will respond to Christ's person and work by denying themselves (Matthew 16:24, Mark

8:34, Luke 9:23), picking up their cross (Matthew 10:38, 16:24, Mark 8:34, Luke 9:23), and lovingly (Luke 14:26-27, James 4:7) and obediently (2 Thessalonians 1:8, Romans 1:5) submit (James 4:6, Matthew 11:28) and commit their life to Jesus (Matthew 10:37-39, 16:24-26, Mark 8:34-37, Luke 9:23-26, 14:25-33) and trust in Him only for salvation (Romans 10:13, John 3:16, John 3:36, Acts 4:12). Thus, conversion is the turning away from sin in repentance and to the Lord Jesus Christ in faith for salvation (Acts 20:21, 1 Thessalonians 1:9, Ephesians 4:22-24, Colossians 3:9-10, Mark 1:15).

Therefore, when Peter is commanding the audience to "repent" and "turn back," he's calling for true repentance and saving faith in the Lord Jesus Christ which results in conversion.

This is a call to trust Jesus as Lord and Christ. The audience is being called to repent, surrender, and trust Jesus as their Lord and Christ. Peter is telling them to abandon Judaism for Christ. Peter is telling them to stop following the Pharisees and Sadducees. Peter is telling them to be completely identified and submitted to Jesus. Peter is telling them to abandon the works-righteousness system of Judaism. The Jews would know that identifying with Jesus would potentially mean accepting the same fate the religious community and leaders gave to Jesus. This is no small repentance. This is a complete abandonment of the Jewish system. This is surrender to Jesus as the Lord and Messiah. This is willingness to pay the price for being associated with Jesus. The Pharisees had already determined that Jesus was not the true Messiah so any such allegiance to Jesus Christ would be tantamount to worshipping a false god and was worthy of death (Deuteronomy 13:6-15). As we learned in Chapters 5 and 6, this was the call to deny yourself, hate your own life, take up your cross and follow Jesus (Matthew 16:24-26, Mark 8:34-37, Luke 9:23-26, 14:25-33).

Sixteenth, let's note that there is the promise of forgiveness of sins associated with this gospel call. The word "blotting out" comes from *exaleiphó* which means to "wipe out," "erase," or "obliterate." It gives the idea of something being completely erased. For those that have come to Christ in true repentance and saving faith, they will be forgiven all their past, present, and future sins. In fact, *exaleiphó* is written in the aorist tense and infinitive mood. This simply means that if one comes to Christ in true repentance and faith, they will once for all have their sins forgiven and blotted out. Thus, we see that this gospel call to repentance carries with it the promise of forgiveness of sins.

Seventeenth, let's notice that when one comes to true repentance and faith in Christ, there are times of refreshing. This word "refreshing" comes from *anapsuxis* and carries the idea of "breathing easy" or "a recovery of breath" which is refreshing. The reason there would be times of refreshing would be because one's sins have been forgiven, they have been reconciled to God through Christ, there is no fear in judgment and condemnation. To surrender and now be at peace and in the kingdom of the King of kings and Lord of lords is to breathe easy and be refreshed.

One last point is that there is much commentary written about eschatology, the Messianic kingdom, and other prophecies in Acts 3:20-21. For the purposes of this book, it would not be advantageous to discuss these topics, but they do warrant consideration and attention in one's personal study.

Acts 3:22-24 – *Moses said, 'The Lord God will raise up for you a prophet like me from your brothers. You shall listen to him in whatever he tells you. And it shall be that every soul who does not listen to that prophet shall be destroyed from the people.' All the prophets who have spoken, from Samuel and those who came after him, also proclaimed these days.*

Eighteenth, we see that Peter has identified Jesus as "the" prophet that was prophesied in Deuteronomy 18:15. Therefore, we can know that Jesus was and is the fulfillment of Deuteronomy 18:15

Nineteenth, Peter warns that those who would not listen to Jesus and obey Him, would be destroyed. Thus, there is a promise of condemnation and hell for those who reject Christ. As we noted earlier, the punishment for sin is hell is a place of God's full wrath and is a place of blackest darkness (Jude 13, Matthew 22:13), filled with furious and concentrated fire everywhere (Matthew 5:22, 5:29, 13:42, 13:50), where there is weeping and anger against God for the unrepentant Christ-rejecting (Matthew 11:20-24) and Christ-neglecting sinners (Hebrews 2:1-3) where they will spend all eternity paying for every sin they've ever committed (Revelation 20:12) with no hope of escape (Luke 16:26), and only the expectation of excruciating torments to their body, soul, and spirit (Matthew 10:28) and an undying conscience that will haunt them day and night, forever and ever, with no reprieve (Luke 16:25). Thus, Peter warns of destruction and hell for those who will not repent and put their faith in Jesus Christ.

Acts 3:25-26 – *You are the sons of the prophets and of the covenant that God made with your fathers, saying to Abraham, 'And in your offspring shall all the families of the earth be blessed.' God, having raised up his servant, sent him to you first, to bless you by turning every one of you from your wickedness.*

The last point we should see is that the Abrahamic Covenant was fulfilled in Christ. Paul elaborates on how Christ is the fulfillment of the Abrahamic Covenant and how all nations would be blessed though Christ. In Galatians 3:16, Paul says this of the promise God made to Abraham which was in Christ, "Now the promises were spoken to Abraham and to his seed. He does not say, 'And to seeds,' as one would in referring to many, but rather as in referring to one, 'And to your seed,' that is, Christ." Paul is referencing back to the Abrahamic Covenant in Genesis

12:7 where the LORD promises to bless Abraham's descendants. However, in Galatians 3:16, Paul narrows down *"seeds"* to *"seed."* He is deliberate to note that all promises and blessings would come through the one seed Jesus Christ. All nations would be blessed through Jesus Christ.

The Abrahamic Covenant included the LORD circumcising Abraham to Himself, circumcising Israel to Himself, circumcising the land of Israel to Himself, and a promise that all nations would be blessed through Christ who would circumcise the heart (Genesis 12-15, Deuteronomy 10:12-16, 30:6). Christ is the one who circumcises the heart where it says in Colossians 2:11, "In him also you were circumcised with a circumcision made without hands, by putting off the body of the flesh, by the circumcision of Christ." Likewise, in Romans 2:28–29, Paul says this regarding circumcision of the heart, "For no one is a Jew who is merely one outwardly, nor is circumcision outward and physical. But a Jew is one inwardly, and circumcision is a matter of the heart, by the Spirit, not by the letter. His praise is not from man but from God." Therefore, we see that circumcision of the heart is performed by Christ and with the Holy Spirit, not with human hands and that all who have had a heart circumcision are Abraham's offspring and heirs according to the promise as it says in Romans 4:16, "Therefore, the promise comes by faith, so that it may be by grace and may be guaranteed to all Abraham's offspring – not only to those who are of the law but also to those who have the faith of Abraham." Therefore, Peter is stating that the promise of the Abrahamic Covenant to be blessed is found in God's servant, Jesus Christ.

As we close this chapter, we gain an even greater understanding of how Peter presented the gospel and gave a gospel call. Peter indicted the crowd of their sins, he warned of judgment and not having one's sins forgiven, he demonstrated that Jesus was the Christ prophesied from the Old Testament, he demonstrated that the prophets foretold that Christ would suffer which pointed to

Christ's propitiating and expiating work, he called for repentance and faith, he demonstrated that Jesus was the fulfillment of the Abrahamic Covenant and the means by which all nations would be blessed. Once again, we have a faithful explanation of the gospel by Peter as well as a faithful gospel call of repentance toward God and faith in Jesus Christ and a promise of the forgiveness of sins to all those who would come to Christ in faith.

CHAPTER 9

Peter's Sermon to the Sanhedrin

Acts 4:12 – *And there is salvation in no on else, for there is no other name under heaven given among men by which we must be saved.*

As we enter this chapter, we've had the opportunity to see Peter give two messages to two large crowds. In this chapter, we are going to see Peter give a message to the Jewish leaders. Thus far, we've seen Peter's Spirit filled messages. If we've paid careful attention, we see that Peter is bold and indicts the crowd of their sins and calls them to repentance and faith in the Lord Jesus Christ. We also see that Peter consistently teaches the person and work of the Lord Jesus Christ and also points back to the Old Testament Scripture to demonstrate that Jesus is the fulfillment of the prophecies of the Messiah. We also see that Peter warns of judgment and destruction for rejecting Christ. Thus, we've come to understand that Peter's first two messages contain a presentation of the gospel along with gospel calls or gospel invitations. Before we get into the text of interest, Acts 4:7-12, it would be helpful to get a running start. Therefore, we'll briefly review Acts 4:1-6 first.

After Peter has finished preaching to the crowd, the priests, the captain of the temple, and the Sadducees come to arrest Peter and John for preaching about Jesus and the resurrection from the dead (Acts 4:1-3). The Sadducees possessed much power and authority during this time. They were not well liked by the people because they were pro Rome. They also stood in opposition to the Pharisees in that they did not believe in a resurrection from the dead and they did not agree with the oral tradition of the Pharisees. The Sadducees also gave the preeminent attention to the Torah, or the first five books of the Bible. Therefore, because the Sadducees did not believe in the resurrection from the dead and Peter was preaching the resurrection in Jesus, we read in Acts 4:2 that they were "greatly annoyed because they were teaching the people and proclaiming in Jesus the resurrection from the dead." The word "greatly annoyed" comes from *diaponeomai* and it means "to be worn out," "be greatly troubled," or properly "to bring on exhausting, depleting grief which results in piercing fatigue." Thus, the Sadducees came with the *sagan*, the captain of the temple police, to arrest Peter and John. The proclamation of Peter proclaiming Christ's resurrection and the resurrection from the dead would be aggravating for the Sadducees as this completely undercut their false teaching on the resurrection and heralded Jesus as Lord and Christ whom they had put to death by crucifixion. Therefore, Peter and John were put into custody (Acts 4:4). Additionally, we see that because of this spirit filled teaching by Peter, that more people were coming to faith in Christ and the number had grown to five thousand (Acts 4:5).

The next day, there is a gathering of the most prominent Jewish leaders which include the rulers, elders, scribes, and high priests (Acts 4:5-6). Therefore, we see that John and Peter were surrounded by the Jewish elite leaders, teachers, scribes, high priests, and most likely, members of the Sanhedrin. This would certainly have been an intimidating position for John and Peter. As we know, Caiaphas oversaw the unjust trials of Jesus as the high priest. Annas was the father-in-law of Caiaphas and he was very influential with the Jewish leaders (John 18:13). Therefore,

Peter and John had been assembled in a very similar manner as Jesus where the Jewish rulers will begin questioning them. Peter and John were two disciples of the Lord Jesus Christ that had been arrested, detained, and were now going to speak for their Lord in front of some of the same Jewish leaders who had unjustly put Jesus on trial and crucified Him.

Acts 4:7 – *And when they had set them in the midst, they inquired, "By what power or by what name did you do this?"*

First, let's see that the Jewish rulers were very calculated in their question. It was no secret how the lame man was able to miraculously walk. If the temple guard wanted a testimony from the lame man who had been healed, they could have received a testimony from the lame man who would tell them, "It was in the name of Jesus Christ of Nazareth that I could stand and walk" (Acts 3:6). If the Jewish rulers and leaders wanted to get a testimony from the crowd on how the man was healed, they could have gathered a testimony from those in the crowd and the testimonies would have stated the following, "this man was given perfect health by faith in the name of Jesus" (Acts 3:16). If the Jewish leaders wanted a testimony from the lame man or the crowd, they would have also received a testimony that Peter indicted them and the Jewish leaders for denying Jesus (Acts 3:13), that Peter indicted them because they denied the sinless and Holy One of God (Acts 3:14), that Peter indicted them because they killed the Author and Creator of life (Acts 3:15), that Peter indicted all of them for acting in ignorance (Acts 3:17), that Peter testified there was forgiveness of sins that would come from the Lord through repentance (Acts 3:19, 20), that Peter testified that Jesus was the foretold prophet from Deuteronomy 18:5, that there was judgment and destruction for those who did not obey the prophet (Acts 3:22-23), and that Peter testified Jesus was the fulfillment of the Abrahamic Covenant and the means by which they would be blessed if they turned from their wickedness and to the Prophet, the Lord Jesus Christ (Acts 3:25-26). In fact, the Jewish rulers would have had all night to deliberate over the line of questions they desired to ask. Therefore, the question was meant to bring to the forefront, their testimony of Jesus Christ.

Second, Peter was given a chance to preach to the whole Jewish leadership. The Sanhedrin was made up of 71 members. The Great Sanhedrin would take appeals from cases which were passed to them by lesser courts. To put it in modern terms of American jurisprudence, this was the Federal Supreme Court. There were seventy-one judges on the Great Sanhedrin in the case of an even vote so that the seventy-first member could be the tiebreaker. In the modern American era, judges that are on the Supreme Court have not only attended the best law schools, they have also served on smaller circuits, gained experience, and are considered experts in the law. In the same way, The Sanhedrin was made up of extremely knowledgeable Jewish leaders who were knowledgeable in Old Testament Scripture and the law. Unlike Jesus, who would stand His unjust trials and remain silent as a sheep before its shearers (Isaiah 53:7), Peter was going to give a testimony of the Lord Jesus Christ.

Acts 4:8-9 – *Then Peter, filled with the Holy Spirit, said to them, "Rulers of the people and elders, if we are being examined today concerning a good deed done to a crippled man, by what means this man has been healed*

Third, let's note that when Peter is going to give his message, he is filled with the Holy Spirit. A good short, definition of *being filled with the Holy Spirit* is as follows: **Being filled with the Holy Spirit is being submitted, affected, and influenced by the Holy Spirit to do His will.** Only believers can be filled with the Holy Spirit. Therefore, when Peter gives this speech, he is being controlled by the Holy Spirit.

Fourth, let's note that Peter realizes he's being persecuted and intimidated. Peter and John have been detained and are now in the process of being interrogated. In fact, when it says the rulers and elders were interrogating them, the word for "interrogating" is *anakrinó* which means "to distinguish by vigorously judging 'down to up'" or "careful evaluation and judgment." This word gives the idea that Peter and John were being scrutinized greatly, but also unjustly. Peter knows that they are being examined unjustly because they were arrested and put in custody so the Jewish rulers could ask them how the lame man was healed. There was no just cause to have them arrested and put in custody for helping someone. Additionally, these were the same men who oversaw the unjust trials of the Lord. The same way they saw the Jewish leaders treat the Lord Jesus Christ, is the same treatment they were receiving. They were essentially being asked how they helped a lame man which was no crime at all. This is the persecution and intimidation that both Peter and John were facing.

Fifth, let's remember what Jesus promised would happen when they were persecuted. If we think back to Matthew 10 where Jesus sends out His disciples, we see this promise being given in Matthew 10:17-20, "Be on your guard; you will be handed over to the local councils and be flogged in the synagogues. On my account you will be brought before governors and kings as witnesses to them and to the Gentiles. But when they arrest you, do not worry about what to say or how to say it. At that time you will be given what to say, for it will not be you speaking, but the Spirit of your Father speaking through you." Therefore, we see the Holy Spirit was working in and through Peter to give a testimony of Jesus Christ (John 15:26-27). It was the Holy Spirit who would prove the Jewish rulers wrong about sin, righteousness, and judgment (John 16:8). The Holy Spirit was going to work in and through Peter to glorify the Lord Jesus Christ (John 16:14).

Acts 4:10 – *let it be known to all of you and to all the people of Israel that by the name of Jesus Christ of Nazareth, whom you crucified, whom God raised from the dead – by him this man is standing before you well.*

Sixth, let's note that Peter is specific in who healed this man. The one who healed the lame man was Jesus Christ of Nazareth. This is the Jesus who grew up in Nazareth, who was the son of Mary, and who had brothers and sisters (Mark 6:1-3). This is the Jesus who was attested to the people of Israel by God with mighty works, wonders, and signs (Acts 2:33). This is the Jesus who the Jewish leaders crucified (Acts 2:23). This is the Jesus who was raised from the dead (Acts 2:24). This is the Jesus who is both Christ and Lord (Acts 2:36). This is the Jesus who baptizes with the Holy Spirit (Luke 3:16). This is the Jesus who John the Baptist pointed to who was the Lamb of God who takes away the sin of the world (John 1:29). This is the Jesus who claimed to be equal with God the Father (John 5:17-18). Please note that Peter's answer wasn't "I do not know him." Note the Spirit-filled boldness, the Spirit-filled conviction, and the Spirit-filled courage of Peter to call Jesus "Christ." The High Priest asked Jesus if He was the Messiah or Christ, the Son of God and when Jesus affirmed that He was, the leaders charged Jesus with blasphemy and testified that He was worthy of death (Matthew 26:61-66). So, Peter faced with this same dilemma gives a bold testimony of Jesus and calls Him "Christ."

Seventh, let's note that Peter indicts the Jewish leaders for crucifying Jesus, the Messiah. This was a recurring theme with Peter. It was critical to demonstrate the necessity of the cross and the suffering Servant. It was necessary to demonstrate that Christ was a propitiation which gave expiation for sins. The person and work of Jesus needed to be continually proclaimed. Jesus needed to be born of a virgin (Matthew 1:23), so we could be born of God (John 3:3, 7). Jesus needed to be born a man (Matthew

1:23), so we could be born again (John 3:3, 7). Jesus needed to be the Son of Man (Luke 19:10), so that we could be sons of God (1 John 3:1). Jesus needed to be rejected by God (Isaiah 53:3), so we could be resurrected by God (1 Corinthians 15:52). Jesus needed to be despised (Isaiah 53:3), so we would not be damned (Romans 1:18–32). Jesus needed to be crushed by God (Isaiah 53:5, 10), so we would not be cursed by God (Galatians 3:13). Jesus needed to be crucified (Isaiah 53:5), so we could be justified (Romans 3:24). Jesus needed to be forsaken (Matthew 27:46), so we could be forgiven (Isaiah 53:12). Jesus suffered (Isaiah 53:11), so we would be saved (Matthew 1:23). Jesus needed to suffer the wrath of God (Isaiah 53:10), so He could show forth the riches of God (Ephesians 2:7). Jesus needed to be resurrected (Isaiah 53:11), so we could be perfected (Hebrews 10:14). Jesus needed to bear reproach (Hebrews 13:13), so we could be redeemed (Romans 3:24). Jesus offered himself as a sacrifice (Hebrews 9:26), so we could be saints (2 Corinthians 5:21). The cross was and is crucial to the gospel. Therefore, Peter preached the importance of the crucified Christ. Christ came to save sinners. Christ came to seek and save the lost. Christ came to save the worst of sinners. Peter needed to convict the Jewish leaders of their sin and explain how the cross of Christ provided reconciliation between holy God and sinful man. Peter also needed to convict the Jewish rulers of their horrendous sin of killing Jesus Christ.

Eighth, let's note that Peter proclaims the resurrection of Christ. Without the resurrection of Jesus, Christ would have just been an ordinary man that died and stayed dead. Without the resurrection of Jesus, the Christian faith would amount to nothing. Without the resurrection of Jesus, there would be no hope in Jesus as He would have no power over death as He couldn't raise Himself from the dead. Without the resurrection of Jesus, God the Father would have sinned in selecting a Savior who sinned and could not raise Himself from the dead. However, Jesus was resurrected from the dead on the third day by His own power

(John 10:18), by God the Father (Galatians 1:1) and God the Holy Spirit (Romans 8:11), which affirmed His person, His teachings, and salvific work for sinners (Romans 4:25). The Triune God raised Jesus from the dead. As we noted in the previous chapter, the resurrection was God's ultimate validation of Christ's salvific work for sinners. The resurrection of the Lord Jesus Christ is God's ultimate testimony that those who die in Christ will be resurrected as Christ was (1 Corinthians 15:21-23).

In fact, Peter refers to Christ's resurrection in his infamous baptism verse where he says in 1 Peter 3:21, "Baptism, which corresponds to this, now saves you, not as a removal of dirt from the body but as an appeal to God for a good conscience, through the resurrection of Jesus Christ, who has gone into heaven and is at the right hand of God, with angels, authorities, and powers having been subjected to him." Peter is explaining that the Flood and ark correspond to baptism in that the water in the Flood was used as the agent of destruction, wrath, and judgment but was not the saving agent. However, the ark was the saving agent in which eight persons went into the ark and were rescued from destruction, wrath, and judgment. So, just like the ark was the means to protect the eight persons from the wrath of God, so the sinner makes a demand to God for a good conscious through Jesus Christ who took the wrath of God on the cross for sinners, who died, rose again, and is empowered with all authority to judge and to forgive, to condemn and to save, to punish and to pardon.

Likewise, Peter is clear that this baptism is not a water baptism or a ceremonial washing. He makes this abundantly clear where he says, "Not as a removal of dirt from the body." Peter lived amongst wide spread ceremonial washings which provided absolutely no salvific merit (Matthew 15:1-20). The baptism that Peter spoke of was a baptism which appealed to God through the Lord Jesus Christ to escape the judgment and wrath of God through faith in Jesus Christ who took the judgment and wrath of God for sinners, died, was resurrected, ascended into heaven, is presently enthroned at the right hand of the Father, and who could provide shelter from the wrath that was to come (1 Thessalonians 1:10).

Ninth, let's note how purposeful Peter is to confront the error of the Sadducees. As we noted earlier, the Sadducees did not believe in the resurrection from the dead. Jesus would confront the Sadducees on this very issue and would prove that the Torah spoke of the resurrection which proved the Sadducees wrong (Matthew 22:23-33). Peter did not tread lightly around this doctrinal issue. Peter didn't look for points of common agreement. No! Peter declared that there was a resurrection of the dead in His Lord, God, and Savior. Not only this, we read in Matthew's account of the gospel that many of the saints were raised and coming out of their tombs after Christ's resurrection (Matthew 27:52-54). Therefore, Peter boldly declared the resurrection from the dead in Jesus (Acts 4:2).

Acts 4:11 – *This Jesus is the stone that was rejected by you, the builders, which has become the cornerstone.*

Tenth, we see that Peter testifies that Christ is the cornerstone and charges the Jewish leaders with rejecting God's Christ. As we learned earlier as we looked at Psalm 118:22, the word "cornerstone" comes from *akrogóniaios* which can mean "belonging to the extreme corner." The corner stone needed to have the correct angles so all the angles of the building would be symmetrical. The angle of the cornerstone would determine the angle of every other stone laid against it. Thus, the cornerstone was essential to the construction of the building. As we learned earlier, the person and work of the Lord Jesus Christ is the cornerstone and very foundation of the church and whoever believes in Him will not be put to shame. Paul proclaimed this very truth that Christ is the head of the church (Colossians 1:18, Ephesians 1:22-

23). Peter speaks of Christ as the precious cornerstone where he says this in 1 Peter 2:6-7, “For it stands in Scripture: ‘Behold, I am laying in Zion a stone, a cornerstone chosen and precious, and whoever believes in him will not be put to shame.’ So the honor is for you who believe, but for those who do not believe, ‘The stone that the builders rejected has become the cornerstone,’ and ‘A stone of stumbling and a rock of offense.’” In other words, the Jewish leaders who were responsible for the spiritual leadership of Israel should have been pointing everyone to Christ, but rather, they rejected this cornerstone. Rather than embrace the Messiah through faith, they called Him Beelzebul, they asked for more miracles, they did not believe His works or words, and they ultimately beat Jesus to death and had Him crucified. They ended up rejecting and killing the very cornerstone that was to be their salvation. To them, Christ was a stumbling block and a rock of offense rather than the chosen and precious cornerstone. Therefore, we see Peter indict them again for rejecting God’s Christ. Peter also affirms that Jesus is the chief cornerstone on which the church is built.

Acts 4:12 – *And there is salvation in no one else, for there is no other name under heaven given among men by which we must be saved.*

Eleventh, we see that Jesus is the only means of salvation. Peter makes a declarative statement here. Heaven has provided one means by which sinful men can be reconciled to a holy God. There is one mediator between God and man, the man Christ Jesus that offers salvation (1 Timothy 2:5). When Peter says there is no other name under heaven given to men by which we must be saved, he means to say that that there is no one and nothing that heaven has provided for the salvation of men other than the Lord Jesus Christ.

A brilliant theologian and pastor has said that the Christian faith is one of positive confirmation and absolute denial. This simply means that the Christian faith will proclaim the way of salvation through Jesus Christ, but it will also deny that any other means of salvation outside of the Lord Jesus Christ. Let's look at a few examples of such absolute denial using Peter's language from Acts 4:12. There is condemnation for those who hope in Allah for salvation. There is condemnation for those who seek salvation in Islam. There is condemnation for those who seek salvation in Buddhism. There is condemnation for those who seek salvation in Taoism. There is condemnation for those who seek salvation in Shintoism. There is condemnation for those who seek salvation in Sikhism. There is condemnation for those who seek salvation in Zoroastrianism. There is condemnation for those who seek salvation in Judaism. There is condemnation for those who seek salvation in Hinduism. There is condemnation for those who put their hope in Sun Myung Moon for salvation. There is condemnation for those who seek salvation in Christian Science. There is condemnation for those who seek salvation in Scientology. There is condemnation for those who seek salvation in Mormonism which teaches a false Christ. There is condemnation for those who seek salvation in the Jehovah's Witness church that teaches a false Christ.

We could even be more specific on absolute denial in churches that would declare themselves a part of the Christian faith. There is condemnation for those who hope in good works plus the Lord Jesus Christ for salvation. There is condemnation for those who hope in water baptism plus Christ for salvation. There is condemnation for those who hope that Mary will be a co-mediatrix along with Christ for salvation. There is condemnation for those who hope in indulgences plus Christ for salvation. There is condemnation for those who hope in taking communion plus Christ for salvation. Salvation is in Christ and Christ alone. Peter goes right to the heart of the gospel. Peter's declaration is that the

Lord Jesus Christ is the only name that heaven has given to mankind for salvation. The Biblical person and work of Jesus Christ is the only means for salvation.

Twelfth, let's notice that Peter has confirmed their condemnation if they do not repent and embrace Christ through faith. We can know for certain that since Jewish leaders have rejected and continue to reject the Lord Jesus Christ, Peter is declaring that they are not saved and will not be saved. Thus, Peter's message ends with a confirmation of Christ as the only means of salvation and condemnation for all those who will not repent and embrace Jesus as Lord and Christ through faith.

Lastly, we see that after Peter has given this message to the Jewish leaders, the Jewish leaders solemnly charge John and Peter not to speak or teach in the name of Jesus. However, we see Peter and John give this answer in Acts 4:19-20, "Whether it is right in the sight of God to listen to you rather than to God, you must judge, for we cannot but speak of what we have seen and heard." Since Jesus is the Way and the Truth and the Life, Peter and John could not obey the charge from the Jewish leaders (John 14:6). Jesus testified that His disciples would be His witnesses in Jerusalem, Judea, Samaria, and to the farthest part of the earth (Acts 1:8). Since Jesus is the only means by which men can be saved, Peter and John were compelled to continue preaching the Lord Jesus Christ.

The apostles would continue preaching and declaring the good news of Jesus Christ which would lead them to be imprisoned again and brought before the council again (Acts 5:12-28). The Jewish council would remind the apostles that they were commanded to stop preaching and teaching the good news of Jesus Christ and Peter would give this statement in Acts 5:29-31:

"We must obey God rather than men. The God of our fathers raised Jesus, whom you killed by hanging him on a tree. God exalted him at his right hand as Leader and Savior, to ***give repentance*** *to*

Israel and forgiveness of sins. And we are witnesses to these things, and so is the Holy Spirit, who God has given to those who obey him."

In Peter's short response back to the Jewish leaders. We once again see Peter preaching Jesus's crucifixion, resurrection, and exaltation. We see Peter preach Jesus as Lord with all authority as He is at God's right hand. We see Peter preach Jesus as Prince and Savior. We see Peter indict the Jewish leaders of their sin. We see Peter preach repentance for the forgiveness of sins in Jesus. Thus, we see Peter continuing to give the gospel of the person and work of the Lord Jesus Christ and call for repentance towards God and faith in the Lord Jesus Christ.

As we close this chapter, we see the Spirit-enabled preaching of Peter. Peter preached on sin and indicted the leaders and the crowds of their sin. Peter preached judgment. Peter preached on the person of Jesus which included Him being Lord, being the promised Christ, being the Son of God, being the baptizer with the Holy Spirit, being the Son of David, being the Author and Creator of life, being the foretold prophet of Deuteronomy 18:5, being the fulfillment of the Abrahamic Covenant, and more. Peter preached the work of Jesus which includes His sinless life, His miracles, His teaching, His substitutionary propitiation for sin on the cross, His death, His burial, His resurrection, His ascension, His present enthronement, His sovereign authority to rule and judge, His return to restore all things, and more. Peter preached repentance and faith in the Lord Jesus Christ for the forgiveness of sins. Peter preached the gospel. As we understand Peter's theology of repentance toward God and faith in the Lord Jesus Christ, we see how his gospel calls and gospel invitations were always tied to the proclamation of the gospel of the Lord Jesus Christ.

Chapter 10

Simon the Sorcerer – Baptized & Believed, but not Saved

Acts 8:13 – *Even Simon himself believed, and after being baptized he continued with Philip. And seeing signs and great miracles performed, he was amazed.*

As we enter this chapter, we've learned and studied three of Peter's gospel messages to three different crowds. We've come to understand the content of Peter's gospel presentation and we've also come to understand Peter's gospel calls or invitations for repentance toward God and faith in the Lord Jesus Christ. In this account, we are going to look at Peter's confrontation with Simon Magus or Simon the Sorcerer. Luke is very intentional to place this narrative in the book of Acts to record the account of a false convert. The Lord promised there would be those who would identify with Him and the church but would not be truly born again or truly converted. Jesus promised that there would be good soil and bad soil (Matthew 13:1-9, 18-23). Jesus promised that there would be wheat and tares (Matthew 13:24-30). Jesus promised that there would be good fish and bad fish (Matthew 13:47-50). Therefore, the account of Simon the Sorcerer is important to expose the nature of false converts. This account is also important as we'll see the contrast between true conversion and false conversion, true repentance and false repentance, and saving faith and non-saving faith.

Acts 8:9 – *But there was a man named Simon, who had previously practiced magic in the city and amazed the people of Samaria, saying that he himself was somebody great.*

The very first thing that we note about Simon is that he practiced magic. There is much commentary and speculation written about the extent of Simon practicing magic. The word "magic" comes from *mageuó* which means to "practice sorcery" or "magic." There are some commentators that would speculate that this magic was demonic sorcery. Other commentators would suggest that Simon used sleight of hand trickery. In either case, we see that Simon was someone that practiced either demonic sorcery or tricked people with sleight of hand. In either instance, this would be sinful deception at best or demonic sorcery at worst. Both scenarios describe a sinful deceptive man or a sinful idolatrous man.

The second thing that we see about Simon is his absolute lack of humility where it says he declared that he was great. As we learned earlier, Jesus came to proclaim good news to the poor, blind, prisoners and the oppressed (Luke 4:18-19). We learned that the very first Beatitude was poverty of spirit (Matthew 5:3). We learned that this type of poverty of spirit is a picture of a person reduced to total destitution who crouched in a corner begging as he held out one hand for alms and hid his face with the other hand because he was ashamed of being recognized. This is the bankruptcy of the inner man. This is the bankruptcy of the inner man's spirit. This is bankruptcy of the inner man's spirit over sin. To commit one sin is to be rich in trespasses. To commit one sin is to be rich in wickedness. To commit one sin is to be rich in abomination against the Lord. To commit one sin is to be the wealthiest owner of what God hates. Therefore, we can understand that Simon was in bondage to sorcery and in bondage to pride.

Acts 8:10 – *They all paid attention to him, from the least to the greatest, saying, "This man is the power of God that is called great."*

The third point we should see is that Simon loved the praise of men. There is much written in commentaries about what Simon taught and the claims he made to deity. For the purposes of this book, we won't review the specific claims he made by the early church fathers and others. However, what is important to see is that Simon accepted the attention that he was receiving and he welcomed the testimonies that he was power of God that is called Great. If we simply remember the words of the Lord as He confronted the Pharisees, we can recall His statement on humility in Matthew 23:12 where He says, "Whoever exalts himself will be humbled, and whoever humbles himself will be exalted." Simon had no interest in humility. Rather, he enjoyed the exalted claims he received from the people.

Acts 8:11 – *And they paid attention to him because for a long time he had amazed the people with his magic.*

The fourth point that we should see about Simon is he loved preeminence. As we noted earlier, there is much speculation on whether this magic was a demonic demonstration of power or if this was simply sleight of hand. Regardless, we see that his magic amazed the people. The word for "amazed" is *existémi* and it means "to be astonished," "to be amazed," "to be beside oneself," "to be flabbergasted," or "to be overwhelmed." Simon's magic exalted himself, gave himself prestige, and gave himself honor. It's very clear that Simon loved the preeminence he received by his ability to amaze the crowds.

Acts 8:12 – *But when they believed Philip as he preached good news about the kingdom of God and the name of Jesus Christ, they were baptized, both men and women.*

The fifth point we see is Philip came preaching the gospel. In fact, Luke gives Philip an honorable title in Acts 21:8 where he calls him, "Philip the evangelist". Philip was going about preaching the gospel. As we learned earlier, the kingdom of God is the same as the kingdom of heaven and in this sense, is used to describe the sphere of salvation. The individuals who have inherited eternal life and salvation are those who have entered the kingdom of God. Therefore, we can understand that Philip was preaching the bad news of sin, death, hell, and judgment and he was also preaching the good news of the person and work of the Lord Jesus Christ and how to enter the kingdom of God through repentance toward God and faith in the Lord Jesus Christ (Mark 1:15, Matthew 4:17).

The sixth point we see is that there was a group of people that believed Philip and his message and responded by being baptized. It would be reasonable to assume that Peter's very same message to the Jewish crowd on the day of Pentecost was the same gospel call that Philip issued. The audience in Samaria would need to so identify with Jesus that they would deny themselves, take up their cross, and follow Christ. The Samaritans would surely know of Christ being crucified by the Jewish leaders and the consequences of declaring Jesus as Lord and Christ. It would be reasonable to assume that Philip called the Samaritans to Christ exactly how Peter called people to Christ because Peter imitated Christ's call in Matthew 16:24-26, Mark 8:34-37, Luke 9:23-26. This gospel invitation would confront them with the decision to publicly declare Jesus as Lord and Christ even if it costs them their family and relationships, their personal ambitions, their personal sins, and their personal belongings. Therefore, the response of some of the Samaritans to be baptized because of their belief in the gospel of the Lord Jesus Christ would indicate that Philip issued a gospel call to repent and be baptized for the forgiveness of sins and thus, receive the free gift of the Holy Spirit which was similar to Peter.

Acts 8:13 – *Even Simon himself believed, and after being baptized he continued with Philip. And seeing signs and great miracles performed, he was amazed.*

The seventh point we should see is that Simon believed the gospel that Philip preached and responded to Philip's message by being baptized. At this point in the verse, we are not told whether or not Simon possesses saving faith. It's only when we start examining Acts 8:17-24 that we realize that Simon never had saving faith and was never justified by faith. In Matthew 13, the Lord explained that there would be some who would receive the word with joy, but had no root. This type of person would endure for a while and when tribulation or persecution would come on account of the word, they would fall away (Matthew 13:20-22). We also see that there are people who hear the word but the cares of the world and deceitfulness of riches choke the word, and it proves unfruitful (Matthew 13:22). What we see from Simon is that he believed, he responded to the message by being baptized, and he continued with Philip. In fact, the word "continued on" comes from *proskartereó* which means "to persist," "to persevere in," "to continue steadfast," or "to continue with intense effort." This word is not a picture of someone following along drudgingly. No, it's a picture of someone who is following in strong devotion. Therefore, the initial testimony of Simon is that he would have appeared to be a true convert.

The eighth point we should see is that Simon was amazed at the signs and great miracles that Philip performed. We noted earlier that the crowds were amazed by Simon's magic. Here, we see that Simon is amazed by the signs and miracles that Philip has performed. The Scripture doesn't tell us the specific signs and miracles that Philip was performing. However, in Acts 5:12-16 we read that some of the signs and wonders that were being performed were healing the sick and those with unclean spirits. If these were the same signs and miracles that Philip performed, Simon would have realized the true power of God. He would have realized he had an inferior power as compared to the power of God that was working through Philip as he preached the gospel. Simon would have realized that he had no ability to perform the same types of signs and wonders. Simon was amazed because the signs and wonders he had seen were things that he had no power to perform and he saw the true power of God working through Philip.

Acts 8:14-15 – *Now when the apostles at Jerusalem heard that Samaria had received the word of God, they sent to the Peter and John, who came down and prayed for them that they might receive the Holy Spirit*

The ninth point we should see is that there was apostolic confirmation to validate that the Samaritans had truly and savingly believed the good news preached by Philip. Thus, Peter and John were sent to substantiate that the Samaritans were included in Christ's church. The Jews and the Samaritans did not look favorably upon one another and so it was important to authenticate their inclusion into the church by the apostles. We'll even see in Chapter 11 that Peter needed to be told three times by the Holy Spirit that Gentiles were to no longer be called unclean. Therefore, this confirmation by the apostles was necessary as the gospel was spreading, the church was growing from Jerusalem and in all Judea and Samaria, and to the ends of the earth (Acts 1:8).

The tenth point we should see is that this is not the normal way one receives the Holy Spirit. As noted above, this is a time of transition in the church which needed apostolic confirmation.

Scripture is abundantly clear on when someone receives the Holy Spirit. Jesus said that those who believed in him would receive the Holy Spirit (John 7:38-39). Paul wrote in his epistle to the Ephesians that they were sealed or received the Holy Spirit when they heard the gospel and believed in Christ (Ephesians 1:13). Likewise, Paul tells the Galatians that they received the Holy Spirit through faith in Christ (Galatians 3:2, 14). Therefore, it would be appropriate to understand this receiving of the Holy Spirit by the apostles laying their hands on the Samaritans as a time in transition in the church. The ordinary means to receiving the Holy Spirit is when one comes to saving faith in the Lord Jesus Christ and they are immediately justified by faith, receive, and are indwelt by the Holy Spirit.

Acts 8:16 – *for he had not yet fallen on any of them, but they had only been baptized in the name of the Lord Jesus. Then they laid their hands on them and they received the Holy Spirit*

The eleventh point we should see is that Luke is purposeful to distinguish between water baptism and the baptism with the Holy Spirit. Here we see that there is a distinction between water baptism in the name of the Lord Jesus and having the Holy Spirit falling on someone, or rather, being baptized with the Holy Spirit. Luke makes this distinction, John sees this distinction, and Peter sees this distinction. Therefore, Luke is purposeful to call out the contrast of baptism with water which is performed by man and the baptism of the Holy Spirit which is performed by God.

The twelfth point we should see is that the apostles confirmed that the Samaritans had indeed received the gospel message from Philip and savingly believed it. We remember that in verse 14 that Peter and John had gone to confirm if those in Samaria had truly received the word of God or gospel. That is to say, they went to confirm that the Samaritans savingly believed the gospel. When the apostles laid their hands on the Samaritans, the

Samaritans who had savingly believed, received the Holy Spirit. Please note the apostles weren't there to confirm whether they had been baptized with water. No, they went there to confirm the Samaritans had truly believed the gospel. Most likely, the manifestation that they had received the Holy Spirit may have likely been speaking in tongues, or known languages, and praising God. This is exactly what happened for the Jews in Jerusalem on the day of Pentecost where they spoke in known languages and were praising God (Acts 2:3-11). It is what happened to the first Gentile believers (Acts 10:45–46). It was the same thing that happened with the believers in Ephesus (Acts 19:6). Therefore, it is likely that the signs that accompanied the Samaritan's inclusion into the church and receiving the Holy Spirit are the same signs the first Samaritan believers received, the same signs the first Gentile believers received, and the same signs the Ephesians first received which was speaking in other known languages and praising God.

Acts 8:18-19 – *Now when Simon saw that the Spirit was given through the laying on of the apostles' hands, he offered them money, saying, "Give me this power also, so that anyone on whom I lay my hands may receive the Holy Spirit."*

This is where we'll transition into the evidence that although Simon believed and was baptized, he was not saved and did not possess saving faith. The first point we'll see is that Simon did not receive the Holy Spirit. Although we see that there were other Samaritan believers who received the Holy Spirit and truly believed the gospel, we see that Simon did not receive the Holy Spirit, and thus, did not savingly believe in the Lord Jesus Christ.

The second point we should see is that Simon had a false view of how the Holy Spirit was received. Simon thought that it was possible to receive the Holy Spirit by giving the apostles money. Of course, this is where we get the term simony which refers to the buying or selling of ecclesiastical privileges. Thus, we see that Simon had a wrong view of how the Holy Spirit is received which would also demonstrate that he had a wrong view of salvation.

The third point we should see is that Simon desired the power of the Holy Spirit. As we noted earlier, Simon practiced sorcery. Simon declared that he was someone great. Simon sought the preeminence that came with practicing sorcery and amazing the crowds. Thus, it makes sense that Simon asked for the very same power that amazed him. He was not interested in humbling himself. He was not interested in becoming poor in spirit. He did not see himself as the poor, blind, a prisoner, and oppressed. He did not see the magnitude of his sin. No, he was interested in obtaining greater power. Obtaining greater power would lead to greater preeminence, greater self-exalting claims, and greater pride.

Acts 8:20 – *But Peter said to him, "May your silver perish with you, because you thought you could obtain the gift of God with money!"*

The fourth point we should see is that the apostle Peter shows us the true condition of Simon. Peter tells Simon that he is perishing. Peter's statement to Simon could even be said this way, "Simon, may you and your silver go to hell." Peter would know better that money doesn't buy your way into heaven (Matthew 19:16-30). Peter knew that God would not be bought off with money. This was the absolute perversion of Simon's heart. Peter affirms that Simon is not in the kingdom of God by stating that Simon should perish along with his money. Simon showed his absolute depravity thinking he could buy God with money. Yes, Simon believed the gospel, but it is abundantly clear he did not possess saving faith. Peter makes this absolutely clear.

Acts 8:21 – *You have neither part nor lot in this matter, for your heart is not right before God*

The fifth point we should see is that Simon has no part or share in the gospel. The word for "matter" actually comes from the original word *logos*. *Logos* can also mean "word" or "the Word." In the original language, there is the definite article "the" in front of *logo*. It is true that this could be translated as "matter." It could also be translated as "word" as well. In fact, Peter could have easily said to Simon, "You have neither part nor lot in **the Word**." Simon has no part or lot in the gospel. Simon has no part or lot in the kingdom of God. Simon has no part or lot in the kingdom of heaven. Simon has no part or lot in the fellowship of the saints. Simon has no part or lot in the saving message of God's Word. Simon has absolutely no share or part in the ministry, kingdom, gospel, or salvation.

The sixth point we should see is that Simon's heart is not right before God. So not only has Peter declared that Simon has no share in the matter or God's Word, but his heart is also not right before God. This is simply another way of saying that Simon has an unregenerate heart. Simon has an unconverted heart. Simon has an uncircumcised heart. Therefore, Peter gives another declarative statement that Simon is not saved.

Acts 8:22 – *Repent, therefore, of this wickedness of yours, and pray to the Lord that, if possible, the intent of your heart may be forgiven.*

The seventh point that we should see is that Peter calls Simon to repentance. In fact, Peter gives the command to repent in the aorist imperative. As we noted earlier, the aorist imperative calls for a specific, definite, and decisive choice. It often expresses a note of urgency. The aorist imperative communicates a sense of getting something done, once for all, and swiftly. As we learned earlier in John the Baptist's message. This was a heart repentance that would change one's mind about one's sinfulness and about Jesus. This was to elevate one's sin and bring down low one's self-will, self-righteousness, and pride and to turn to the Lord Jesus Christ. Peter calls Simon to repentance!

The eighth point we should see is that Peter commands Simon to pray to the Lord for forgiveness because the intent and disposition of Simon's heart is wicked. The word for "pray" comes from *deomai* which means to "entreat," "beg," "request," "beseech," or "pray." This word carries with it the sense of pleading, beseeching, or begging and emphasizes the existence of a need that must be met. It means much more than simply asking. In fact, *deomai* is written in the aorist imperative as well and carries the sense of needing to carry this command out with a great sense of urgency. Therefore, we see that Peter sees that Simon's heart is wicked, unregenerate, unconverted, and damned. He is commanding Simon to repent and go directly and urgently to the Lord so that he may be forgiven and saved. Peter is warning Simon that Simon's heart is wicked and needs to be forgiven lest he perish.

Acts 8:23 – *For I see that you are in the gall of bitterness and in the bond of iniquity.*

The ninth point we should see is that Simon is full of bitterness. Peter tells Simon that Simon is in the gall of bitterness which explains Simon's unregenerate condition. The word for "bitterness" comes from *pikria. Pikria* originally referred to something that was sharp or bitter and what was painful to the feelings. It was also used to describe inedible or poisonous fruits. In the New Testament *pikria* is used to describe animosity, resentfulness, harshness, or an openly expressed emotional hostility against an enemy. It is settled hostility that poisons the inner man. It is used to express when somebody does something which isn't liked and there is ill will against someone. Peter sees that Simon is openly bitter and resentful. Perhaps Simon is resentful because he is being called to repent. Perhaps Simon is bitter because he thought he could buy the Holy Spirit with money. Perhaps Simon is bitter because he realizes that he doesn't have the power he desired. Regardless, we see that Peter notes this attitude of Simon and that Simon is bitter.

The tenth point we should see is that Simon is in bondage to unrighteousness. The word "unrighteousness" comes from *adikia* with *a* meaning "not" and *dike* meaning "justice." Properly it means the opposite of justice which would be unrighteousness or the violation of God's standards. Therefore, we see that Simon is in the bondage of unrighteousness. Why does Peter tell Simon to repent and earnestly pray to the Lord that the Lord may forgive Simon? We find the answer in John 8:36 where Jesus says, "So if the Son sets you free, you will be free indeed." What is the only way to be free from the bondage of unrighteousness? The answer is to repent and turn away from his sin and self-righteousness and go the opposite direction toward God, to deal directly and earnestly with the Lord, and call on the name of the Lord for salvation and to put his faith in Christ alone. Only the Son of God can deliver Simon, forgive his sins, impute His perfect righteousness to Simon and justify him before the throne of God.

Acts 8:24 – *And Simon answered, "Pray for me to the Lord, that nothing of what you have said may come upon me."*

The eleventh point we should see is that Simon would not repent and be humbled before the Lord. Rather than obeying Peter's command to repent and earnestly ask the Lord for forgiveness, Simon rejects this command and gives a command back to Peter that Peter should pray for him. Simon wasn't interested in being humbled. Simon wasn't interested in dealing directly with the Lord. Simon wasn't the sinner who would say to the Lord, "God, have mercy on me, the sinner" (Luke 18:9-13). Simon refused to see his own sinfulness and the holiness of Christ and would not say, "I am a sinful man" (Luke 5:8). Simon would not repent, would not humble himself, and would not go to the Lord for the forgiveness that he needed.

As we close this chapter, it is vitally important to see that although Simon the sorcerer believed and was baptized, Scripture clearly indicates that he was not saved. This is all to say that Scripture continually gives warnings about the nature of saving faith and true conversion. Scripture clearly warns that there is a faith that saves and a faith that does not save (James 2:14-26). There is a faith that justifies and there is a faith that does not justify. There is a demon faith that intellectually believes the truth, emotionally shudders at the truth, but does not volitionally obey the truth. There is a demon faith that agrees with the truth, trembles at the truth, but does not lovingly and submissively obey the truth. So, we see that Simon believed and was baptized (Acts 8:13), but he was not saved (Acts 8:17-24). Does Acts 8:13 contradict Mark 16:15-16 which says, "And he said to them, 'Go into all the world and proclaim the gospel to the whole creation. Whoever **believes and is baptized will be saved**, but whoever does not believe will be condemned'"? Not at all. Simon the Sorcerer simply possessed a non-saving or non-justifying faith. The Bible warns against false conversion (Matthew 7:21-28), false repentance (Luke 3:3-17), and non-saving faith (John 12:42) with continuous repetition and fervency. Those who come to true faith in the Lord Jesus Christ will be saved.

Chapter 11

Peter's Sermon to Cornelius

Acts 11:15-16 – *As I began to speak, the Holy Spirit fell on them just as on us at the beginning. And I remembered the word of the Lord, how he said, 'John baptized with water, but you will be baptized with the Holy Spirit.'*

Peter's "baptism now saves you" verse is one of the most quoted verses to support baptismal regeneration. It is important to note that Peter had the same understanding as Matthew, Mark, Luke, the apostle John, John the Baptist, Paul, and Jesus when it came to water baptism and baptism with the Holy Spirit. It is also important to know what the role of the baptism with the Holy Spirit is in conversion. In Acts 10, it becomes extremely clear that Peter was very aware that there was a difference between water baptism and baptism with the Holy Spirit and he was also aware of who baptizes with the Holy Spirit and who could only baptize with water. Luke is very careful to record this account of Peter's distinction so we will look to Acts 10-11 to reveal Peter's understanding of baptism with the Holy Spirit and its role in conversion. However, before we get started, let's revisit the definition of the baptism with the Holy Spirit. In this definition, we'll see that the baptism with the Holy Spirit includes the Holy Spirit working through God's Word of the good news of Jesus Christ to regenerate man, God granting repentance to man, God granting to man saving faith in the Lord Jesus Christ, the Holy Spirit uniting man to Christ, and the Holy Spirit indwelling man:

The baptism with the Holy Spirit is the sovereign monergistic work of salvation performed by God the Father, God the Son, and God the Holy Spirit. The Holy Spirit is given from the Father to the Son (John 14:16, 15:26; Luke 11:13) and the Son pours out or gives the Holy Spirit in the Father's name (Matthew 3:11–12; Mark 1:8; Luke 3:16, 24:49; John 1:31–33; 14:16, 26; 15:26; 16:7; Acts 1:4–5, 2:17–18, 10:44–48, 11:16, Titus 3:6). The Holy Spirit then regenerates or causes man to be born again (John 3:3–10, Titus 3:5, Ezekiel 36:25–27) through hearing the Word of God/Gospel (James 1:18, Ephesians 1:13, Romans 1:15– 17, 10:17, 1 Corinthians 1:21) which gives spiritual life to the previously spiritually dead man (Ephesians 2:1–3, Colossians 2:13). God then grants man the ability to repent which is a gift (Acts 11:18, 2 Timothy 2:25) and put saving faith in Jesus Christ which is also a gift (Ephesians 2:8–9, Philippians 1:29, John 7:38–39). Man is then justified by grace through faith in Christ (Titus 3:7), receives and is indwelt by the Holy Spirit (Galatians 3:2, 3:14; Ephesians 1:13; 1 Corinthians 6:19), and the Holy Spirit spiritually unites/immerses man with Jesus Christ and puts the man into the body of Christ (1 Corinthians 12:13, Romans 6:3–4). Baptism with the Holy Spirit is not water baptism, and water baptism is not baptism with the Holy Spirit for only Christ can baptize with the Holy Spirit and man can only baptize with water (Matthew 3:11–12; Mark 1:8; Luke 3:16; John 1:31–33, 3:8, 7:38–39, 14:15–17, 26; 15:26, 16:7; Acts 1:4–5, 2:17–18, 10:44–48, 11:16; 1 Corinthians 1:17). Baptism with the Holy Spirit is a one-time, instantaneous, and salvific work of God (1 Corinthians 12:13).

Acts 10 is the account of the first Gentile conversion and Peter was privileged to experience this conversion. Acts 10 begins with Cornelius, a centurion in the Italian Regiment (Acts

10:1). Scripture explains that Cornelius was a Gentile and a devout and God-fearing man (Acts 10:2). Cornelius' faithfulness was seen as a memorial offering before God and he had received a vision and saw an angel of God who ordered him to send men to Joppa to bring Peter to his house (Acts 10:3–8).

The following day, Peter also had a vision where he saw heaven opened and something like a large sheet being lowered down to earth (Acts 10:9–11). It contained all kinds of animals, which included unclean animals as well as animals that conform to the Jewish dietary laws (Acts 10:12). This happened three times and Peter had wondered what the meaning of the vision meant (Acts 10:14–16). There are a couple of suggestions to what this vision may have meant. The first explanation is that this vision did away with the Jewish dietary laws. The voice told Peter to "Get up, Peter. Kill and eat." In Matthew 15:17–20, Jesus says, "Don't you see that whatever enters the mouth goes into the stomach and then out of the body? But the things that come out of a person's mouth come from the heart, and these defile them. For out of the heart come evil thoughts—murder, adultery, sexual immorality, theft, false testimony, slander. These are what defile a person; but eating with unwashed hands does not defile them." After Jesus gave the explanation that food doesn't enter the heart, but the stomach and then is expelled, He declared all foods clean (Mark 7:19). In the original language it says, "Purifying all the food." Thus, the first interpretation is that in this vision, Jesus communicated the cessation of the dietary laws.

The second interpretation sees this vision as also having to do with Jews and Gentiles. In Leviticus 11, the LORD describes clean and unclean food. In this passage, there are reptiles such as the gecko, the crocodile, the sand reptile, and the chameleon. Likewise, the LORD also calls the eagle, the vulture, the buzzard, the red kite, the falcon, and more birds unclean. In Acts 10:15, the voice spoke to Peter saying, "Do not call anything impure that God has made clean." The interpretation sees the clean animals as the Jews and the unclean animals as being the Gentiles. It is important to note that the sheet comes from heaven which signals that the church was born from heaven and includes both Jew and Gentile. Peter's vision was meant to communicate that the church, which came from heaven, was to include both the Jew and Gentile. Thus, both interpretations of the dream would be fitting. After the vision, Cornelius' men found Peter at Simon the tanner's house (Acts 10:17–18). The men explained the vision that Cornelius had, and Peter invited Cornelius' men into his house (Acts 10:19–23).

The next day, Peter went with the men to Cornelius' house (Acts 10:24–26). When entering Cornelius' house, he interprets the vision that he had where he says in verse 28, "But God has shown me that I should not call anyone impure or unclean." Peter communicates to the Gentiles in Cornelius' house that he is not to regard them as unclean anymore. Cornelius goes on to describe his vision to Peter (Acts 10:30–34). Peter then launches into the gospel message.

Peter explains that there is peace through Jesus Christ who is Lord of all (Acts 10:36). Thus, Peter is giving a message of reconciliation and explaining that Jesus Christ is the sovereign Lord entrusted with all authority in heaven and on earth. Peter will then explain how this good news was first preached by John the Baptist starting with his message of baptism for the forgiveness of sins (Acts 10:37). Of course, Cornelius would know that this was a radical call to repent from the heart, elevate and confess sin, bring down all self-righteous, self-exaltation, and self-will and embrace the Messiah, Jesus Christ. Peter explains God anointing Jesus of Nazareth (Acts 10:38). We can remember that Jesus was anointed by the Holy Spirit at His baptism and that the Father proclaimed that Jesus was His beloved Son with whom He was well pleased. This would also speak of Christ's sinless nature. Peter also explains Jesus' divine power over the devil which included casting out demons, healing the sick, and performing miracles which all attested to His claims and His teaching. Peter explains Jesus' crucifixion (Acts 10:39). The crucifixion would explain why the Messiah needed to suffer which would speak of Jesus' sinless nature and the need to be a substitutionary propitiation to satisfy the righteous wrath of God toward sinners which would allow Him to forgive sins. Peter explains Christ's resurrection (Acts 10:40). This would demonstrate God's approval of the Son's intercessory work for sinners and the demonstration of Christ having the victory over sin and Satan. Peter explains Christ's post-resurrection appearances which testifies that He was a first-hand eyewitness to the resurrection of Jesus Christ (Acts 10:41). Peter explains Christ as Lord and Judge of all people which demonstrates that Christ is empowered with all authority to save and condemn (Acts 10:42–42). Finally, Peter explains Christ as the only means for forgiveness of sins (Acts 10:43).

While Peter had given the presentation of the gospel of Jesus, the Holy Spirit came on all who heard the message (Acts 10:44). Let us note that this is the baptism with the Holy Spirit. The Gentiles heard the good news of Jesus Christ, had believed, and thus received the promised Holy Spirit for believing in Christ (John 7:38–39). The Holy Spirit was poured out by God the Father through His Son, Jesus Christ. Peter had no control of the Holy Spirit. Cornelius had no control over the Holy Spirit. It was the salvific work of the Triune God to pour out His Spirit on Cornelius' household. The Jews who were present were astonished that the Holy Spirit had been poured out to the Gentiles as was evidenced by the speaking in tongues (Acts 10:45–46). The same sign of speaking in tongues, or known languages, was given to the Gentiles and they responded in praise to God (Acts 10:46). This is exactly what happened for the Jews on the day of Pentecost where they spoke in known languages and were praising God (Acts 2:3-11). This is what happened when Paul was in Ephesus and told the Ephesians that they were to believe in Jesus and when he laid hands on them, they began speaking in tongues or known languages and prophesying or speaking forth the praises of God (Acts 19:6). Thus, we can see that as the church was growing from Jerusalem to Samaria to Caesarea to Ephesus, there were signs given to demonstrate that those who were not Jewish were to be included into the church. It's important to note that this was a time of transition in the New Testament to show the inclusion of Gentile nations into Christ's church. There is much written about speaking in tongues as it relates to the baptism with the Holy Spirit. For the purposes of this book, we won't dive into this subject, but what is important to note is that all true believers are baptized with the Holy Spirit which is always connected with believing the gospel.

Peter makes an amazing statement following the conversion of the Gentiles. Peter says in Acts 10:47–48, "'Can anyone withhold water for baptizing these people, who have received the Holy Spirit just as we have?' And he commanded them to be baptized in the name of Jesus Christ. Then they asked him to remain for some days." Peter has just made a distinction between baptism with the Holy Spirit and water baptism. Peter recognizes that *baptism with the Holy Spirit* is a salvific work of God to bring someone to faith in Jesus Christ where they receive and are indwelt by the Holy Spirit. As Peter has recognized this, he commands them to be baptized in the name of Jesus Christ. Just after the Gentiles had received the baptism with the Holy Spirit, Peter commands them to be baptized with water in the name of Jesus Christ. There is no doubt that Peter would have made strong and clear distinctions between the baptism with the Holy Spirit and water baptism which we'll see in Acts 11.

In Acts 11, the apostles and brothers throughout Judea heard that the Gentiles had received the Word of God. The Jews, or the circumcision party, began to criticize Peter (Acts 11:1–3). However, Peter begins describing his vision to the men and going to Cornelius' house (Acts 11:4–12). Picking up in Acts 11:14,

Peter explains how Cornelius stated, "He will declare to you a message by which you will be saved, you and all your household." As we noted earlier, this was Peter's gospel message. In verses 15–16, Peter says, "As I began to speak, the Holy Spirit fell on them just as on us at the beginning. And I remembered the word of the Lord, how He said, 'John baptized with water, but you will be baptized with the Holy Spirit.'" Peter's theology in verses 15 and 16 cannot be understated. As Peter began to speak the gospel, the Gentiles were baptized with the Holy Spirit. Peter goes on to make an important point. Peter notes that Jesus said, "John baptized with water, but you will be baptized with the Holy Spirit." Peter manifestly saw that that man can only baptize with water and Christ is the one who baptized with the Holy Spirit. He heard this from both Jesus and John the Baptist. In fact, in verse 17, Peter says, "If then God gave the same gift to them as he gave to us when we believed in the Lord Jesus Christ, who was I that I could stand in God's way?". Peter would have fully agreed with Jesus when Jesus said this to Nicodemus about controlling the Holy Spirit in the new birth in John 3:8, "The wind blows where it wishes, and you hear its sound, but you do not know where it comes from or where it goes. So it is with everyone who is born of the Spirit." Simply put, Peter is saying he could not stand in God's way. Peter couldn't control the Holy Spirit, stop the Holy Spirit, coerce the Holy Spirit, or command the Holy Spirit. He simply gave the gospel and Christ baptized with the Holy Spirit. Furthermore, immediately after Peter realized the Gentiles had been baptized with the Holy Spirit, he ordered them to be water baptized.

Lastly, those who were with Peter recognized that the baptism with the Holy Spirit was God granting repentance that leads to life (Acts 11:18). Therefore, the baptism with the Holy Spirit in just this portion of Scripture includes God pouring out the Holy Spirit, God granting repentance, God granting faith in His Son, man receiving the Holy Spirit, and man being indwelt by the

Holy Spirit. Additionally, we know from previous chapters that God the Holy Spirit regenerates man which allows man to repent and put saving faith in Christ. We also see that this baptism with the Holy Spirit is a one-time instantaneous salvific work of God.

As we end this chapter, Peter had very clear theology on baptism with the Holy Spirit and clearly differentiated this with water baptism. Luke, who wrote the account of Acts is also careful to point out Peter's recognition and distinction. The point of this chapter is not to get bogged down in understanding the baptism with the Holy Spirit, although this is important. Rather, it is to demonstrate Peter's theology on conversion. Peter simply preached the gospel and it was the work of God to save man through the gospel message. It was God who poured out the Holy Spirit upon those who heard and believed the gospel. It is God who regenerates. It is God who grants repentance. It is God who grants faith in His Son. Let us remember that as true believers in Christ, it is our responsibility to share the gospel to all nations. It is God who works through His gospel to save. Finally, let us remember that Peter quoted the Lord when saying, "'John baptized with water, but you will be baptized with the Holy Spirit.'" Man cannot baptize with the Holy Spirit and give salvation. Only Christ can baptize with the Holy Spirit and give salvation.

CHAPTER 12

Peter's Confession at the Jerusalem Council

Acts 15:8-9 – *And God, who knows the heart, bore witness to them, by giving them the Holy Spirit just as he did to us, and he made no distinction between us and them, having cleansed their hearts by faith.*

There have been church councils that have needed to gather to come together and confirm important doctrinal truths throughout church history. The Jerusalem Council was one such council that needed to confirm how man was saved. They needed to confirm how a sinful man could be reconciled to a holy God. They needed to confirm if man could be saved by the law or if man was saved by grace. They needed to confirm if the circumcision was necessary for salvation. They needed to confirm if one needed to keep the law of Moses to be saved. Thus, this was a critical gathering. Either salvation was by grace through faith in Christ or salvation was by the law through works. Therefore, the outcome of this council was vitally important to the church.

As we go through this chapter, it is important to recap what we have learned about conversion. We've learned about John the Baptist's baptism of repentance. We've learned about regeneration or being born again from Jesus' dialogue with Nicodemus. We've looked at two of Christ's gospel calls where He calls sinners to self-denying, cross-bearing repentance and submissive and preeminent loving faith in Him. We've seen Peter issue gospel calls. We've learned what the baptism with the Holy Spirit is. We've seen Peter confront false converts. Thus far, we've learned quite a bit on the soteriology or the theology of salvation. Below is a summary of definitions of what we've learned regarding soteriology:

- *Baptism with the Holy Spirit:* is the sovereign monergistic work of salvation performed by God the Father, God the Son, and God the Holy Spirit. The Holy Spirit is given from the Father to the Son (John 14:16, 15:26; Luke 11:13) and the Son pours out or gives the Holy Spirit in the Father's name (Matthew 3:11–12; Mark 1:8; Luke 3:16, 24:49; John 1:31–33; 14:16, 26; 15:26; 16:7; Acts 1:4–5, 2:17–18, 10:44–48, 11:16, Titus 3:6). The Holy Spirit then regenerates or causes man to be born again (John 3:3–10, Titus 3:5, Ezekiel 36:25–27) through hearing the Word of God/Gospel (James 1:18, Ephesians 1:13, Romans 1:15–17, 10:17, 1 Corinthians 1:21) which gives spiritual life to the previously spiritually dead man (Ephesians 2:1– 3, Colossians 2:13). God then grants man the ability to repent which is a gift (Acts 11:18, 2 Timothy 2:25) and put saving faith in Jesus Christ which is also a gift (Ephesians 2:8–9, Philippians 1:29, John 7:38–39). Man is then justified by grace through faith in Christ (Titus 3:7), receives and is indwelt by the Holy Spirit (Galatians 3:2, 3:14; Ephesians 1:13; 1 Corinthians 6:19), and the Holy Spirit spiritually unites/immerses man with Jesus Christ and puts the man into the body of Christ (1 Corinthians 12:13, Romans 6:3–4). Baptism with the Holy Spirit is not water baptism, and water baptism is not baptism with the Holy Spirit for only

Christ can baptize with the Holy Spirit and man can only baptize with water (Matthew 3:11–12; Mark 1:8; Luke 3:16; John 1:31–33, 3:8, 7:38–39, 14:15–17, 26; 15:26, 16:7; Acts 1:4–5, 2:17–18, 10:44–48, 11:16; 1 Corinthians 1:17). **Baptism with the Holy Spirit** is a one-time, instantaneous, and salvific work of God (1 Corinthians 12:13).

- **Regeneration**: is the sovereign monergistic work of God the Holy Spirit in giving spiritual life to spiritually dead and sinful man so that man is enabled to repent and respond in saving faith to Jesus Christ.
- **Repentance**: is a gift from God and radical change in mind (Acts 5:31, 11:18, 2 Timothy 2:25) where the sinner understands his sin against God and is thus, poor in spirit (Matthew 5:3, Luke 18:9-14), has godly sorrow and mourns over his sin against God (Matthew 5:4, 2 Corinthians 7:10), and turns away from his sin and sinful former way of life (Ephesians 4:22) and toward God for righteousness and salvation (Matthew 5:5-6, Luke 3:3-17, Acts 17:30, 20:21, 1 Thessalonians 1:9).
- **Saving faith**: is a gift from God (Ephesians 2:8-9) where a sinner has knowledge of Jesus' person and work where a sinner will respond to Christ's person and work by denying themselves (Matthew 16:24, Mark 8:34, Luke 9:23), picking up their cross (Matthew 10:38, 16:24, Mark 8:34, Luke 9:23), and lovingly (Luke 14:26-27, James 4:7) and obediently (2 Thessalonians 1:8, Romans 1:5) submitting (James 4:6, Matthew 11:28) and committing their life to Jesus (Matthew 10:37-39, 16:24-26, Mark 8:34-37, Luke 9:23-26, 14:25-33) and trusting in Him only for salvation (Romans 10:13, John 3:16, John 3:36, Acts 4:12).
- **Conversion**: is the turning away from sin in repentance and to the Lord Jesus Christ in faith for salvation (Acts 20:21, 1 Thessalonians 1:9, Ephesians 4:22-24, Colossians 3:9-10, Mark 1:15).

As we jump into this chapter, let's keep these definitions at the forefront of our minds as we build on the foundation we've built.

Acts 15:1 – *But some men came down from Judea and were teaching the brothers, "Unless you are circumcised according to the custom of Moses, you cannot be saved."*

First, we see that there is an issue where men are teaching that circumcision is necessary for salvation. In the New Testament, we see much discourse over the role of circumcision, the Abrahamic Covenant sign, and its role in salvation. We also see that Paul had to deal with the belief and teaching that physical circumcision had salvific merits throughout the course of his ministry. Many of Paul's epistles dealt with this topic (Romans 2:28–29, 1 Corinthians 7:19, Galatians 1–6, Ephesians 2:11, Philippians 3:2–3, Colossians 2:11–12, Titus 1:10). Paul would continually defend and explain that circumcision was a sign and seal of the Abrahamic Covenant to point to the meaning of the promise to Abraham and the need for a spiritual heart circumcision performed by the Lord. Circumcision was meant to be a sign which signified that God had cut away Abraham for Himself (Genesis 12:2), cut away a people for Himself (Genesis 13:14-17), cut away a nation for Himself (Genesis 12:2), cut away a land for His people (Genesis 17:8), and cut away the foreskin of the heart to have a people for Himself (Deuteronomy 10:12-16, 30:6). As we come to the New Testament, we see that this heart circumcision is done by Christ (Colossians 2:11) and through the Spirit (Romans 2:28-29). Therefore, we see how aggressive these false teachers were who tried to persuade others that they needed to be physically circumcised to be saved. In this verse we see that there were those who came from Judea and were giving a false gospel that one needed to be physically circumcised to be saved.

To understand how Jews perceived circumcision as carrying salvific merit, there are some historical books and works that can be referenced to understand what the Jews believed about physical circumcision. For example, the book of Jubilees is a noncanonical book that was written towards the end of the BC era. In the Book of Jubilees it says the following, "And every one that is born, the flesh of whose foreskin is not circumcised on the eighth day, belongeth not to the children of the covenant which the Lord made with Abraham, but to the children of destruction; nor is there, moreover, any sign on him that he is the Lord's, but (he is destined) to be destroyed and slain from the earth, and to be rooted out of the earth, for he hath broken the covenant of the Lord our God." Furthermore, it goes on to state, "And now I announce unto thee that the children of Israel will not keep true to this ordinance, and they will not circumcise their sons according to all this law; for in the flesh of their circumcision they will omit this circumcision of their sons, and all of them, sons of Beliar, will leave their sons uncircumcised as they were born. And there will be great wrath from the Lord against the children of Israel, because they have forsaken His covenant and turned aside from His Word, and provoked and blasphemed, inasmuch as they do not observe the ordinance of this law; for they have treated their members like the Gentiles, so that they may be removed and rooted out of the land. And there will no more be pardon or forgiveness unto them [so that there should be forgiveness and pardon] for all the sin of this eternal error." This is essentially saying that circumcision put them in the LORD's covenant while uncircumcision put them outside of God's covenant. While there is certainly precedence concerning God's anger and wrath for not giving the sign of circumcision to the male members of Israel (Exodus 4:24–26), these statements certainly tied circumcision to forgiveness of sins and being in the Abrahamic Covenant. They also tied uncircumcision to breaking God's covenant, being outside God's covenant people, being sons of Beliar/

Belial, and not being forgiven. Therefore, we can see that there was rabbinic writing and teaching that supported circumcision carrying salvific merit.

In the *midrashim*, which are ancient commentaries of the Old Testament, Rabbi Levi said this regarding circumcision, "In the age to come Abraham will sit at the gate of Gehenna [hell], and he will not permit a circumcised Israelite to go down there. Then what will he do for those who sinned too much? He will remove the foreskin from infants who died before they were circumcised and will place it over [Israelite sinners] and then lower them into Gehenna." Here, we see a statement that Abraham guards hell so that those that have undergone circumcision will not receive eternal punishment. Rabbi Menachem wrote in his commentary on the Book of Moses, "Our Rabbins [rabbis] have said that no circumcised man will ever see hell." In the Jalkut Rubem it stated, "Circumcision saves from hell" (num 1). In the Midrash Millim it was written, "God swore to Abraham that no one who was circumcised should be sent to hell" (fol. 7, col. 2). The book of Akedath Jizehak taught that "Abraham sits before the gate of hell, and does not allow that any circumcised Israelite should enter there" (fol. 54, col. 2). Thus, we can clearly see how circumcision, the sign of the Abrahamic Covenant, was taught as a means of salvation.

We have an account from Paul in his epistle to the Galatians where Paul needed to correct Peter who was leading others astray by his actions and causing others to believe circumcision was necessary for salvation. Apparently, there were men that were sent to the Galatian church by James who was a leader in the Jerusalem (Galatians 2:12). These men were claiming to be Christians, claiming allegiance to Christ, and said that they were being sent by James. The hypocrisy that Peter was showing was that he would withdraw from the Gentiles when the Judaizers came. The hypocrisy in this is that the Judaizers didn't associate with Gentiles as the Judaizers saw the Gentiles as unclean pagans.

Furthermore, since the Judaizers believed that one needed to be circumcised and follow Jewish rituals to be saved, they would not have believed the Gentiles to be true converts. Thus, when Peter withdrew from the Gentiles when the Judaizers came, Peter was affirming through his actions that the Judaizers were correct in their teaching, which was absolutely devastating to the teaching of justification by faith.

The hypocrisy of Peter led other Jews astray as well such as Barnabas. Therefore, Paul's reaction to Peter was that Paul opposed Peter to his face where it says in Galatians 2:11, "But when Cephas came to Antioch, I opposed him to his face, because he stood condemned." This was a strong reaction from Paul to Peter for Peter misleading others. The original word that has been translated to "opposed" is *anthistémi,* which carries the idea of "opposing someone and taking a complete stand against," "forcefully declare one's personal conviction," and was used as a military term to mean "to strongly resist an opponent." Paul even says that Peter stood "condemned," which is translated from *kataginóskó,* which means "to be decisively guilty on the basis of direct personal acquaintance." *Kataginóskó* is not the same word used for condemnation or final judgment which Paul uses in Romans as *katakrima*. We know that Peter was not eternally condemned as Peter was an apostle and was recommissioned by the Lord.

Peter was knowingly wrong. Peter had enough time with the Lord to know that circumcision was not a means to salvation. Peter was warned to watch out for the teaching leaven of the Pharisees (Matthew 16:6, 12, Luke 12:1, Mark 8:15). Peter knew that he was supposed to be on guard against the false teaching hypocrisy of the Pharisees and by withdrawing from the Gentiles when the Judaizers came, Peter was affirming the teaching of the Judaizers through his withdrawal.

The false teaching that the Judaizers were propagating attacked the subjective response of repentance toward God and faith in the Lord Jesus Christ. The Judaizers replaced repentance and faith in Christ with circumcision and ceremonies plus Christ. We should see how dangerous it is to tolerate a false gospel. We should see how dangerous it is to give cadence or acceptance to those who preach a false gospel. This example in the life of Peter and Paul is an example of dealing with one who is affirming a false gospel through their actions. When one either teaches a false gospel or affirms it, that person must be dealt with urgently, firmly, and boldly.

Acts 15:2 – *And after Paul and Barnabas had no small dissension and debate with them, Paul and Barnabas and some of the others were appointed to go up to Jerusalem to the apostles and the elders about this question.*

Second, we see that there was a debate between salvation through the law and salvation through faith in Christ. These men who came from Judea were teaching that in order to be saved one needed to be circumcised, and this caused debate and disagreement. Paul and Barnabas had a large dissension with these false teaching heretics. In fact, the word for "dissension" comes from *stasis* which can mean "insurrection," "dissension," "uproar" or "strife." This false gospel was a direct attack on the gospel of being saved by grace through faith in Christ. Therefore, Paul and Barnabas fiercely stood their ground and debated these false teachers. Additionally, we see that this issue caused Paul, Barnabas, and others to go up to Jerusalem to meet with the apostles and elders to address this dispute.

Acts 15:3-4 – *So, being sent on their way by the church, they passed through both Phoenicia and Samaria, describing in detail the conversion of the Gentiles, and brought great joy to all the brothers. When they came to Jerusalem, they were welcomed by the church and the apostles and the elders, and they declared all that God had done with them.*

Third, we see that Paul, Barnabas, and the others were declaring the conversion of Gentiles to other believers as they went to Jerusalem. What is most important about this is the detail Luke gives on their travel back. As we learned earlier, the Jews did not like the Samaritans. However, we read in Acts 8 that Samaritans were included in Christ's church. Phoenicia was a Gentile area and so Paul, Barnabas and the others were describing the conversion of Gentiles to other Gentiles in Phoenicia. This conversion to the Lord was by grace through faith, in Christ. Additionally, we see that Paul, Barnabas and the others had described to the apostles, the elders, and the Jerusalem church that the Gentiles were being converted. The Jerusalem church was then told all that God was doing through their ministry.

Acts 15:5 – *But some believers who belonged to the party of the Pharisees rose up and said, "It is necessary to circumcise them and to order them to keep the law of Moses."*

Fourth, we see dissension arise on how someone is saved. It is likely that Paul, Barnabas, and the others were declaring that Gentiles were being saved by grace through faith in Christ. Their testimony on how Gentiles were being saved is likely what caused this statement. Whether these believers were truly converted and had been greatly deceived or whether they were false converts, these "believers" claimed that it was necessary for these Gentiles to be circumcised and keep the law of Moses. They were teaching the necessity of circumcision and adherence to the law of Moses. The word "necessary" comes from *dei* which means "necessary" or "absolutely necessary." Therefore, what these "believers" were saying was that circumcision was necessary for salvation as well as keeping the Law of Moses. This would mean that for one to be saved, they needed to keep all of the Sabbath laws perfectly, keep all of the dietary restrictions perfectly, keep all of the burnt offering regulations perfectly, keep all of the guilt offering regulations perfectly, keep all of the appointed Festivals perfectly (Passover and Unleavened Bread, Offering of Firstfruits, Weeks, Trumpets, Day of Atonement, Tabernacles), keep all of the restrictions on skin diseases perfectly, keep the Ten Commandments perfectly, keep all of the regulations of bodily discharges perfectly, keep the purification after childbirth perfectly, and more.

This is the way the law works. If you put just one hope of salvation in circumcision you are on the hook for everything else the law requires. The same is true of water baptism. If you put just one hope of salvation in water baptism, even in the New Testament, you are on the hook for perfectly keeping all other aspects of the law. The law damns men. The law curses men. The law shows forth the perfect character and nature of God. However, putting one's hope of salvation in ceremonies, rituals, or sacraments is the way of the law. This is what was at stake. Just putting one toe in the water of ceremonialism, sacramentalism, ritualism is tantamount to diving in headfirst into the damning curse of keeping the entire law perfectly.

Acts 15:6 – *The apostles and the elders were gathered together to consider this matter.*

Fifth, we see that this matter was of the utmost importance. If salvation could be achieved through circumcision, then what was the point of Christ coming? If salvation could be achieved through burnt offerings, then why would God send His Son to suffer the wrath of God in place for sinners? If salvation could be achieved through baptisms and ceremonial washings, then why was Christ's baptism part of His perfect work needed to fulfill all righteousness on behalf of sinners (Matthew 3:13-15). If salvation could be achieved through Sabbath observances, then why did Christ speak of a greater rest for the soul that was offered in Him (Matthew 11:28-30). If salvation could be achieved through the law, then Paul would be exactly right where he said this in Galatians 2:21, "I do not nullify the grace of God, for if righteousness were through the law, **then Christ died for no purpose**." Therefore, not only did this question carry with it the question of how sinful man is reconciled to a holy God, it carried with it far more theological ramifications. For the purposes of this book, we won't go through the plethora of ramifications, but here are a few of the theological implications if man could be justified through the law: Christ would have died for nothing, God the Father would have made a mistake sending His Son as a sinless propitiation for sins, God would violate His own character and attributes by not justly punishing the sinner for violations against His law, Jesus' teaching would be a lie, and Jesus would not be the Way, the Truth and the Life as there would be another way to salvation. As you can see, there was much at stake in this matter of how man is reconciled to God. The gospel of the Lord Jesus Christ was at stake.

Acts 15:7 – *And after there had been much debate, Peter stood up and said to them, "Brothers, you know that in the early days God made a choice among you, that by my mouth the Gentiles should hear the word of the gospel and believe."*

Sixth, we see Peter give a firsthand testimony of a Gentile conversion. There was much discussion that took place over this question. However, we see Peter stand up to give a testimony. Peter's testimony on this matter is just as important as His testimony on who Jesus was in Matthew 16:16. Peter is going to bring them right back to his experience with Cornelius. As we learned earlier, Peter needed to be told that the Gentiles should not be called unclean (Acts 10:28). Peter would go to a Gentile's house and proclaim the gospel (Acts 10:34-43). As Peter delivered this gospel, the Gentiles were baptized with the Holy Spirit and were justified by faith and received the Holy Spirit (Acts 10:44-45). Peter declared this very truth in Jerusalem and declared that the Gentiles had received the gift of the Holy Spirit by believing in the Lord Jesus Christ and that God had granted repentance to the Gentiles (Acts 11:1-18).

Peter is bringing them right back to the first Gentile conversion. Peter could have easily asked this question, "How was Cornelius and those in his household saved? How did Cornelius and those in his household receive the Holy Spirit? What saving message did they believe to receive the Holy Spirit? Was Cornelius justified by works or by faith?" Paul was in the crowd that day. Perhaps we should learn from Paul what he thought about the power of believing the gospel for salvation versus trying to find salvation in water baptism where he says, "For Christ did not send me to baptize but to preach the gospel, and not with words of eloquent wisdom, lest the cross of Christ be emptied of its power. For the word of the cross is folly to those who are perishing, but to us who are being saved it is the power of God." Likewise, Paul could have given this statement on the efficacy of physical circumcision for salvation in Galatians 6:15, "For neither circumcision counts for anything, nor uncircumcision, but a new creation." The Jerusalem church should have known that Peter's report on Cornelius and his household demonstrated that salvation came through faith in Christ.

If there was ever an opportunity to express that salvation came through any other means, this was the opportunity to clarify this. The apostles were present. Paul was present. Barnabas was present. Elders of the Jerusalem church were present. If salvation could be achieved through water baptism, this would have been the opportunity to clarify this. If salvation could be achieved through the Lord's Supper, this would have been the opportunity to clarify this. If salvation could be achieved through anointing someone with oil, this would have been the opportunity to clarify this. If salvation could be achieved through confirmation, this would have been the opportunity to clarify this. If salvation could be achieved through the Levitical system and keeping the law of Moses, this would have been the opportunity to clarify this. However, we will see Peter stand firm on how one is saved.

Acts 15:8 – *And God, who knows the heart, bore witness to them, by giving them the Holy Spirit just as he did to us*

Seventh, we see that God is the one who knows whether one has saving faith in the Lord Jesus Christ and He freely gives the Holy Spirit to such people. Peter simply gave the gospel to Cornelius, but it is God who knows and changes the heart. God is the one who knows the genuineness of one's faith. God is the one who knows the genuineness of one's heart. God is the one who knows the genuineness of one's repentance. God is the one who knows the genuineness of one's belief. What did we learn with Simon the Sorcerer's faith? Simon believed and was baptized, but he was not saved for he did not possess a saving faith (Acts 8:9-24). However, we saw that God knew the hearts of the Samaritans and gave the Holy Spirit to those who had saving faith. Cornelius and those in his household were given the Holy Spirit because they had come to saving faith in the Lord Jesus Christ. Anyone who comes to saving faith in the Lord Jesus Christ will be given the Holy Spirit and indwelt by Him.

Acts 15:9 – *and he made no distinction between us and them, having cleansed their hearts by faith.*

Eighth, we see that God justifies someone by faith and not by anything external. When Peter says that "he made no distinction between us and them," he is saying that God does not look at anything external. God looks at the heart (1 Samuel 16:7). God is the one who knows the heart (Luke 16:15). God is the one who is greater than our hearts and knows all things (1 John 3:20). Peter is saying that God doesn't make distinctions or judgments based on anything external such as circumcision, race, ethnicity, or any of the like. No, as we learned above, God looks at the heart and knows the heart. Therefore, when one comes to saving faith in the Lord Jesus Christ, regardless of anything external, He gives them His Holy Spirit and justifies them. God does not cleanse or justify the heart by any other means. As we know, man's original and natural disposition is utterly sinful, depraved, and turned away from God. Therefore, when we see that when one's heart is justified by faith, we can easily understand that the faith which justifies is a faith where the heart turns away from sin and self-righteousness in repentance and toward the Lord Jesus Christ in faith for salvation. Likewise, all true or saving repentance is a believing repentance that always turns away from sin and self-righteousness and turns to Christ in faith for salvation.

Acts 15:10 – *Now, therefore, why are you putting God to the test by placing a yoke on the neck of the disciples that neither our fathers nor we have been able to bear?*

Ninth, we see that God's testimony on salvation has already been demonstrated. If we look back to Pentecost, we see that the believers were given the Holy Spirit and justified by faith in the Lord Jesus Christ. If we look back to the Samaritans in Acts 8, we see that they were given the Holy Spirit and justified by faith in the Lord Jesus Christ. If we look back to Cornelius and his household in Acts 10-11, we see that they were given the Holy Spirit and justified by faith in the Lord Jesus Christ. How much evidence needed to be demonstrated that the Holy Spirit was given to those who had saving faith in the Lord Jesus Christ? How much evidence needed to be given that the Holy Spirit and justification before God was not given through baptisms, circumcision, law observance, ritualism, legalism, and the like? There was a clear demonstration of how someone was justified before the throne of God and this was through faith in the Lord Jesus Christ.

Tenth, let's see that any means of being saved outside of faith in the Lord Jesus Christ is a damning yoke that no man can bear. Scripture is abundantly clear that man is not justified by works, rituals, sacraments, ceremonies, and the like (Matthew 5:17-20, Romans 3:20, 4:9-12, 4:15 Galatians 2:16, 5:1-6 6:12-13, James 3:2). To put someone under a system of sacramentalism, ritualism, ceremonialism, or works is to put them under neck-breaking condemnation that will never justify anyone before the throne of God and will reconcile no one to God. Water baptisms as a means for salvation is a return to the Mosaic Covenant of works (Hebrews 9:10). Water baptisms is a return to the Mosaic Covenant that can never perfect those who draw near (Hebrews 10:1-2). Anything outside of saving faith in the Lord Jesus Christ is damning.

Acts 15:11 – *But we believe that we will be saved through the grace of the Lord Jesus, just as they will.*

The last point we see is that man is saved through the grace of the Lord Jesus Christ. Salvation is all a work of God. Man contributes nothing. If we think back to our definitions of regeneration, repentance, faith, and baptism with the Holy Spirit, we clearly see how salvation is by grace. Man does nothing to cause himself to be born again, it is simply the work of God the Holy Spirit in giving man new birth. Likewise, repentance is a gift and granted by God. Faith is a gift and granted by God. The Baptism with the Holy Spirit is a sovereign monergistic work of salvation which is unaffected by the will and works of man (John 1:13, Acts 10-11). Man does absolutely nothing to save himself. It is God who saves man. The only thing that man does is sin and do the very things God hates. Therefore, salvation is unmerited, unearned, and undeserved. Salvation is simply God saving unworthy, guilty, damned, and sinful men who possess no redeeming quality. Therefore, we can see that all glory for the salvation of sinful men will be to the glory of God alone (Romans 11:33-36).

As we close this chapter, we see the magnitude of answering the question on how sinful man is reconciled to a holy God. When we think about conversion, our understanding goes hand in hand with the person and work of the Lord Jesus Christ. When we think about conversion, our understanding of the person and work of the Lord Jesus Christ comes from what we know about the inerrant, infallible, authoritative, inspired, and all sufficient Word of God found in Scripture. When we think about conversion, we see that repentance toward God and faith in the Lord Jesus Christ was preached by John the Baptist, Jesus, Peter, Paul and the New Testament speaks in unanimity on salvation. When we think about conversion, we see that God causes a man to be born again and turn in repentance to the Lord Jesus Christ in faith. When we think about conversion, we see that there is a true conversion and a false conversion. When we think about conversion, we see that there's a false repentance and a true repentance. When we think about conversion, we see that there is a saving faith and a non-saving faith. When we think about conversion, we see gospel calls or invitations to deny yourself, take up your own cross, and follow Christ. When we think about conversion, we see gospel calls to hate your own life, take up your cross, and follow Christ. When we think about conversion, we need our understanding to be informed by Scripture.

CHAPTER 13

Peter's Condemnation of False Teachers

2 Peter 2:1—But false prophets also arose among the people, just as there will be false teachers among you, who will secretly bring in destructive heresies, even denying the Master who bought them, bringing upon themselves swift destruction.

The Second Book of Peter was written for the purpose of exposing, thwarting, and defeating the proliferation and invasion of false teachers into the church. Peter wrote this letter with the intention to provide instructions and explanations on how to protect his listeners against false teachers and their lies. Although Peter does not identify the specific destructive heresies, he does give a general characterization and that false teachers have destructive heresies, deny Christ, and twist Scripture. Of particular importance is Peter's emphasis on knowledge. Peter links knowledge of God and of the Lord Jesus Christ to receiving grace and peace (2 Peter 1:2). Peter links knowledge of God to being able to live a godly life (2 Peter 1:3). Peter links knowledge of the Lord Jesus Christ to prevent living an idle and unfruitful life (2 Peter 1:8). Peter links knowledge of the Lord Jesus Christ and living a godly life to assurance of salvation (2 Peter 1:10–11). Peter talks about knowledge of the Lord's coming (2 Peter 1:16). Peter links lack of knowledge with blaspheming (2 Peter 2:12). Peter talks about the damning results of apostasy where a false teacher has full knowledge of the Lord Jesus Christ, but turned from the knowledge of Jesus Christ (2 Peter 2:21). Peter links growing in the knowledge of the Lord and Savior Jesus Christ to not being led astray by false teachers (2 Peter 3:17–18).

As we transition into Peter's portrait of false teachers, we can see that Peter has spent time ensuring that everyone know their salvation which would come from knowing the gospel (2 Peter 1:3–11). Peter will then remind his people to remember, recall, and retain the truth (2 Peter 1:12–15). Peter then confirms the truths of the gospel are not man-made but from God (2 Peter 1:16). He defends his apostleship by being an eyewitness account which would affirm the transfiguration of Jesus (2 Peter 1:16). He confirms the Lord's second coming (2 Peter 1:16). He confirms Jesus being the Son of God by hearing the Father's affirmation of the Son (2 Peter 1:17). He confirms hearing the voice of the Father (2 Peter 1:18). He confirms the importance of Scripture, more specifically, the Old Testament which confirms prophecies that were foretold (2 Peter 1:19). He confirms that Scripture is all inspired by God and not from man (2 Peter 1:20), and that all Scripture was written by man as they were inspired by the Holy Spirit (2 Peter 1:21). This transitions us into his teaching on false teachers.

It is probably good to stop and reflect at this point as we approach Peter's description of false teachers. Thus far, we have sought to understand the gospel and the gospel call. We've studies both the bad news as well as the good news. Once we've understood the bad news, we are able to see how good the good news of the gospel really is. We started with some definitions of the bad news as well as the good news which are as follows:

- **The Bad News**: Man has sinned which is breaking God's law by either not doing what God's law demands (James 4:17) or doing what God's law prohibits (James 2:10) by any thought (Matthew 5:28), word (Matthew 5:22), deed (Matthew 5:39), or intent (Matthew 6:1) which God hates (Psalm 5:5, 11:5), abhors (Psalm 5:6), is angered with (Psalm 7:11), is ready to destroy and punish (Psalm 7:12-13), which is being at warfare with Him (James 4:4), which God considers an abomination (Proverbs 22:12), and which God considers evil (Psalm 7:9). Because God hates sin , He must deal with sin according to who He is. Because God is infinite (1 Timothy 1:17), loving (Psalm 136, 1 John 4:17), just (Genesis 18:25, Deuteronomy 32:4, Job 34:10, Jeremiah 17:10, Ezekiel 18:1–32), good (Psalm 25:8, Mark 10:18), faithful (Lamentations 3:22–23), omniscient (Psalm 147:5, Hebrews 4:13), immutable (James 1:17, Numbers 23:19), omnipresent (Jeremiah 23:23–24), and holy (Isaiah 44:6, 45:5), He must punish sin. For God to leave sin unpunished would violate and act in opposition to His character. The punishment for sin is hell which is a place of God's full wrath and is a place of blackest darkness (Jude 13, Matthew 22:13), filled with furious and concentrated fire everywhere (Matthew 5:22, 5:29, 13:42, 13:50), where there is weeping and anger against God for the unrepentant Christ-rejecting (Matthew 11:20-24) and Christ-neglecting sinners (Hebrews 2:1-3) where they will spend all eternity paying for every sin they've ever committed (Revelation 20:12) with no hope of escape (Luke 16:26), and only the expectation of excruciating torments to their body, soul, and spirit (Matthew 10:28) and an undying conscience that will haunt them day and night, forever and ever, with no reprieve (Luke 16:25).
- **The Gospel**: The gospel is the good news of salvation that God has authored and owns (Romans 1:1). God had

promised this plan of salvation through His prophets and Holy Scripture and has fully revealed the good news of salvation through Scripture (Romans 1:2) which is the authoritative, inspired, inerrant, infallible, and all-sufficient Word of God (2 Peter 1:20-21, 2 Timothy 3:16-17). The good news concerns the person and work of the Lord Jesus Christ. Jesus is the Jewish Messiah and Son of the Living God (Matthew 16:16, Romans 1:1-4). Jesus is God and He is coequal and coeternal with God the Father and God the Holy Spirit (John 5:17-18, 10:30, 10:38, 14:10). Jesus is the eternal, only begotten, one-of-a-kind, Son of God (John 3:16). Jesus is the Anointed One of God (Luke 4:18-19). Jesus is the Savior of the world (Luke 2:11). Jesus is the Creator and Sustainer of the Universe (John 1:1-14). Jesus is the King of Israel (John 1:49). Jesus is the Son of David (Matthew 1:1-16, Luke 3:23-38). Jesus was born of a virgin (Matthew 1:23, Galatians 4:4). Jesus was the Word made flesh (John 1:14). Jesus was physically born into this world as a man (Matthew 1:25). Jesus is thus truly God and truly man (Philippians 2:5-11). The work of Jesus is that Jesus lived a sinless life (Matthew 26:59-60, 1 Corinthians 5:21) and fulfilled all righteousness found in the law and prophets (Matthew 5:17-20, Luke 24:44-46). He declared Himself to be the Christ (Matthew 16:16), the only begotten Son of the Living God through His teaching (John 3:16, Matthew 22:41-46), which was attested to by His miracles and display of divine power (John 10:37-38). Jesus offered himself as a spotless and blameless sacrifice for sin (John 1:29, 1 Peter 1:19) to propitiate the righteous anger of God by taking all the sins of God's people (John 10:11, Romans 3:25, Isaiah 53, 1 Peter 2:24) and, thus, the full wrath of God that was due to man (Matthew 26:39, 27:45-46, Luke 22:44). His sacrifice propitiated the righteous anger of God and reconciled (Romans 5:10-11) and brought peace from man to God and God to man (Matthew 27:51-53, John 19:30, Romans 5:1, 1 Peter 2:25). His substitutionary sacrifice and death also redeemed sinful man to Holy God by forgiving man's sin (Hebrews 8:12, Ephesians 1:7) and imputing Christ's righteousness to man (1 Corinthians 5:21, Isaiah 53:1-12, Romans 4:3-5). Jesus was resurrected from the dead on the third day by His own power (John 10:18), by God the Father (Galatians 1:1) and God the Holy Spirit (Romans 8:11), which affirmed His person, His teachings, and salvific work for sinners (Romans 4:25). He ascended to the right hand of the Father (Luke 24:51) and is empowered with all authority to bring about the plan of salvation for all His people (Matthew 28:18) by causing them to be born again (John 3:1- 10) and justified by His grace (John 3:16, 3:18, 3:36). He will also return to bring all His own to heaven with Him (John 6:37- 40, 14:1-3) to be glorified (John 17:24) while also judging and condemning Satan, demons, and sinful man to hell (Matthew 25:31-46, Revelation 20:7-15). The benefits of the person and work of Christ are available to those who respond to the gospel call of repentance towards God and faith in the Lord Jesus Christ (Mark 1:15, Acts 20:21). Repentance is a gift from God and radical change in mind (Acts 5:31, 11:18, 2 Timothy 2:25) where the sinner understands his sin against God and is thus, poor in spirit (Matthew 5:3, Luke 18:9-14), has godly sorrow and mourns over his sin against God (Matthew 5:4, 2 Corinthians 7:10), and turns away from his sin and sinful former way of life (Ephesians 4:22) and toward God for righteousness and salvation (Matthew 5:5-6, Luke 3:3-17, Acts 17:30, 20:21, 1 Thessalonians 1:9). Saving faith is a gift from God (Ephesians 2:8-9) where a sinner has knowledge of Jesus' person and work where a sinner will respond to Christ's person and work by denying themselves (Matthew 16:24, Mark 8:34, Luke 9:23),

> picking up their cross (Matthew 10:38, 16:24, Mark 8:34, Luke 9:23), and lovingly (Luke 14:26-27, James 4:7) and obediently (2 Thessalonians 1:8, Romans 1:5) submitting (James 4:6, Matthew 11:28) and committing their life to Jesus (Matthew 10:37-39, 16:24-26, Mark 8:34-37, Luke 9:23-26, 14:25-33) and trusting in Him only for salvation (Romans 10:13, John 3:16, John 3:36, Acts 4:12). Thus, conversion is the turning away from sin in repentance and to the Lord Jesus Christ in faith for salvation (Acts 20:21, 1 Thessalonians 1:9, Ephesians 4:22-24, Colossians 3:9-10, Mark 1:15).

Only after we understood the gospel can we begin to understand false teachers. We need to understand the essential components of the bad news: sin, death, and hell. We needed to understand the **essential components of the gospel: authored by God, found in Scripture, objective person of Jesus, objective work of Jesus, and the subjective response to the objective person and work of Jesus which is repentance and faith in Jesus**. False teachers cannot be identified aside from knowing the gospel. Peter knows this and was desiring that his people would continue on in the truth of what they had learned. One of the reasons this chapter is at the end of the book is for this sole reason. Apart from a scriptural understanding of the gospel, it would be impossible to detect error. As we transition into 2 Peter 2, let's keep this in mind as we seek to better understand Peter's theology of a false teacher.

2 Peter 2:1—*But false prophets also arose among the people, just as there will be false teachers among you, who will secretly bring in destructive heresies, even denying the Master who bought them, bringing upon themselves swift destruction.*

The first point to emphasize is that false teachers will be among Christians. This is not speaking of false religions outside of Christianity. No, this is speaking of false teachers being amongst believers. Peter knew of the history of false prophets rising up among the Israelites. There were certainly many instances where the people of Israel were led astray by false teachers or false prophets such as Korah, Dathan, and Abiram opposing Aaron and Moses (Numbers 16:1–49), the prophets of Baal on Mount Carmel (1 Kings 18), the false prophets who prophesied good news to King Ahab (1 Kings 21), the false prophets during Jeremiah's time prophesying peace when there was no peace (Jeremiah 6:13–17, 23:9–32), the false prophets of Isaiah's time prophesying peace when there was no peace (Isaiah 44:24–26), the false prophets during Ezekiel's time prophesying peace when there was no peace (Ezekiel 13:1–16), and many more instances.

The lexicon describes a *pseudoprophétés* or a false prophet as "one who in God's name teaches what is false" or "someone pretending to speak the word of the Lord (prophesy) but in fact is a phony (imposter), acting as a wolf in sheep's cloth." The lexicon describes a *pseudodidaskalos* or a false teacher as "a teacher of false things" or "a spurious teacher (i.e., propagator of erroneous Christian doctrine)." A good starting definition of a *false teacher* would be as follows and will line up with Peter's definition: **A false teacher is one who holds to, unrepentantly, and persistently teaches and preaches a false gospel that damns men's souls by attacking, twisting, misinterpreting, adding to, or leaving out the essential components of the gospel or essential components of the bad news of sin, death, and hell. A false teacher could also be one who teaches the true gospel but lives a life in contradiction and opposition to the gospel and thus, blasphemes the gospel through their life** (Galatians 1:6–9, Matthew 15:14, 23:13–15; 2 Peter 2:1–22, 3:16; Luke 11:52; Jude 4).

Peter would have known the same truths as Paul that false teachers could spring up from inside the church (Acts 20:29–30), from outside the church (Acts 20:29), that they would teach different objective truths about the person of Jesus (2 Corinthians 11:4), that they would teach different objective truths about the work of Jesus (2 Corinthians 11:4), that they would have different and deceptive spirits (2 Corinthians 11:4), that they would be deceitful and would disguise themselves as apostles of Christ (2 Corinthians 11:13), that Satan was in false religion and disguised himself as an angel of light (2 Corinthians 11:14), that those who serve Satan would disguise themselves as servants of righteousness (2 Corinthians 11:15), and that they would have smooth and flattering speech (Romans 16:18). Peter knew the same thing. In fact, as we learned earlier, Peter needed to be corrected by Paul in Galatians when Peter's actions with the Judaizers were causing people to be led astray.

Jesus spoke much about false teachers and false prophets. Jesus warned that there would be false prophets that looked like true teachers (Matthew 7:15-20). Jesus warned of the dangerous influence of false teachers and their teaching (Matthew 16:5-12, Mark 12:38-40). Peter would have seen Christ denouncing false teachers (Luke 11:37-54, Matthew 23:1-36, Matthew 15:1-20, Luke 16:14-15). Peter would know that false teachers would receive a greater condemnation (Mark 12:40). Peter saw that false teaching and false gospels were being propagated in the early church (Acts 15:1-13).

The second point to notice is that the false teachers will secretly introduce their destructive heresies. The phrase *secretly bring in* comes from *pareisagó,* which is a compound word of *pará*, which means "*from* close beside," and *eiságō,* which means "introduce." Properly, it means to "introduce from close beside (i.e., enter by stealth)." This secretly introduced heresy could be a simple misinterpretation (Luke 11:52), man-made rule or oral tradition (Mark 7:9), a twisting of Scripture (2 Peter 3:16), or adding to or taking away from Scripture (Revelation 22:18–19). There is often just enough truth in the lie to pass as something that may be truth. Peter is warning the believers that this is not going to be obvious. This is going to be very subtle. This is going to be hard to detect. This is going to require knowledge of the truth and careful examination. Just as the Bereans were commended for comparing Paul's message with Scripture (Acts 17:10–12), it is also required of believers to pay attention to the message and what is being taught because Peter is stating that the heresies are going to enter stealthily. Jude adds a little bit in Jude 4, where he says, "For certain people have crept in unnoticed who long ago were designated for this condemnation, ungodly people, who pervert the grace of our God into sensuality and deny our only Master and Lord, Jesus Christ." So, both Peter and Jude warn that false teachers enter stealthily and introduce their heresies stealthily as well.

The third point to note is that the heresies that they introduce are destructive heresies both for themselves and their listeners. Destruction comes from *apóleia* and it means "destruction, causing someone or something to be completely severed." It does not mean annihilation but rather speaks of the complete loss of well-being. This word *apóleia* is often used to describe destruction which is eternal destruction or eternal misery. Jesus spoke of how false teachers were outside the kingdom and kept others outside the kingdom of heaven when he denounced the Pharisees in Matthew 23:13 where He said, "But woe to you, scribes and Pharisees, hypocrites! For you shut the kingdom of heaven in people's faces. For you neither enter yourselves nor allow those who would enter to go in." The Pharisees and scribes were literally shutting up the kingdom of heaven right in man's face. This was an objective picture of someone earnestly seeking the Lord and coming right up to the line and having a door slammed in their face. This is a brutal picture of someone about to enter through a wide-open door and then having a false teacher continually slam the door shut right in the face of those entering. This is a graphic and violent picture of the effort that false teachers go to which keeps people out of the kingdom of heaven. When we look at the last half of the verse, it says, “For you neither enter yourselves nor allow those who would enter to go in.” These, false teachers are accursed and damned by God for a false gospel (Galatians 1:8-9). They are accursed because they’ve given a false or a different gospel that damns men’s souls. They are accursed because they make Christ’s salvific work of no profit for those who are trying to enter the kingdom of God (Galatians 5:2). They sever and completely cut people off from Christ and they make people full-fledged pagans (Galatian 5:4, 12). Once again, this is not random. This is not a mistake. This is not isolated. No, this is purposeful. This is deliberate. This is continual. This is habitual. This is constant. This is a fixed position. Jesus is talking in the present tense. These false teachers are purposefully teaching a false gospel. These false teachers are deliberately teaching a false gospel. These false teachers continually teach a false gospel. These false teachers are habitually teaching a false gospel. These false teachers will not change and do not relent. When the door is open, they move to shut it. When someone is close to entering, they slam the door close. When someone sees the light on the other side of the door, they slam it shut and keep the light out. This portion of Scripture makes it clear that false teachers are those who do not enter the kingdom by holding to and teaching a false gospel that will damn men’s souls and damns their own souls.

The fourth point is that heresies comes from *hairesis* and means a self-chosen opinion, a religious or philosophical sect, discord, or contention. This stresses a personal aspect of choice. The word *hairesis* evolved to mean a self-willed opinion. A self-willed opinion stands in opposition to the submission to the power of truth, and leads to division and the formation of sects. Paul helps us understand the extent of this self-chosen opinion or religious sect where he says in Titus 3:10–11, "As for a person who stirs up division, after warning him once and then twice, have nothing more to do with him, knowing that such a person is warped and sinful; he is self-condemned." The phrase *who stirs up division* comes from *hairetikos,* which carries the same meaning as *hairesis.* Therefore, it should be noted that these heresies aren't minor. No, these heresies are eternally destructive to those who hear them and are eternally destructive to those who teach them. Those who teach these heresies are self-condemned.

The fifth point we should see is these teachers have no submission to the Lord. There is a difficult phrase to dissect in this verse which is *even denying the master who bought them.* When Peter is saying that they are "even denying the master who bought them," he is saying that although they claim to be Christ's, they deny Him by their teaching or manner of life. They contradict and deny the Lord by their actions and teaching. One of Jesus' most compassionate invitations to accept Him as Lord and Savior comes in Matthew 11:28–30, where He says, "Come to me, all who labor and are heavy laden, and I will give you rest. Take my yoke upon you, and learn from me, for I am gentle and lowly in heart, and you will find rest for your souls. For my yoke is easy, and my burden is light." Notice in Matthew 11:29, Jesus says, "Take my yoke upon you, and learn from me." This is a picture of submission. Farmers back in the ancient world knew the frustration of trying to plow a field or transport a cart with a stiff-necked animal. An animal that refused to bow his head in submission to the yoke was useless to perform any real work. When someone accepts Jesus as their Lord and Savior, there is a bowing of the head and a submission to Christ's yoke. When Jesus stops, you stop. When Jesus goes, you go. When Jesus commands you to pick up the pace, you will pick up the pace. When Jesus commands that you turn to the left, you'll turn to the left. This is not perfect obedience, but Peter is saying that there is no submission with these false teachers. As we learned just above, these false teachers have self-willed opinions and religious sects which goes hand in hand with no submission to the Lord. Jude helps clarify this a little more where he says in Jude 4, "For certain people have crept in unnoticed who long ago were designated for this condemnation, ungodly people, who pervert the grace of our God into sensuality and deny our only Master and Lord, Jesus Christ." Jude gives the same picture of these false teachers who enter the church stealthily but deny the Lord and Master, Jesus Christ. This is to say that they claim allegiance to Christ, but by their teaching and actions, they deny Him. Paul likewise gives the same idea where he says in Titus 1:16, "They profess to know God, but by their actions they deny Him. They are detestable, disobedient, and unfit for any good work." Therefore, we can understand that Peter is saying these false teachers claim allegiance to Christ but deny Him through their teaching and lives. Let's also note that this verse does not suggest that these false teachers are Christians. We'll see this as we transition to the sixth point which is that they bring destruction upon themselves.

Sixth, let's notice that they will be destroyed. Peter says, "bringing upon themselves swift destruction." Not only do these false teachers introduce destructive heresies which damn their hearers, they bring destruction upon themselves. *Tachinos* is translated to "swift" and carries with it the idea of something or an event being swift, quick, or impending. Jude gives this same picture in Jude 23 where he says, "Save others by snatching them out of the fire; to others show mercy with fear, hating even the garment stained by the flesh." This carries the idea that these false teachers are right on the precipice of entering eternal punishment and need to be rescued. However, it is also a dangerous task to reach your hand in the fire to help pull them out as they are deceitful and misleading. They are like unmarked graves and they can defile you by their teaching (Luke 11:44). Thus, false teachers teach a false gospel that ultimately curses and damns them. Peter fully agrees that such a teaching that produces a false gospel is a teaching that will damn the one who teaches it.

2 Peter 2:2—*And will follow their sensuality, and because of them the way of truth will be blasphemed*

It is quite clear that false teachers will teach false doctrines that will damn men's souls. Up until this point, we haven't necessarily discussed a false teacher's actions or walk of life. However, Peter's statement in verse 2 explains that a teacher's walk of life can also be an indication of whether or not they are a false teacher. Paul said this very thing to Timothy where he says this in 1 Timothy 4:16, "Keep a close watch on yourself and on the teaching. Persist in this, for by so doing you will save both yourself and your hearers." Paul's exhortation was that Timothy carefully watch over his walk of life as well as his doctrine for the sake of Timothy's life as well as those around him. The wickedness that is produced out of a false teacher is not the product of sound doctrine, but of "destructive heresies."

Seventh, let's notice that teaching destructive heresies can lead to following sensuality. *Sensuality* has been translated from *aselgeia,* which means "licentiousness," "wantonness," or "outrageous conduct, conduct shocking to public decency." Paul gives a picture of what these false teachers may look like in 2 Timothy 3:1–7, where he says, "But understand this, that in the last days there will come times of difficulty. For people will be lovers of self, lovers of money, proud, arrogant, abusive, disobedient to their parents, ungrateful, unholy, heartless, unappeasable, slanderous, without self-control, brutal, not loving good, treacherous, reckless, swollen with conceit, lovers of pleasure rather than lovers of God, having the appearance of godliness, but denying its power. Avoid such people. For among them are those who creep into households and capture weak women, burdened with sins, and led astray by various passion, always learning and never able to arrive at a knowledge of the truth." Paul gives another picture of false teachers in 1 Timothy 6:3–5, 9–10 where he says, "If anyone teaches a different doctrine and does not agree with the sound words of our Lord Jesus Christ and the teaching that accords with godliness, he is puffed up with conceit and understands nothing. He has an unhealthy craving for controversy and for quarrels about words, which produce envy, dissension, slander, evil suspicions, and constant friction among people who are depraved in mind and deprived of the truth, imagining that godliness is a means of gain. But those who desire to be rich fall into temptation, into a snare, into many senseless and harmful desires that plunge people into ruin and destruction. For the love of money is a root of all kinds of evils. It is through this craving that some have wandered away from the faith and pierced themselves with many pangs." In 2 Timothy 2:16, Paul gives another description of false teachers where he says, "Avoid godless chatter, because those who indulge in it will become more and more ungodly." Again, Paul describes false teachers in Titus 1:10 where he says, "For there are many who are insubordinate, empty talkers and deceivers, especially those of the circumcision party. They must be silenced since they are upsetting whole families by teaching for shameful gain what they ought not to teach." Jude also provides a characterization of false teachers in his epistle. Therefore, when Peter says that false teachers will blaspheme the way of truth through their sensuality, we can understand the outward sensual behavior and internal motives of a false teacher could encompass the following behaviors and attitudes from Paul and Jude's description:

- Lovers of self—someone preoccupied with their own selfish desires (2 Timothy 3:2)
- Lovers of money—someone in love with personal gain of money or wealth (2 Timothy 3:2)

- Boastful—an empty pretender, bragger (2 Timothy 3:2, Jude 16)
- Proud—arrogant, going beyond what God directs (2 Timothy 3:2)
- Abusive to parents—slanderous and evil-speaking toward parents (2 Timothy 3:2)
- Disobedient—unwilling to be persuaded by God (2 Timothy 3:2)
- Ungrateful—without God's grace which results in unthankfulness (2 Timothy 3:2)
- Unholy—having utter disregard of what is sacred (2 Timothy 3:2)
- Unloving—devoid of natural affection (2 Timothy 3:3)
- Unappeasable—unable to be pleased or satisfied (2 Timothy 3:3)
- Slanderous—falsely accusing (2 Timothy 3:3)
- Without self-control—powerless, inclined to excess, lacking self-restraint (2 Timothy 3:3)
- Brutal—not tame; savage, fierce (2 Timothy 3:3)
- Not loving good—someone who is hostile to the things of God (2 Timothy 3:3)
- Treacherous—betraying or being a traitor (2 Timothy 3:4)
- Reckless—impulsive, rash, reckless, headstrong brought on by unbridled passion (2 Timothy 3:4)
- Swollen with conceit—having a cloudy mindset or moral blindness resulting from poor judgment which brings further loss of spiritual perception (2 Timothy 3:4)
- Lovers of pleasure—loving the bodily or natural senses of pleasure (2 Timothy 3:4)
- Not lovers of God—not a lover of God or the things of God (2 Timothy 3:4)
- Having a form of godliness but denying its power—outward moralism but not true believers and no inward reality

of the power of the Holy Spirit or partakers in God's divine nature (2 Timothy 3:5)

- Creep into houses and capture weak women—taking advantage of the weak and vulnerable (2 Timothy 3:6)
- Learning but never able to come to a knowledge of the truth—learners but do not possess saving knowledge (2 Timothy 3:7)
- Teaches a different doctrine that doesn't agree with Christ's teaching (1 Timothy 6:3)
- Is inclined toward meaningless debates and questions and idle speculations (1 Timothy 6:4)
- Argue over words—argue over terminology and minor doctrinal subjects (1 Timothy 6:4)
- They have a corrupted mind—unregenerate mind that does not have in mind the things of God (1 Timothy 6:5)
- They are deprived of the truth—do not have the truth of God's word and more specifically, the gospel (1 Timothy 6:5)
- They engage in godless chatter—empty discussion or discussion of vain and useless matters (2 Timothy 2:16)
- Insubordinate—not subject to rule, not submissive to God and unwilling to come under Christ's Lordship, not submissive to God's plan with a defiant attitude (Titus 1:10)
- Empty talkers—an idle talker, one who utters empty senseless things (Titus 1:10)
- Deceivers—leading others into delusion or away from the truth (Titus 1:10)
- Relying on dreams—they give undue preeminence to their personal dreams rather than give the preeminence which is only due to Scripture (Jude 8)
- Fruitless trees and twice dead—they appear to provide a spiritual need but provide nothing because they are spiritually dead (Jude 12)
- Murmurer—one who discontentedly complains (Jude 16)

- Discontent—complaining over allotted portion (Jude 16)

It's important to note that a false teacher may not have all these characteristics or traits. However, these traits are important in helping discern the outward fruit of a teacher's life to determine if they are a false teacher. It's also important to note that Paul describes them as "having an appearance of godliness, but denying its power." Paul is simply saying that they act religious, they may act moral, but they lack the transformation and power that comes from the regenerating work of the Holy Spirit and the indwelling power and presence of the Holy Spirit that accompanies the life of a believer. Jude says they have "crept in unnoticed." Jude is simply stating that they came in unnoticed which speaks of their ability to blend into the church. Jesus also says in Matthew 23:27 that they may have outward morality where He says, "Woe to you, scribes and Pharisees, hypocrites! For you are like whitewashed tombs, which outwardly appear beautiful, but within are full of dead people's bones and all uncleanness." Here, both Jesus and Paul note that they are going to be hard to spot and will have a form of godliness and be dressed with morality and religious acts. Therefore, outward sensuality can be a strong indication of someone being a false teacher, but this may not always be the case as we've seen that outward morality is an effective means to hide a false teacher.

Eighth, we should see that false teachers who follow their sensuality will blaspheme the way of the truth. The word *blaspheme* comes from *blasphémeó*. *Blasphémeó* refers to speaking evil against or refusing to acknowledge good; hence, *blaspheming* reverses that which is good. Blaspheming the way of the truth can be understood from two different perspectives and both would be correct. The first way a false teacher could blaspheme the way of the truth by their sensuality is by giving the correct doctrine, but having their life disagree with the correct doctrine. For example, a pastor who said that one must repent and put their faith in Jesus but was actively committing adultery with another woman would certainly be blaspheming the way of truth because, by his actions, he is claiming he belongs to God but his life vehemently opposes the truth. This could cause his listeners to dismiss the true doctrine by the hypocrisy of his life. Another way a false teacher could blaspheme the way of the truth is by teaching a false doctrine which accepts a sensuous lifestyle and, thus, blasphemes the gospel call to saving faith or blasphemes the believer's sanctified walk of life. In both cases, whether the false teacher gives true doctrine and lives sensuously or gives false doctrine and lives sensuously, this blasphemes the way of truth of how someone understands to come to Jesus in a saving way or how a believer is to live their sanctified Christian life.

2 Peter 2:3 – *And in their greed they will exploit you with false words. Their condemnation from long ago is not idle, and their destruction is not asleep.*

As we see above, there are many reasons why false teachers may continue in their false doctrine. This could be for love of money, job security, pride, love of prominence, comfort, keeping friends, and a host of other factors. In any case, it is God who knows the heart. In Proverbs 21:2, it says, "Every way of a man is right in his own eyes, but the LORD weighs the heart." We don't know what the reason is for false teachers and their motives, but we can be assured they have their own reasons for teaching their damning doctrines.

Ninth, Peter notes that the false teachers will continue in their false doctrine because of greed. *Greed* has been translated from *pleonexia,* which means "covetousness" or, properly, "the desire for more things (lusting for a greater number of temporal things that go beyond what God determines is eternally best)." As mentioned above, it's impossible to know the true motive of a false teacher, but the text strongly suggests that the false teacher is unwilling to give up the damning doctrine for their own covetous reasons.

Tenth, we should see that they deceive through false words. The word *false* is actually *plastos* in the original language, which means "formed, molded," "shaped according to a mold," or "made-up, fabricated." It carries with it the idea of molding at will to suit one's vain imaginations. Once again, this is fake or molded theology. This is not God's Word. False teachers may use words in the Bible and may use Biblical terminology, but what they speak is not actually God's truth. As we noted above, these false teachers are self-willed and deny submission to the Lord through either their actions or teachings. The false words are just an outcome of their self-will and unsubmissive hearts and minds. False teachers may use the same terminology, but they have a different dictionary. False teachers may use the same words as true teachers, but the words have different meanings which are false.

Eleventh, we see that they exploit their listeners through their false words. The word *exploit* comes from *emporeuomai,* which carries the idea of "a place for trading or doing business." Peter is saying here that they take advantage of their listeners for money. The outrageous televangelists who have huge mansions and private jets would certainly fall in this category but Peter would also have in mind those who make their living off false teaching. For example, it's not necessarily that these false teachers are getting rich off their trade but, rather, they are able to get what they want through their profession. This certainly carries the heavy implication that false teachers do this for money. As we noted earlier, false teachers can certainly be covetous for money, but they can also be covetous for power, prestige, preeminence, comfort, friends, and more.

Twelfth, we see that their condemnation is confirmed. As we learned earlier, those who teach destructive heresies are those who preach a different or false gospel (Galatians 1:8–9). Those who teach a false gospel are accursed and headed for destruction

(Galatians 1:8–9, Matthew 23:13–15). It should be noted that these false teachers are those who hold to and persistently teach and preach a false gospel.

2 Peter 2:4-10 – *For if God did not spare angels when they sinned, but cast them into hell and committed them to chains of gloomy darkness to be kept until the judgment; if he did not spare the ancient world, but preserved Noah, a herald of righteousness, with seven others, when he brought a flood upon the world of the ungodly; if by turning the cities of Sodom and Gomorrah to ashes he condemned them to extinction, making them an example of what is going to happen to the ungodly, and if he rescued righteous Lot, greatly distressed by the sensual conduct of the wicked (for as that righteous man lived among them day after day, he was tormenting his righteous soul over their lawless deeds that he saw and heard); then the Lord knows how to rescue the godly from trials, and to keep the unrighteous under punishment until the day of judgment, and especially those who indulge in the lust of defiling passion and despise authority*

Thirteenth, we should see that unrepentant false teachers will not escape judgment and condemnation. Peter makes an argument from the greater to the lesser that if God has judged and condemned angels, the ungodly world, and whole cities, false teachers will be judged and condemned as well. His first illustration is that of angels who sinned during the time of Noah and were cast into the deepest pit of hell (2 Peter 2:4, Jude 6, 1 Peter 3:19-20). His second illustration is that God saved only eight people and killed the rest of the ungodly world by a flood (2 Peter 2:5). Peter's third illustration is that God saved only three people in Sodom and Gomorrah while causing sulfur and fire to rain down and kill everyone in these immoral cities (Genesis 19:23-30). Therefore, if God has judged angels who are greater than men and sent them to hell, if God has judged the entire ungodly world by the flood, and if God has judged the wicked and rampant sinfulness of an entire city by causing fire and sulfur to rain down and kill all but three people, then God will judge false teachers. This is Peter's point. He is simply stating that false teachers will not escape judgment and condemnation.

2 Peter 2:10-19 – *and especially those who indulge in the lust of defiling passion and despise authority. Bold and willful, they do not tremble as they blaspheme the glorious ones, whereas angels, though greater in might and power, do not pronounce a blasphemous judgment against them before the Lord. But these, like irrational animals creatures of instinct, born to be caught and destroyed, blaspheming about matters of which they are ignorant, will also be destroyed in their destruction, suffering wrong as the wage for their wrongdoing. They count it pleasure to revel in the daytime. They are blots and blemishes, reveling in their deceptions, while they feast with you. They have eyes full of adultery, insatiable for sin. They entice unsteady souls. They have hearts trained in greed. Accursed children! Forsaking the right way, they have gone astray. They have followed the way of Balaam, the son of Beor, who loved gain from wrongdoing, but was rebuked for his own transgression; a speechless donkey spoke with human voice and restrained the prophet's madness. These are waterless springs and mists driven by a storm. For them the gloom of utter darkness has been reserved. For, speaking loud boasts of folly, they entice by sensual passions of the flesh those who are barely escaping from those who live in error. They promise them freedom, but they themselves are slaves of corruption. For whatever overcomes a person, to that he is enslaved.*

Fourteenth, let's note that Peter goes on to describe these false teachers in great detail in 2 Peter 2:10-19. They are those who indulge in defiling lust and passion (2 Peter 2:10). The word for "defiling" comes from *miasmos*. *Miasmos* means "defiling" or "pollution." This word comes into the English language as miasma which is a highly unpleasant or unhealthy smell or vapor. As we learned earlier, Satan is the god of this age and the prince of the power of the air. These false teachers walk in the pollution of the worldly system. These false teachers walk in the pollution of abhorrent and false Christianity. These false teachers don't fight the worldly system or false Christianity. No, they live, breathe, eat, sleep, and revel in worldliness or abhorrent doctrine.

These false teachers despise Christ's Lordship (2 Peter 2:10). The word for "despise" comes from *kataphroneó* and it means to "scorn," "disregard," "esteem lightly," "hold in contempt," or "disdain." Additionally, the word for "authority" comes from *kuriotés* and means "lordship." As we saw above, these false teachers will claim allegiance to Christ, but by their actions or their doctrine, they deny the Lord. They despise when their systematic theology disagrees with the Lord's teaching. They scorn having to obey the Lord. They lightly esteem the Lord's commands. They create their own self-willed interpretations of Scripture that contradict God's Word. As we learned earlier, their ultimate rejection of authority is God's Word. When they encounter a verse they don't understand, they twist it. When they're shown their sin, they justify it. They are skilled at rejecting God's authority in various ways.

These false teachers blaspheme fallen angels and Satan even though the demons and Satan are more powerful than them (2 Peter 2:10-11, Jude 8). Not even angels pronounce blasphemous judgement against the devil or evil angels (Jude 8-9). However, these false teachers are bold which means that they are darers who foolishly ignore what should make them afraid (2 Peter 2:10). They are so foolish and arrogant that they do not even realize that they are the ones being deceived by the devil and demons. Rather than using discernment and wisdom, they are self-willed and arrogant. They are audacious and exalt themselves and speak blasphemously against fallen angels, but they will never humble themselves. They have no concern or care for their error or walk of life.

These false teachers are like irrational animals which means that they function on a fleshly level and are without reason and operate contrary to reason (2 Peter 2:12). The word "irrational" comes from *alogos* which means, "without reason," "contrary to reason," or "absurd." They are irrational like animals and cannot rationalize from God's point of view and His divine reason (2 Peter 2:12, Jude 10). Rather, they operate, rationalize, and behave against divine reason. They operate as unregenerate people and lack divine transformation. They may speak of God, Jesus, the Bible, and church, but they ultimately lack the reality of a regenerated life. They cannot discern and perceive the things of the Spirit of God (2 Corinthians 2:14). They cannot discern or perceive the things of God because they are unregenerate and do not have the mind of Christ (1 Corinthians 2:16). They are unregenerate and irrational because God has not put his laws into their minds and written it on their hearts (Hebrews 8:10).

These false teachers are utterly worthless (2 Peter 2:12). Peter describes them as an animal that has been born to be captured and destroyed. Unlike animals who serve a purpose when they're caught and killed for food, these false teachers only serve a benefit when they die which puts an end to their false teaching. The greatest benefit these false teachers provide is when they die and stop propagating damning doctrine that damns other men's souls. The greatest benefit these false teachers provide is when they are eventually captured and sent to hell.

These false teachers speak blasphemously, irreverently, and slanderously about divine truth in willful ignorance (2 Peter 2:12, Jude 10). Not only are they self-willed and arrogant, but we see that they boldly proclaim their false teaching in ignorance and with irreverence. Although they're shown to be wrong, they irreverently continue in their error. They will be destroyed in their destruction. The end result of their damning doctrine or immoral life will be destruction, not salvation.

These false teachers revel in the daytime meaning they live outright debauched, indulgent, and sinful lives in public without hiding (2 Peter 2:13). Not only do they revel audaciously by living immoral and indulgent lives, but they also revel in their deceptions. Rather than be concerned and repentant about living an outright immoral life or spreading a damning false gospel, they make their immoral lives public, and they boldly proclaim their damning false gospels. Not only do they boldly proclaim their damning doctrines, but they also put them in catechisms, creeds, and confessions for everyone to see.

These false teachers are blots and blemishes meaning they are spiritually dirty, foul, diseased, and polluted (2 Peter 2:13). They aren't characterized as children of God. No, they are characterized as a stain, a blemish, a disgrace, and a blot. They are a disfiguring spot amongst the true church. They are a moral blemish amongst true believers. They are a contamination amongst the saints.

These false teachers have eyes full of adultery meaning they view women as potential adulterers or as sexual objects (2 Peter 2:14). They devise ways to seduce women. They devise ways to prey on women to fulfill their sexual desires. They devise ways to talk flirtatiously with women. They devise ways to manipulate women. They are masters of severing marriages. They are experts in finding vulnerable women. They are skilled in taking a conversation to debase and immoral levels. They specialize in meeting secretly with women under the guise of trying to help them. They cannot stop devising ways to feed their insatiable adulterous heart.

These false teachers never cease from sin (2 Peter 2:14). The word for "insatiable" comes from *akatapaustos* which means "not ceasing from" or "not abandoning." There is nothing that stops these false teachers from their sins. This word gives the idea that they are relentless in their sin. They cannot be commanded, coerced, or convinced to stop their sin. If they are commanded to stop preaching a false gospel, they double down on their damning doctrine. If they are confronted and shown their error, they persist on in their error. They cannot stop and cease from their sin because they are enslaved and in bondage to their sin (John 8:34). They are adept in justifying their sin, downplaying their sin, and ignoring their sin. These fall teachers will talk of their self-righteous deeds but never their sinfulness.

These false teachers have hearts trained in greed meaning they can never have enough pride, power, preeminence, money, materials, and authority (2 Peter 2:14). The word for trained comes from *gumnazó* which means "to exercise," "to train." They are those who are exercised in covetousness. Their church is never big enough. Their salary is never compensating enough. They need more recognition. They need more praise. They need more followers. They need more fame. Their hearts will never be satiated or content.

These false teachers entice and deceive unstable souls or rather, people (2 Peter 2:14). They don't prey on the strong man of God. Rather, they look for those whom they can deceive. They look for the unlearned. They look for those who are weak in Bible knowledge. They look for those who are easily influenced. They look for those who can be easily deceived. These cowardly false teachers prey on the weak, not the strong.

These false teachers are accursed children (2 Peter 2:14). As we noted above, these false teachers give false gospels that damn those who embrace their heresy, and they damn their own souls for unrepentantly teaching destructive doctrines. They are not blessed, they're cursed. They are not counseled by God, they're cursed by God. They are not making diminutive doctrinal error, they are making damned disciples.

These false teachers love the prosperity that comes with leading others astray (2 Peter 2:15-16). Balaam led the people of

Israel into sin where the men began to commit sexual immorality with the women of Moab (Numbers 25:1-9, 31:15-16). They are willing to forsake the truth for temporary gain. They are willing to find ways to compromise for the sake of temporary profit.

These false teachers are waterless springs, clouds, and mists meaning that they appear to provide a spiritual need but fail to deliver what they promise (2 Peter 2:17, Jude 12). Just as a spring or a cloud would be welcoming in the desert climate, so these false teachers make promises but end up delivering nothing just like a waterless spring or cloud with no rain or water. The only thing they can provide is a façade of Christianity without providing deliverance. They provide religiosity but no reconciliation with God.

These false teachers are doomed to go to hell (2 Peter 2:17). There is a place of gloom and utter darkness that has been reserved for them. The word for "gloom" comes from *zophos* and means "darkness," "murkiness," or "gloom." It's a type of appalling gloom that is so dark and foreboding it can be felt. It is meant to convey the idea of an indescribable despair. This, of course, is hell (Matthew 22:13). There is a reserved place in hell for these false teaching heretics of unquenchable fire, foreboding darkness, indescribable despair, and unfathomable torment.

These false teachers are boastful and speak vain and purposeless words that cannot save (2 Peter 2:18). They can appeal to the flesh with their empty, arrogant, and enticing words. They are not ashamed to give their damning doctrine. They will speak with much bravado and persuasion, but the false gospel they proclaim cannot save. They may give smooth words of flattery and deceptive speech that sounds religious (Romans 16:18), but in the end, it will damn those who embrace their doctrine. Are these false teachers ashamed? Are these false teachers remorseful? Are these false teachers apologetic? Are these false teachers embarrassed? No, they are false teachers. As the prophet Jeremiah said about these false teachers in Jeremiah 6:15 and 8:12, "they did not know how to blush."

These false teachers promise freedom but are slaves which means they appear to provide spiritual freedom and knowledge but fall short of their promises and deliver bondage to false religion (2 Peter 2:19). The only thing they can deliver is bondage to their damning doctrine. The only thing they can deliver is a false religious Christianity that is void of salvation.

2 Peter 2:20-22 – *For if, after they have escaped the defilements of the world through the knowledge of our Lord and Savior Jesus Christ, they are again entangled in them and overcome, the last state has become worse for them than the first. For it would have been better for them never to have known the way of righteousness than after knowing it to turn back from the holy commandment delivered to them. What the true proverb says has happened to them: "The dog returns to its own vomit, and the sow, after washing herself, returns in the mire."*

Fifteenth, we should see that false teachers will not take correction. They will not submit to the Lord. They are self-willed. They are driven by their own desires. They will not repent. In fact, Peter says of them in 2 Peter 2:19–21, "For if, after they have escaped the defilements of the world through the knowledge of our Lord and Savior Jesus Christ, they are again entangled in them and overcome, the last state has become worse for them than the first. For it would have been better for them never to have known the way of righteousness than after knowing it to turn back from the holy commandment delivered to them. What the true proverb says has happened to them: `The dog returns to its vomit, and the sow, after washing herself, returns to wall in the mire.'" Peter is describing those false teachers who knew the truth, but then decided to turn back to false teaching. Those who knew the whole truth of the gospel but decided to return back to the vomit of a false gospel. This is a graphic and ugly picture. It would not be uncommon in the ancient world to see a dog vomit and eat his own vomit. The vomit would be foul, potentially carry disease, and would smell. The picture is of a dog who vomits and then returns and smells, licks, chews, and swallows its own vomit. Here, Peter pictures false teachers the same way. They are pictured as filthy animals who lick up vile, putrid, and worthless false doctrine. Likewise, pigs returning to the mire pictures the same grotesque nature of false teachers. It is one of pigs returning to a pile of mud, manure, and urine and rolling around in a vile sludge of filth. In the very same way, false teachers are pictured as those wallowing in a vile sludge of abhorrent doctrine that damn their souls and damn the souls of their listeners. These false teachers aren't just making a onetime choice. No, they have purposefully, deliberately, and decisively chosen to continue teaching a false gospel. These false teachers will be beaten with more blows (Luke 12:47). These false teachers will endure the most severe punishment for their treachery (2 Peter 2:17).

2 Peter 3:16—*as he does in all his letters when he speaks in them of these matters. There are some things in them that are hard to understand, which the ignorant and unstable twist to their own destruction, as they do the other Scriptures.*

Peter will also state that Paul says things that are "hard to understand." The phrase *hard to understand* comes from *dusnoétos. Dusnoétos* is a compound word with *dys* meaning "difficult" and *nōetos* meaning "understanding." *Dusnoétos* properly means "difficult to grasp; hard to mentally process, i.e., what is intellectually difficult to capture the true sense of." Peter was not saying that Paul was hard to understand, but rather, the truths contained within his epistles or writings were spiritually lofty and weighty. Peter was not throwing a slanderous accusation at Paul regarding his letters or teaching, but rather that the things of God can be hard for the human mind to comprehend. We can know this as Peter says in verse 15, "Paul wrote to you according to the wisdom given to him." Therefore, we can know that it was not Paul that was difficult to understand, but the lofty and high wisdom of God.

Sixteenth, let's notice that Peter says the ignorant and unstable twist to their own destruction. *Ignorant* comes from the original word *amathés,* with *a* being a negative prefix and *manthanó* meaning "to learn." Properly, they are unlearned and, thus, ignorant. *Unstable* comes from *astériktos,* with *a* meaning "not" and *stērízō* meaning "confirm." Properly, this is one who was not established (unstable), describing someone who (literally) does not have a staff to lean on—hence, a person who cannot be relied on because they are *not steady* (do not remain fixed, i.e., unstable). These false teachers were unlearned and unstable. Let's think back to what we learned in the previous chapter. We learned that these false teachers were self-willed and stiff-necked. These false teachers claimed allegiance to Christ but, by their teaching and/or walk of life, denied Him. As you'll remember, in Matthew 11:29, Jesus said, "Take my yoke and learn from me." These teachers did not want to learn from Christ and did not want to submit. Thus, Peter's description of them makes perfect sense as they will not submit and will not learn, thus, they are unlearned and unstable.

Seventeenth, we should see that Peter understood Paul's writing. Although Peter says that Paul's writings are hard to understand, he does not say they are impossible to understand. No, Peter makes a very clear and fine distinction that he is not the one who doesn't understand, but rather, it is the unlearned and unstable who do not understand Paul's writings.

Eighteenth, we should see what happens when the unlearned and unstable come to hard-to-understand sayings of Paul. They twist Paul's words to their own destruction. The word *twist* comes from the original word *strebloó,* which means to "twist," "torture," or "pervert with language." *Streblē* refers to an instrument of torture and implies "to torture; put to the rack" (i.e., to twist or dislocate like limbs on a torture rack). Peter is saying that when these false teachers come to a hard-to-understand saying of Paul, they will inevitably torture or twist the Scripture and provide a false meaning. This certainly carries with it the idea of misinterpretation of Scripture as in Luke 11:52 where Jesus says, "Woe to you, lawyers! For you have taken away the key of knowledge. You did not enter yourselves, and you hindered those who were entering." This is very similar to Satan twisting Scripture during Jesus' temptation. For example, Satan quotes Psalm 91:11–12, where it says, "For he will command his angels concerning you to guard you in all your ways. On their hands they will bear you up lest you strike your foot against a stone" and uses this verse to justify tempting God when this verse is used for trusting God. Another example is taking Matthew 7:1, where it says, "Judge not, that you be not judged." Here, Jesus is speaking of self-righteous, hypocritical judgments. This verse is often misquoted as an authoritative verse to never judge anyone's actions, lawlessness, or sin. However, Jesus commands in Matthew 7:6 that we do not give to dogs what is sacred and throw our pearls to swine. Therefore, Jesus does command that we be discerning and judge without self-righteousness, without hypocrisy, and without final judgment of others. Another example of twisting Scripture is using John 3:5 as a verse to justify baptismal regeneration where Jesus says, "Truly, truly, I say to you, unless one is born of water and the Spirit, he cannot enter the kingdom of God." In the John 3:5 example, pastors and priests who twist this verse to mean baptismal regeneration completely ignore that Nicodemus was a premier teacher of the Pharisees and was a legalist and ritualist and they also ignore how Jesus emphasizes the sovereign monergistic work of God in regeneration in John 3:3, 6, 7, and 8. These are examples of how Scripture can easily be twisted to suit one's own desires. The context in this verse is that the false teachers will twist a portion of Scripture that will ultimately lead to a false gospel and, thus, will damn them and damn those who believe it.

Nineteenth, we should note that this twisting of Paul's hard-to-understand sayings results in the false teacher's own destruction. As we learned earlier, the definition of a *false teacher* is as follows: **A false teacher is one who holds to, unrepentantly, and persistently teaches and preaches a false gospel that damns men's souls by attacking, twisting, misinterpreting, adding to, or leaving out the essential components of the gospel or essential components of the bad news of sin, death, and hell. A false teacher could also be one who teaches the true gospel but lives a life in contradiction and opposition to the gospel and thus, blasphemes the gospel through their life. False teachers are damned, and they damn those who embrace their false doctrine.**

Twentieth, let's note that Paul's letters are placed in the category of Scripture. Peter implies this when he says wisdom was given to Paul (2 Peter 3:15). Peter says that the unlearned and unstable twist Paul's words as they do with other Scripture. Peter is essentially putting Paul's letters and teachings as equivalent to Scripture. This is an important passage which authenticates Paul's letters as Scripture.

Lastly, let's note that false teachers can distort and twist Scripture to such a degree that they create a false gospel which will inevitably distort and twist other Scripture. Peter makes this abundantly clear when he says, "The ignorant and unstable twist to their own destruction, as they do the other Scriptures." Paul spoke of this permeating influence of false teaching in Galatians 5:9 where he says, "A little leaven leavens the whole lump." When there is a false gospel, this will inevitably lead to more error. A false gospel must inevitably bend and twist other portions of Scripture to accommodate the falsehood.

Thus, Peter would describe false teachers as false prophets (2 Peter 2:1), bold (2 Peter 2:10), self-willed (2 Peter 2:10), irrational creatures (2 Peter 2:12), blasphemous (2 Peter 2:2, 10), ignorant (2 Peter 3:16), defiled (2 Peter 2:10), deceptive (2 Peter 2:13), covetous (2 Peter 2:3), accursed (2 Peter 2:14), un-submissive (2 Peter 2:1), Lordship scorning (2 Peter 2:10), unrepentant (2 Peter 2:21-22), unceasing from sin (2 Peter 2:14), adulterous (2 Peter 2:14), right way forsaking (2 Peter 2:15), waterless springs (2 Peter 2:17), hell bound (2 Peter 2:17), slaves of corruption (2 Peter 2:19), vomit eating (2 Peter 2:22), excrement wallowing (2 Peter 2:22), and only good when dead creatures who will be eternally destroyed and condemned (2 Peter 2:1, 3, 9, 12). What a picture the apostle Peter draws of these vile and despicable false teaching heretics!

Teaching sacramental conversion and salvation amounts to a false gospel. Teaching sacramental conversion and salvation amounts to a works-salvation (Galatians 2:21). Teaching sacramental conversion and salvation is a false gospel and really is no gospel at all (Galatians 1:6-7). Teaching sacramental conversion and salvation is to be accursed (Galatians 1:8-9). Teaching sacramental conversion and salvation is to teach a perverted and corrupted false gospel (Galatians 1:7). Teaching sacramental conversion and salvation is a destructive heresy (2 Peter 2:1). Teaching sacramental conversion and salvation is to twist Scripture to one's own destruction (2 Peter 3:16). Teaching sacramental conversion is a damning yoke that no man can bear (Acts 15:10).

Let us learn from Peter what true conversion unto the Lord Jesus Christ is. Let us learn from Jesus, John, Paul, the New Testament writers, and the Holy Spirit on the dangers of false teaching. Let us learn that Jesus is the Way, the Truth, and the Life and that no one comes to the Father except through Him (John 14:6). Let us learn from Peter and Jesus that the response to the gospel was one of repentance toward God and faith in the Lord Jesus Christ. Let us learn from Peter and Jesus that the saving faith or faith that justifies is a submissive, meek, loving, repentant, and humble faith in the Lord Jesus Christ (James

4:7–10; Matthew 4:17, 5:3–6, 16:24–26; Mark 1:15, 8:34–37; Luke 3:3–17, 9:23–26, 13:1–5, 14:25–33; John 12:24–26). All praise and honor be given for the glory of God and the building up of Christ's church. Amen.

Prayer

"Father, do the work that I cannot do. In your mercy, use your Word to save the blind and hard-hearted in sacramental churches. Open their eyes, give them the new birth, grant repentance, and author in them saving faith. Do this all for the glory of your beloved Son, the Lord Jesus Christ. Amen."

Notes

1. Robert L. Thomas and Stanley N. Gundry, *The NIV Harmony of the Gospels* (San Francisco, California: Harper & Row, 1988), 000–000.

2. Steve Lawson, "The Perfect Sacrifice of Christ" sermon, November 24, 2010.

3. Steve Lawson, "The Perfect Sacrifice of Christ, Part 1" sermon, January 2, 2005.

4. Steve Lawson, "The Perfect Sacrifice of Christ, Part 2" sermon, February 6, 2005.

5. Steve Lawson, "The Perfect Sacrifice of Christ, Part 3" sermon, April 3, 2005.

6. Alfred Edersheim, *The Life and Times of Jesus the Messiah* (London: Longmans, Green Co., 1923), 000–000.

7. Houser, Shelley Helzerman. "An Estimate of the Value of Two Boatloads of Fish, as Recorded in Luke 5:1-11." *Usi*, Dec. 2017, www. Academia.edu/35395818/An_Estimate_of_the_Value_of_two_boatloads_of_Fish_As_Recorded_in_Luke_5_1_11.

8. John Macarthur, "Behold! The Lamb" sermon, September 29, 2012.

9. Steve Lawson, "Christ Our Substitute" sermon, January 1, 2014.

www.ingramcontent.com/pod-product-compliance
Lightning Source LLC
LaVergne TN
LVHW020528100826
845148LV00010B/1392

* 9 7 8 1 6 3 3 5 7 2 9 7 3 *